W9-ASG-807

THE DYNAMICS OF RELIGION

PETER SLATER

The Dynamics of Religion

Meaning and Change in Religious Traditions

ST. JOSEPH'S UNIVERSITY   STX
BL51.S558 1978
The dynamics of religion :

3 9353 00075 0370

BL
51
.S558
1978

Published in San Francisco by
HARPER & ROW PUBLISHERS
New York • Hagerstown • San Francisco • London

179208

THE DYNAMICS OF RELIGION: Meaning and Change in Religious Traditions. Copyright © 1978 by Peter Slater. All rights reserved. Printed in the United States of America. No part of this book may be used or reproduced in any manner whatsoever without written permission except in the case of brief quotations embodied in critical articles and reviews. For information address Harper & Row, Publishers, Inc., 10 East 53rd Street, New York, NY 10022. Published simultaneously in Canada by Fitzhenry & Whiteside, Limited, Toronto.

FIRST EDITION

Designed by Leigh McLellan

LIBRARY OF CONGRESS CATALOGING IN PUBLICATION DATA

Slater, Peter, 1934–
    The dynamics of religion.

    Includes bibliographical references.
    1. Religion—Philosophy. 2. Religions. I. Title.
BL51.S558   200'.1   78–4426
ISBN 0–06–067389–3

    78 79 80 81 82 10 9 8 7 6 5 4 3 2 1

IN MEMORY OF ALYS SLATER

Contents

Preface

THIS BOOK is written for all who are interested in questions concerning meaning and purpose in life. They may or may not be traditionally religious. But they can scarcely avoid noticing the changes which have occurred in the meanings and purposes of all the major traditions. Such changes take many forms and each religion undergoes many transformations in the course of its history. So it is also with us as individuals. No child simply repeats the faith of the parents. No parent simply lives by the faith formed in childhood. Yet neither religious leaders nor academics have much to say to those who are interested in religious questions, but feel the pressure of the changing contexts in which such questions are asked. Far too many cheap shots are taken at religion and facile defenses made of traditional beliefs by people who gloss over the constantly changing attitudes and expectations of believers. If nothing else, I hope that this book will leave readers truly sensitive to the dynamic nature of religious life and thought. Without such sensitivity there is little hope of understanding religion.

To my mind understanding means knowing how to go on acting or thinking in a certain way when we are on our own.

Understanding how to play chess means knowing how to make our own moves in the game. Understanding a faith means knowing how to develop our own forms of that system of beliefs. The study of religion should teach us what it would mean for us to make the moves of faith, even without a guide. Whether or not we make such moves, however, is a matter of living, not just studying. As each of us lives his or her own life, so each of us finds his or her own faith. Others can help us to understand what we are doing. But the moves must be our own. This book is about such moves. It is an aid to understanding the dynamics of religion, not a substitute for religious living.

The book is about various religious options rather than a plea on behalf of any one of them. But it is a plea to understand religion from within and not just as an object for abstract speculation or disinterested observation. With the possible exception of theology, the disciplines of mind which we bring to religious studies sensitize us to all the nonreligious factors at work in the traditions. These disciplines are necessary if we are to avoid uncritical rehearsals of what each body of faith says about itself. But when our historical, linguistic and psycho-social work of interpretation is done, we still have to see the religious dimension in the lives of such men as Mahatma Gandhi and Malcolm X. In order to do so we must have a theory of religion which takes account of traditional ways of thinking that are religiously motivated. We must see changes in religious life as possible expressions of religious truth, and not always as signs of loss of faith. Too many accounts of religion either ignore the lessons of history or presuppose that everything since Methuselah is bad news.

Since our subject is living faith in whatever form, our theory must take account of data from all the world's religions. When we try to do so we reach beyond the expertise of any single scholar. This fact is often used, especially by philosophers of religion, as an excuse for keeping to the problems of meaning and truth suggested by the statements of conservative theologians. But our interest is not in philosophy or theology in any narrow sense. Consequently, we must risk extending the range of our study to the limits of all available insights into religious life and thought. This does not mean that we should pretend to be African Bushmen if in fact we are urban North Americans. But it does mean that we cannot remain satisfied with lip service mention of other religions, followed by academic business as usual.

I am dissatisfied with the narrow conceptions of religion which stultify many discussions of faith. It is high time that general readers woke up to the fact that the religiously interesting questions today are seldom the conventional ones discussed in the traditional schools. My own experience in public universities has been that, for many students, religious questions are alive but traditional answers are dead. For many others the traditions still live, but in corners cut off from the rest of their experience. I have tried to write for both groups of students and others who share their concerns. Consequently, I turn to stories of faith outside the obviously religious contexts, as well as to developments in the major traditions. As we proceed my own roots in Western ways of thinking will become evident. But I shall try to show how a theory of religion rooted in Western experience may still be used to improve our understanding of other religions.

In order to appreciate the faith of others we do not have to have shared their background. But we do have to know enough of where they come from in order to be able to see where they are going. If we would share their faith we must be prepared to share their sense of destiny. Much of this book is given over to questions of meaning with regard to symbols, stories, and patterns of change. But all of these, on the "religious" level, lead to policies, decisions, and judgments which we make now in order to realize our highest hopes for the future. As I shall argue shortly, it is a mistake to study religion only in its archaic forms, just as it is a mistake to suppose that all philosophy is just as we find it in Plato's dialogues. In order for me to understand what it would mean for me to be religious in one way or another, I have to grasp the consequences of each religious option for my particular lifestyle and future relationships. The religious "level" or "dimension" of our existence involves us in a network of intentions which runs ahead of more restricted levels of meaning and purpose.

For any statement, religious or otherwise, I accept the view that, before we ask whether it is true or false, we must first clarify what we mean by it. But I also accept the view that truth in religion is truth to live by, existential truth—truth that is personally involving and powerful for change. This conception affects my understanding of meaning in religion. The meaning of faith goes beyond that of isolated words or sentences to the contexts in which we become aware of life's deep possibilities. These contexts are ways of life and the stories which communicate them. They are religious when they include some reference to forces and relationships which reach beyond our present perceptions and everyday histories. Our tests for truth begin in the present. But they are conclusive, if at all, only as the outcome of procedures based on what it means to continue on one line of development rather than another. If our interest is in what is true for us, and not just what seemed true to our ancestors, we must articulate principles and focus on processes from the past which point to our future. Otherwise we shall not be talking of ways of *life*. If we would understand the dynamics of living faith we must work with a conception of religion that includes such references and their consequences.

Dynamics of Faith was the title of a book by Paul Tillich. I count myself among his former students and, insofar as there is a method in my thinking, it derives from his so-called method of correlation.[1] Tillich spoke as if our questions are provoked by daily experience, while the answers are translations of those traditionally given in theology. But I agree with those who contend that the questions and answers go both ways. Tillich at his best understood this. He constantly reshaped his theological thinking in response to politics, art, literature, psychology, and personal meetings with leaders of the world religions. I differ from him in that I write as a university teacher of religion, not a professor of theology in a Divinity School. Also, I consider the faith of others important for an understanding of myself and my own tradition, as well as for my appreciation of their points of view. In part this book is my answer to the question "In what sense may theologians like Tillich and Tertullian be said to have shared the same faith, as Tillich the "Christian" and Tagore the "Hindu" did not, even though the former lived centuries apart, while the latter were near contemporaries?" I approach problems of continuity and change in religion often with this question in mind.

The term "transformations" in the title of several chapters

may mislead some readers into expecting what follows to be an overtly "structuralist" study of religion. The kind of change in meaning which primarily concerns me, however, is neither of the kinds discussed by most structuralists. They tend to concentrate either on close historical developments through time (what are called "diachronic" transformations) or, often in reaction against emphasis on these, on the simultaneous permutations possible within any given whole (what are called "synchronic" transformations).[2] The dynamic interplay between questions and answers in religious thinking which interests me is neither simply genetic nor static, but pragmatic and "eschatological" (that is, having to do with thoughts concerning our ends and expectations for our future). In a sequel to this book I shall have to work out these distinctions as they relate especially to our quest for truth in religion. Likewise, I have deferred to another work full description of the Way of Resurrection, the Way of Revolution and the like, which are mentioned in this text. Their elaboration is not necessary to the theory of identity and integrity in religion with which I answer the question of continuity through change.

I believe that religious thinking is an excitingly different kind of thinking which draws from the humanities, the sciences and the social sciences, and on traditional arguments in theology, without being simply an aggregate of these. Thus what follows is neither an exercise in theology nor a conventional history or philosophy of religions. It is an essay on the dynamics of religious life and thought which must be understood before we can correctly use religious terms. It is a critical reflection on where we are going and what we may become, if we adopt a religious way of life. The transcendent reference in such a life carries thought from the wisdom of the ages to situations in which present preoccupations are challenged and priorities for the future are sifted. If we would gain insight into questions of meaning and truth in religion, then we must become clear about the nature of this dynamic context, as well as about the meaning of "meaning" and "truth." It is to this task of appreciating the full range of living religion that this book is primarily directed.

Finally, I wish to acknowledge those who have helped me to understand religion in general and to improve this book in particular. It is written with thanks for the insights and inspiration of many teachers—Raymond Klibansky, John Wild and Rogers Albritton; Henry Chadwick and Paul Tillich; Robert Lawson Slater; Alys Slater; and Helen Slater—concerning, respectively, philosophy, theology, world religions, living religion, and psychology. I am grateful to former students at Haverford College and Carleton University who, in courses on religion and modern culture, first prompted me to put my ideas on paper, and to Thomas Dean and Ernest Best, who encouraged me to think them worth publishing. The reader should be grateful to Charles Davis and Edgar Davidson and to John Loudon (of Harper & Row) for thorough, critical readings of earlier drafts of the published text. Its writing was made possible by a sabbatical leave from Carleton University and grants from the research fund of the Dean of Arts.

PETER SLATER

Carleton University
Spring 1978

CHAPTER ONE

The Dynamics of Religion

ALTHOUGH most of us at some time try to think through our
position on religious questions, religious thinking and the transformations which result from it are seldom the subject of systematic study. Philosophers have wrestled with so-called proofs of
the existence of God and questions concerning how we know
what we do in religion. Theologians have carried on endless
doctrinal disputes and psychologists have guessed at their reasons for doing so. We can find discussions on whether or not it
is rational to be religious or essays on reason in religion which
espouse some particular point of view. But the changes in religious thinking which typically occur as we grow older, or adopt
one religious persuasion instead of another, are rarely formally
considered. There are studies available on brainwashing and adolescent conversion, but few discussions of the normal processes
and developments of thought in life as it affects religion.

This book proposes a model for conceptualizing changes in
religion which should help us to understand better our own
development and that of others of different persuasions. It is
directed toward an interpretation of any and every religious
system, rather than an apologetic for any particular faith. Of

course, my own preferences will become clear as we proceed. But the problems which most concern me are common to all who contemplate ultimate questions, whatever their orientation may be.

The problems which interest me are philosophical in the broad sense, that is, part of a quest for wisdom. They are not the usual proofs and counterarguments found in texts on evil, immortality, and God. They are problems of identity and integrity in religious ways of life. *In particular, I am interested in the dynamics of continuity and change in religion,* how we keep faith with our ancestors or with our own best insights, while also being true to our changing world. I approach these questions from the side of religious studies, particularly with an eye to the commitments of those who continue to be religious through radical changes in life and thought. Consequently, I draw on findings from the social sciences and linguistic analysis. But my interest is in movements of life and thought within and across traditions, rather than in mapping arguments found in single classical texts.

I describe the changes to be discussed as transformations because I believe that the forms or structures of religious existence are necessarily changing, along with the cultural shifts which characterize our life in the world. Even someone who seeks to conform to the patterns of faith prescribed by an earlier prophet or seer is in a different situation from his religious forerunner, if only because he comes after and has a pattern to follow. We are all sons and daughters in religion, even if we never dreamed, as Oedipus did, of murdering our fathers and marrying our mothers. The question is: when we put away childish things do we also put aside our parents' faith? Or is the rejection of previous patterns just another phase in growing up? If we suppose that our answers depend upon how we go about our acceptance or rejection, rather than on any specific conclusions that we may reach, then it becomes important for us to understand some of the processes whereby we develop our identity in religion. To talk of transformations is to stress the processes rather than the deposits of religious thought.

Several writers in recent years have emphasized the dynamic nature of genuine religious thinking.[1] It is important to do so if, as I believe, keeping faith with our predecessors means changing with the times as they did. To give up thinking on our own behalf and simply to repeat the formulae which served them is to express lack of faith. It is to deny the living presence of whatever enlivened their thought, whether that presence be referred to as the Doctrinal Body *(Dharmakaya)* of the Buddha, as the Holy Spirit of the God of Israel, or as the impact of the Ideal on the Actual in the formation of each generation. As we consider the phenomenon of continuity through change we shall have to pay close attention to what it is that is being continued and what it is that keeps a life religious. Failure to recognize this process can foster conservatism for tradition's sake or radicalism for revolution's sake. To keep faith with our spiritual parents in fact requires us to say No to much that they held dear, just as they said No to many of our requests in the interests of our growing up. In short, thinking truly in religion is a dialectical process, and any model of transformations in religion must reflect this fact.

Much confusion, particularly the confusion of true faith with classical forms of religious life, arises from inadequate comprehension of what it means to be religious. If we assume that the classical forms express the *only* ways there are of being religious, then we shall have to regard all change as a loss of faith. But this is to fall into what I call the archaistic fallacy, that is, the explanation of religion wholly in terms of its "primitive" expressions.[2] Apart from anything else, we only know these from a later or different perspective, which tends to be normative for our appraisal of the data.[3] Besides, as the experience of sex reminds us, knowing as a child never suffices for an understanding of adult ways. What comes earlier in our experience is never a sufficient explanation of what follows in later life.[4]

The dynamics of religion must be understood by reference to the present interplay of past and future considerations. This is the thesis which I wish to drive home in this chapter. In particular, no definition of religion is acceptable which neglects its future thrust. This point has only recently been systematically acknowledged by theologians. It seems scarcely to be noticed in textbooks on the philosophy of religion. The weight of tradition has always been recognized, but not the counterweight of hope.[5] Too many accounts of religion are dominated by nostalgia for its classical conceptions. Whether our focus is on individual or communal developments, we cannot assume that we grasp their meaning simply by researching what their root forms meant to our ancestors. Between then and now lies a series of elaborations and interpretations whose history is equally part of religion.[6]

Much of the best religious thinking has been done in cloisters. But, particularly during the medieval period, cloistered thinking was more suited to the working out of a single point of view than to the appreciation of the views of others. Even within a single tradition there is a plurality of ways of living the religious life. If we think of the processes experienced along the way, rather than of summary reports at journey's end, we have to acknowledge many ways of being religious.[7] Each one develops a consistent pattern of expectations and body of past experiences. These provide the present context for decisions concerning the truth of the moment for the believer.

The most useful accounts of meaning in religion recognize that meaning must be related to context.[8] Our context in religious thinking is neither that of the ancient seers nor that of would-be scientists. Too many accounts of "religious language" read like afterthoughts to a philosophy of science. Of course, changes in religious thinking have important similarities with other kinds of transformation in our culture. But dynamic faith includes much more challenging "feedback" concerning our conceptions of meaning and value in life than is the case in investigations of inorganic matter. Religious life requires a blend of poetic imagination, prophetic argument and ecstatic assertion which may be similar to what scientists experience. But an investigator's life may be changed by his religious investigations in ways which are not replicated in the ordinary course of scientific research.[9]

Religious thinking may be understood as a way of thinking through the priorities demanded in religious life. It looks to the question What if? rather than the philosophical So what? That is to say, the consistency sought in religious thinking stems from our need to reach decisions and transpose rules for the future. In this process logical inferences may or may not be ignored, predictions may or may not be fulfilled, provided that the basic concern for religious mastery is met. For example, if preoccupation with logical deductions obstructs his pupil's perception of a problem, a Zen master will not hesitate to resort to paradox and even contradiction. In the same way, Jesus' profundity as a religious thinker comes down to us most clearly through his parables concerning the coming of the "Kingdom of Heaven." In both examples there is a logic to the patterns of questions and answers which will escape anyone mesmerized by a single paradigm for logical reasoning.

I am not claiming here that the "logic" of religious language is unique. Logic is logic whether among the Bantu or in Plato's Academy. But philosophers of religion must look at the patterns of thought and argument found in religious contexts, not just in textbooks on symbolic logic. There is more to logic in life than is dreamed of by some logicians. Also, there is more to arguing cases in religious contexts than is suggested by those who look only to the law for their examples.[10] Thinking again of the Zen master, we must know whether he seeks for us sudden or gradual enlightenment before we gauge what he means. We cannot simply assume that we know what is meant by his sayings and silences. We have to appreciate the priorities and principles shaping what he says, thinks, and does, if we would know his way and "the" way in which he would direct us.

So far we have talked rather indiscriminately of religion and religious thinking. Like talk of God, talk of religion often hides more than it reveals. Consequently some have suggested that we avoid such talk altogether. This policy is supported by the fact that there are no direct translations for our word "religion" in the scriptural languages of the world religions.[11] Moreover, if we want to argue that the "real" religions of Westerners today are certain kinds of Marxism, nationalism, and consumerism, then we might do better to talk of world-views or "pivotal values," and abandon the term "religion" completely.[12] The situation is aggravated by the fact that, at some time or other, almost anything has counted as being religious—sexual orgies, sexual abstinence, construction of idols, destruction of idols, and so on.[13] Nevertheless, I believe that only a mistaken view of language would force us to abandon the term. Were we to do so, we should soon find ourselves in similar difficulties concerning our use of "values" and "ultimacy" and be no nearer to discussing the real issues of meaning and truth.

If we recognize that usage is our best clue to meaning, and that normal English usage leads us to describe as "religious" phenomena which might come under the heading of "dharma" or "li" or "hsiao" elsewhere, then we may proceed with caution. Given that abstract nouns enable us to bring under one heading a variety of experiences, which might equally come under other headings, and knowing that definitions are not substitutes for further thinking, or reified reproductions of what author and reader may have in mind, then I still think it useful to talk of religious thinking and to offer a working definition of "religion." In any case, without further apology, let me give you my working definition and proceed to comment on those aspects important for our discussion of the dynamics of religion.[14]

In my view, *a religion is a personal way of life informed by traditional elements of creed, code, and cult and directed toward the realization of some transcendent end.* As we shall see, by comparison with others, some ways may have only a minimal creedal element, few formal rituals, or only loosely derived moral rules associated with them. The degree of emphasis on any one element reflects whatever is central to the way of life in question. Each way has its own set of priorities, its own centers of concern and action, which constitute the principles of relevance for thinkers in that tradition. Mention of all these elements here warns us against the assumption—all too common in discussions of religious thought —that religious thought can simply be equated with dogma or *dharma*. In fact I regard doctrinal disputes as generally incidental to the main purpose of religious thinking, which is to help us to lead the religious life with the whole self. *Religious thinking takes place in the context of commitment to a course of action* and thus is different, for instance, from metaphysical theorizing as such or mathematical computation. Indeed, as persecutors have always known, it is most akin to political thinking. At its best, it is thought arising from and applied to the basic needs of the moment ("praxis" in Marxist terminology), rather than speculation with occasional practical applications.[15]

The emphasis on tradition in our definition serves to exclude as religious purely individual passions, as in miserliness or alcoholism. A miser may treasure money with an intensity which shames the average temple-goer. Yet his obsession is an aberration rather than an alternative form of religious life. Later we must consider whether or not a Hitler should be regarded as a religious figure. In the search for criteria of truth and falsehood in patterns of faith, mention of tradition reminds us that essential to religion is reference to something wider than the scope of individual ego attachments. I reject any definition which leads us to treat as equally religious every sincere movement among individuals or groups at a given time.

A personal way of life is both individual and communal. Even a pioneer like Gautama teaches *the* Aryan Way, not just his personal *via media*. Even a religious hermit has his conceptions of hermit life shaped by the examples of others. We may discuss marginal cases. But our paradigm must be of movements which, as they gain momentum, establish traditions against which individual claims must be tested. Although I reject the Platonic notion that the body politic can adequately be understood as a giant-sized individual, I believe that the structures of religious thinking found in communities can be interpreted by reference to the structures of individual faith, and vice versa. This is because thinking and speaking are often one and language is almost never wholly private.[16]

Despite the importance of tradition and the communal context, it is nevertheless the call of the future, rather than an appeal to the past, which determines the growing points of a religious way of life. Even for those who embrace a cyclical conception of time and assert the illusoriness of existence, there is, if only metaphorically, a "before" and "after" in the story of faith. The Buddha, for example, may be ultimately the same in nature, conforming to the same pattern, exercising the same skill in means, in every aeon of his manifestations, so that the most accurate visual presentation of "him" may be a wall supporting ten thousand Buddha images, where the individual figure blurs into a unified impression of infinitely enlightening presence. But the story of Gautama, reenacted in the initiations of countless Burmese boys, is first of a home life in which he is treated as a prince, then of disgust at and withdrawal from worldly pleasures, then of reception into the monastic life and finally, it is hoped, of realization "in" Nirvana.[17] It is this hope of Nirvana, whether understood in terms of a futuristic or of a "realized" eschatology, that shows us the horizon of each Buddhist's path, toward which he or she must eventually proceed. It reminds us that religions are ways *to* as well as ways *from* particular states of existence and patterns of experience.

Failure to acknowledge the future orientation and changing patterns of religious ways of life is a major weakness in many definitions of religion. Without recognition of such orientation, we cannot account for the growth of traditions and convergence of conflicting points of view, except in terms of nonreligious factors. A definition which emphasizes only the sacred past, for example, can only describe change as decline. To equate the sacred with the eternal is not much better, if the lessons of eternity are all supposed to have been completed in the past. Novelty in religion then appears not as creativity but as an invitation to disaster. An analysis wholly in terms of origins never allows us to consider the religious motivation of secular concerns.[18] Church Fathers must then be seen only as subject to "nontheological factors." Mahatma Gandhi will be understood wholly in terms of his youthful identity crisis. And so on. As ancestral shadows become more and more normative for religious studies, a Malcolm X or Martin Luther King is left to sociologists and cultural historians for serious investigation. Religious scholars too often become archeologists, rather than arbiters of culture, because their gaze is fixed on the past. Instead of the dynamics of history they focus on the deposits of archaic faith.

Not all references to the future are religious, however. According to my definition only those count which propose to us some transcendent end such as Nirvana. What counts as transcendent is crucial in this context and, as mention of Nirvana reminds us, our conceptions here may be crippled by ambiguities. Just among the schools of Buddhism, for example, Nirvana may be thought of as future or as neither future nor present. In most classical religious philosophies only eternity transcends time. But in revolutionary ideologies the new aeon is as temporal as the old. We shall have to unravel some of these differences after we have explored various symbolic patterns of faith. But even now we can appreciate that much depends upon what we regard as being transcended.

By my definition what is transcended in a religious way of life is the current or prior state of existence of an individual or group. Thus, for example, in religious or quasi-religious forms of Marxism, the present alienated state of owners and workers will be transcended with the realization of a "classless" society. If talk of this future is purely pragmatic, a best guess as to how history may develop, then such talk will not be religious. But if the end in view is discussed symbolically, as significant of a mythical time when evil is eradicated, and reinforced by ritual actions—for example, May Day parades—then it is religious. Indeed, it is more religious than the vestiges of a doctrine of heaven found among some of the lingering Christian groups in Marxist societies. The religious future is a radically new future. In it life will be structured differently than now, when good and evil are mixed. The end is both a goal and a conclusion to the kind of life from which we presently seek redemption.[19]

For those who are still "on the way" a transcendent end is very much future, even though from the perspective of those who have "arrived" the end may have been present from the beginning. Paradoxes abound on this subject, especially in the language of mystics, because what is essentially a dynamic situation may be described from several angles at once. The "signposts" on the way are those who have gone before, so that their experiences tend to be normative. But those who follow must have some inkling of what they seek. In some sense, it is the same end in view for a holy mother and for those who only know enough to call her "holy." Realizations of the end differ in degree, rather than in kind.

Hope for the common end, not just dissatisfaction with the past, shapes the overall sense of direction in a tradition. It is by reference to their common destiny that the faithful on the way get their bearings. This, rather than futile rehashing of past deviations, is what enables them to adjudicate their differences. Thus in the New Testament the typical subject of exhortation is the coming Kingdom of God. In a secular context the subject may be rather the realization of a national dream. But the dynamics of thought and argument in both will be similar, since both Christians and nationalists, in the course of their respective family arguments, have a shared sense of their ending. Implicit in all this is the assumption that the transcendent end is what is of ultimate value to those who are on the way. It is this which defines their sense of priorities.

Whatever we mean by "ultimate," the transcendent end is the

ultimate concern of those who follow a way. In relation to it, all other pursuits are of only relative importance, even though serious striving for this end may be deferred to the distant future.[20] Within a tradition lay people are treated as servants of those who are further along. For the former, masters of the way represent the authoritative assurance that the way is worthwhile and their ultimate expectations may be met. To some of his executioners, for example, Jesus may have seemed a mad prophet. But to his disciples the sense of his loving fellowship with God was a sign that the Kingdom had come. In Chapter Nine we shall have to discuss whether it is possible to pursue simultaneously a variety of goals, no one of which is said to be of sole or absolute value.[21] Before then, however, I shall argue that the major concern in each tradition is the way to the end and the central symbol of this way, for the faithful, is that which, or the one who, focuses their thinking on the way.

Transformations in religious thinking are part of the process of realizing a transcendent end. In other words, there is no salvation without constant conversion.[22] This is so because the state of existence of an individual on the way changes focus as he or she directs this life toward the ultimate goal. How this occurs will be considered in Chapter Eight. Traditionally a new life-style was modeled on that of a religious leader, whose role a disciple was supposed to adopt. Thus every Christian might be exhorted to be a Christ to one's neighbor, every Buddhist should be a future Buddha, and so on. In western cultures today, as Jung remarked, the central image is more likely to be that of the self as an individual, a genuine individual integrating contrasting attributes in a mature way.[23] But in either case, the process is one of centering, or shifting centers, in such a way that one's thoughts and judgments become quite different from what they were before.

Whether for individuals or for groups our clue to the continuing identity of a changing pattern of faith lies in the phenomenon of centering. It is no accident that mandalas, sacred cosmograms centered on a symbol of the transcendent end, are such archetypal images in the history of religions. Particularly in the quest for a personal identity which is religiously satisfying, we find that our story in religion becomes a story of shifting centers and the realization of a centered self. A religious transformation occurs either with a complete change of center, as in fundamental conversion, or with such a change in the surrounding culture as to give new meaning to life centered in a particular way.

Throughout this book I shall adopt a model of the dynamics of religion based on the phenomenon of centering as a way of organizing our data and approaching our problems. What is centered is personal faith, expressed through clusters of symbols. These symbols are carried by paradigmatic stories of ways of life. What I mean by "symbol" will be explained in Chapter Two. How they are clustered is the subject of Chapter Three. The concept of paradigmatic stories expressing ways of life is developed in Chapter Four. Their "intentionality" and the nature of transcendent ends are further explored in Chapter Five. Only after this groundwork is laid do I feel able to expound my theory of identity and integrity in religion, as it bears on the phenomenon of continuity through change. I need the concepts developed in these earlier chapters in order to discuss transformations within and across traditions, personal conversion and "deconversion," in the chapters which follow. *The key to the model is the concept of a master story in each tradition, which retains the same central symbol as an identifying reference, but changes in meaning as its pattern of auxiliary symbols develops.*

In proposing a model of symbols clustered in stories, I do not rule out other models for analyzing transformations in religious life and thought. Indeed, when we come to the question of "decentralization" in Chapter Nine, I shall review the adequacy of this model. Also, I am far from asserting that people consciously think according to the patterns of marginal and central concerns which I shall outline.[24] I offer these as a heuristic device. They help us to understand, on a religious level, the dynamic continuity experienced in traditional ways of life. I think my model appropriate because I believe that, often in religion, we work in a spiral around particular insights and points of view, rather than proceeding in linear fashion from one point to the next.[25] How we later conceptualize and validate particular claims, however, need not be a replica of our procedure when first we arrive at them.

Finally in this chapter we should note that, although what makes a way of life religious is its mixture of traditional elements and transcendent expectations, the actual way is in the present. The processes of religious life and thought necessarily incorporate present conditions into the dynamic structures of existence. Thus religious meaning changes in changing times and religious truth includes an essential reference to contemporary circumstances. If religious stories were simply stories of happy endings, and religious thinking were simply a matter of reverting to unchanging patterns of thought, we might not need to attend to the dynamics of religion. But *religion has to do with penultimate as well as ultimate concerns.* It includes stories of lay people as well as of priests and priestesses. The quest for wholeness is as strong among householders as among maharishis in ashrams or yogis in meditation halls.

Of course, secular experiences and worldly references alone do not constitute a religious outlook. But without these a religion cannot be considered a viable way of being in the world. For a theory of being, this means that references in religious thought must be to the world as well as to God, to the cycle of existences *(samsara)* as well as to bliss at the end (Nirvana), to what the Chinese call the Ten Thousand Things as well as to the Unnamable Tao.[26] For a theory of knowledge, this means that religious perceptions must include insights into the nature of the present world, as well as into the transformed state of one who has realized the end. *A religious outlook includes a way of looking at the world as well as away from the world.* Religious thought reflects this fact.

In short, no living religion can long ignore the findings of contemporary science. This point may not seem obvious when we consider the obduracy of the faithful when prophecy fails.[27] But even those who announce the end of the world on a particular day do so on the basis of their observations of the world, not just on extraterrestrial guesswork. If we think of it as a life-world *(Lebenswelt)*, a setting for historic action, not just an impersonal system of physical forces, then we should appreciate the extent to which ultimate wisdom builds on worldly wisdom concerning natural processes. It is true that human beings have clung to theories of divinity shaped by outmoded cosmologies, long after science had left these behind.[28] But then the urgency in their thinking stemmed from a desire to perpetuate a dogmatic system, rather than from any vivid experience of divine presence. The dynamic of their argument became purely defensive and was perceived as such by others within their own tradition. Because their past ways of thinking ceased to reflect present religious experience, *what once were true statements in religion became false.* Changes in the sciences help to keep alive patterns of faith which otherwise might make of tradition the whole truth.

The terminology which I have favored so far reflects the influence of Wilfred Smith's *The Meaning and End of Religion.*[29] As I made clear earlier I do not accept his strictures on use of the word "religion." But I do accept his contrast between faith and tradition. By "faith" is meant the personal involvement in a way of life which leads to action on live options. A live option, in William James's sense, calls for action even when we cannot foresee the consequences and cannot give conclusive arguments for acting as we do.[30] Faith in this sense implies investment of the whole self and therefore cannot be "blind" faith. It is personal in that it entails putting one's person, including one's body, behind one's statements of faith. It is not common knowledge. One's reason for believing in the viability of a particular way or trusting a particular teacher cannot be made evident to those who are out of sympathy with one's faith. Yet faith seeks understanding, as Augustine taught. Self-knowledge includes awareness of this faith.

Faith shared leads to a history of actions, including statements of faith, which constitutes in time a particular tradition. (Actions shared lead to mutual confidence, which may well be expressed by professing the same faith, for instance in democracy, in equal rights for women, or in the need for enlightenment.) In a sense, a tradition is formed by the "deposits" of past faith. A living religion is a combination of such a tradition with a contemporary faith. This description does not rule out the possibility that a religion is divinely inspired. But it does emphasize the fact that, even so, religion is the cultural expression of particular human interests and convictions. These interests may include the "humanity" of God or dismiss all talk of God as irrelevant. Either way, in order to understand the diversities of faith we have to study their respective cultural and cross-cultural contexts. *The dynamics of religion may be described as the interplay between faith and tradition in each new generation.*

In what follows I shall show how changes in religious life and thought may be understood as transformations within traditions and consider how these may be reformed in response to new insights of religious faith. I shall argue that we must acknowledge the potency of past symbol systems while looking for new symbols of transcendence in the present. We must look to the contexts in which our symbols receive their distinctively religious uses, as well as to the congruence between "sacred" and "profane" experience, in our search for truth in religion. With this much by way of introduction I turn now to the topic of symbols and meaning in life.

CHAPTER TWO

Symbols and Meaning in Life

IN RELIGION, as in war, people are prepared to renounce the comforts of home and to die young. Very few do so, however, for purely abstract reasons. Categories of substance, number and relation, concepts of space and time, have helped people to ponder the nature of "reality," even as their perceptions have given content to their thoughts. But a way of life requires a sense of worth and purpose which engages the stronger emotions and strengthens the weakened will. In religion, concrete symbols rather than abstract concepts are what engage the imagination. In religious thinking, symbols enable us to blend traditional wisdom with fresh hope, to relate present experience to transcendent ends. How symbols may serve to articulate our sense of worth and purpose is the subject of this chapter.

In my usage, religious symbols are those phenomena, events, roles, and persons in everyday life which put us in mind of our transcendent ends or our ways of realizing these. How such symbols are understood varies according to our conceptions of the world and of ultimate wisdom. Often a symbol develops when we see as significant of final value and truth in life something which might, otherwise, be observed to be simply part of the regular sequence of events. For instance, I might see a rain-bow and simply marvel at its colors. Or I might see in it a sign of divine favor and thereafter take rainbows to be symbols of divine support.[1] Our ability to see through the ordinary to the extraordinary frames of reference in religious thinking supplies much of the content of patterns of faith. In this connection I think that the importance of symbols in religion can hardly be overestimated.

Few of us foster our awareness of transcendent ends during housekeeping hours. If, like Mary in the New Testament, we have Martha in the kitchen to prepare our supper,[2] we may be able to become full-time contemplatives. But in our thinking we tend, like lawyers, to settle issues wherever possible by reference only to particular precedents and points of immediate interest. We do not dwell on the principles of love and justice which our rules are meant to exemplify. With regard to the insurability of blacks in urban ghettos, for instance, or the employability of married women, we have only begun to perceive in recent years the relevance of such principles.[3] We may have thought before only prudentially of good and bad risks. In that case we may have had to be educated into realizing that what seems normal to us need not be normative. Once we recognized the existence of institutional racism or male chauvinism we were not discovering new facts. Nor were we reinterpreting their significance on the fact-gathering level important to social statisticians. Rather we were setting them in a context of social relations which evoked a new sense of obligation and reaffirmation of first principles on our part. Then talk of blacks or working women had symbolic force.

Similarly in religion we may find ourselves viewing family celebrations and bereavements in quite conventional ways. We may, for example, accept the convention that all deaths are sad for the dying. The relevance to our own grief of principles deriv-ing, for instance, from what I call the Way of Resurrection may escape us. But then we may set the pattern of our experiences in the context of the Christian master story. The death of the Christ may transform our feeling for the death in the family. Or we might see it in the context of a Buddhist story of rebirth. Either way we shall then regard death, and life before death, in a new light. The symbol of the Cross or the Wheel of Life will refocus our perception of the boundaries between life and death, grief and joy, hope and despair, which we have just crossed in our own experience.

Of course, especially after we have weighed experiences of radical evil, we may conclude that everything is religiously "out of focus." But then we shall find all symbols empty of religious meaning. Our present concern is to understand those who find them significant. To this end we must appreciate how they use the symbols that they do and listen, not just to the average, but especially to the authoritative voices in religious communities.

Emphasis on symbol systems is not new in the study of religion.[4] But the history of discussions of this topic is confusing. Some writers call "signs" what others call "symbols" and vice versa.[5] Some religious philosophers are adamant in rejecting reliance on any language in religion that is "merely" symbolic.[6] Others speak rather of images and "root metaphors."[7] In recent times I. T. Ramsey wrote of models and qualifiers, while others have reaffirmed Thomistic concepts of analogy.[8] Such terms do not denote exactly the same ranges of relationships in religious thinking. Each highlights slightly different features in our experience of life. Generally I follow writers like Tillich and Gadamer in regarding signs as conventional tokens, such as the letter S (Hebrew ש , Greek σ , etc.). By contrast, symbols are thought to express the power of what is symbolized, for instance, fatherhood or motherhood in relation to divine creativity.[9] *The important point in every case is our need to see through our statements of fact to our demand for truth and presentation of values,* that is, to develop cultural connections between the observed and the preferred or morally required.

Those who object to emphasis on the symbolic nature of language in religion often assume that symbolic talk dissipates the immediacy of religious experience. They tend to think only of minor tokens of faith, which they can reject while developing the metaphor of immediacy or a doctrine of analogy. But for Tillich symbols participate in the dynamics of our relationships, which are understood dialectically in terms of nature and culture, experience and reflection, being and becoming. For Tillich, *so far from dissipating the sense of relationship between worshipers and their Lord, or Taoists and their Way, an "active" symbol fosters its realization.*

According to Paul Ricoeur, the function of symbols in religion is to enable us to discover or have revealed to us "the bond between man and what he considers sacred."[10] Concerning the distinction between the sacred and the profane Ricoeur generally follows Mircea Eliade and other historians of religion.[11] In earliest times, says Ricoeur, the bond between man and "the sacred" was expressed through narratives, especially stories of the beginning and end of time. Typically these were myths relating the "crisis" of evil to the continuation of cosmic order. We can classify them according to their appraisals of our situation and the strategies that they proposed. Ricoeur concentrates on Greek tragedies and the Hebrew myth of Adam. He believes that we can trace a progression toward relatively more ethical and less literal conceptions of defilement, sin, and guilt. Without prejudging this question, we can learn from what he tells us of the process whereby "symbols give rise to thought."[12]

Ricoeur assumes that we find it easier to refer to physical objects than to express psychological reactions to them.[13] Our talk of physical objects tends to be "literal," while our expressions of personal attitudes and the like tend to be "symbolic." Mythological language draws on both "objective" and "subjective" references. It develops a "double intentionality" for our symbols, whereby they retain both their literal signification and their metaphorical allusiveness.[14] For example, in discussions of evil, the word "stain" is not a picture of a stain. It is a sign which enables us to refer literally to spots and smudges. This reference is a matter of linguistic convention.

We presuppose linguistic conventions when we evoke religious insight into our relation to the sacred. Thus with regard to moral evil we can express our sense of defilement by talking of a stain on our character. What we use then is not, in Ricoeur's language, a "perfectly transparent" technical sign—"stain"—but an "opaque" and "symbolic sign"—"stain" again—whose meaning is given with and indicated by the literal sign.[15] Through this process an "inexhaustible depth" of meaning is introduced into our vocabulary which particularly suits the mythological function in traditional religion. For later reference, incidentally, we may note that Ricoeur regards the experience of salvation as prior to specific conceptions of evil. Also, he observes that some myths become dominant in religious cultures, changing the import of earlier myths incorporated into a tradition.[16] Thus the full significance of any given symbol cannot be grasped without reference to its place in a particular set of stories. We shall return to these points later.

Ancient myth-makers naturally used the salient features of their world to express their sense of self and situation. The sun, the moon, the waters, and the sky served as gathering points for a "mass of significations" through which they revealed to others their meaning and purpose in life. Whether such meaning is detected in or projected onto such objects is a question which, according to Ricoeur, presupposes a false dichotomy. Of the sky, for example, he comments:

> It is the same thing to say that the sky *manifests* the sacred and to say that it *signifies* the most high, the elevated and the immense, the powerful and the orderly, the clairvoyant and the wise, the sovereign, the immutable. The manifestation through the thing is like the condensation of an infinite discourse; manifestation and meaning are strictly contemporaneous and reciprocal; the concretion of the thing is the counterpart of the surcharge of inexhaustible meaning which has ramifications in the cosmic, in the ethical and in the political (spheres). Thus the symbol-thing is the potentiality of innumerable spoken symbols which, on the other hand, are knotted together in a single cosmic manifestation.[17]

The "literal" serves as a "matrix" for symbolic uses first in speech, later in thought, as people develop their stories and, in due time, their doctrines of sin and salvation, evil and good.

In religion we see creative and redemptive processes at work through such everyday acts as a kiss or the passing of a common cup. Almost anything may become a symbol for some tradition, as in the case of the executioner's cross in Christianity. In Hindu thought, a sound such as "Om" is said to signify all spoken and unspoken Power (Brahman). Yet the same token is used as a talisman on taxis, to bring good luck to the drivers. Beggars' rags have become Buddhist robes, while princely silks have become symbols of decadence. Groups of such objects may be brought together to constitute a sacrament, as in the care of images and feeding of deities. Their significance depends on traditional contexts and the intentionality of a people. Of course, such phenomena as water and light lend themselves naturally to religious usage. But symbols are typically cultural rather than natural objects.[18] Their meaning has to be found in the context of the myths and rituals in which they have their primary use.

As long as there is some consensus concerning the importance of particular objects in our world, or of particular events in our history, a given set of symbols is likely to remain acceptable as the basis for religious discussions. Among those who agree that the world is God's creation, for example, the "hand" of God will in principle be discernible in ordinary processes of growth and decay. Against this background there may still be debate, for instance about what being a part of creation means for those making policies concerning nonrenewable resources.[19] Similarly people may hear God in Christ as they hear stories of Jesus, or glimpse enlightenment as they hear stories of Gautama the Buddha. They will then see God "in" Christ or the Buddha Nature in the Buddha and, on the strength of this "cosmic manifestation," debate the "two natures" of Jesus or the permanence of the Self. But such debates will proceed on the assumption of a common set of significations.

When cultural conflict arises, for example concerning the nature of the world, it is tempting to suppose that what occurs is that some see the world "as" God's creation, while others do not.[20] They experience the same world but interpret their experience differently, because of their different perspectives.[21] But this way of speaking obscures the nature of religious differences. Those who agree that the world is God's creation do not talk of seeing it "as" such. What is evoked in their use of symbols is not their everyday order of perception. But neither is it some esoteric revelation of an unseen agent interfering in world affairs from behind a cosmic screen. Their procedure is that suggested in Buber's account of the difference between I-You and I-It relationships.[22]

If I stop treating you as an object and become open to a personal relationship, I do not then see your body "as" a person hidden beneath your skin. I see *you* and act accordingly. My seeing you is a function of my intentions in relation to you and my actions express my intentions. I see in your actions the quality of relationship that you affirm and vice versa. When I am looking for you in a crowd I may look *at* any number of other people indifferently. But when I see *you* the level of my response will be according to quite another network of relationships. So it is with how we see things in the world.

We can illustrate differences in religious perception by reference to discussion of a famous essay, "Gods," by John Wisdom.[23] In that essay the difference between theists and atheists is brought out by a story about two people returning to their "long neglected garden." Seeing flowers still growing, one concludes that a gardener has tended the plot in their absence. Seeing all the weeds, the other thinks not. After investigating they fail to detect the presence of a gardener. Still the first person insists that a gardener has been at work; only now the conclusion is that this gardener is invisible.

At this point, Wisdom remarks, the two are no longer disagreeing about "the facts." Each sees what the other sees and expects to see nothing else. Their difference concerning the presence of an invisible gardener is due not to a dispute about the facts but to their different "picture preferences." (We are not told *why* they prefer to see things as they do.) Let us call the statement of the first person's preference "the garden story" and see what Antony Flew does with it, when he retells Wisdom's parable.

In Flew's version, the two are explorers who come upon "a clearing in the jungle."[24] Nevertheless, Flew still makes the first person look at the flowers there and say, "Some gardener must tend this plot." After a series of experiments fail to confirm this statement he moves to talk of an invisible gardener. But, Flew asks, what remains of the original assertion? Let us call Flew's version "the jungle story." Now my question is, given that all see the same mix of grasses and flowers, why do some tell garden stories and others tell jungle stories about what they see? Do some look at the flowers and see the plot "as" a garden, where others focus on the grasses and see it "as" a jungle clearing?

If we take such juxtapositions of images as analogies to how we see our world, we might speak of seeing the world "as" a closed physical system or seeing it "as" God's creation. We could then use the garden model or the jungle model to refer to those parts of the universe which seem to us to indicate the nature of the whole. But, apart from difficulties about how we can meaningfully refer to the world as a "whole,"[25] we are in trouble over this metaphor of "seeing as." We do not ordinarily talk of seeing something "as" something else unless we acknowledge some ambiguity about our perceptions. Wisdom's two people simply see their garden with its flowers and weeds. (The impossibility of experiencing without interpreting, incidentally, is nicely pointed up by the automatic description of the grasses as weeds.) Only when the commentators muddy the picture do we fall back on the concept of "seeing as." Also, only then are we arbitrarily told that part of each story is based on "objective" description, the rest on "subjective" preferences.

It is instructive here to consider how in fact we clear up ambiguities. With a genuinely ambiguous picture, such as the drawing of the "duck-rabbit" (note already what the naming implies),[26] we simply draw in the appropriate kinds of bodies.

What is the equivalent move for discussions of the world as God's creation? If we take up the images suggested by the garden and jungle stories, we shall not proceed to look for signs of some mysterious entity, hidden behind the clouds. Rather, acting on the garden story in relation to our plot of flowers and grasses, we might begin to do some weeding. In the process we would soon realize that there is more to making a garden than just pulling out weeds. As we came to appreciate the cycle of the seasons, the alternation of sunshine and rain, and so on, we might come to think of gardening as the kind of activity that life is all about. We should then see *in our work* an indication of a creative process which extends throughout the universe. Gardening then becomes our symbol for what gives meaning to life. In Tillich's terms, the symbol "participates" in the power of what is symbolized so that we gain insight into the nature of this power. We clarify our situation, not simply by observing it dispassionately, but by becoming actively involved in one way of living in the world.[27]

Meanwhile, across the fence, our neighbors are following up the jungle story in relation to their plot. As space allows, they develop a nature trail, teaching their children to distinguish among the many kinds of wild grasses. They too are active in the way that they "let things be," so that they similarly are not disinterested. (We shall not be pleased, however, since their "weeds" will spread to our garden.) As they grow old and listen to other stories, they begin to meditate on the Way ("the Tao") which cannot be named. They too have a vision of the interplay of forces in life and act on their understanding of these.[28]

Now according to both stories we are participants acting to transform our respective plots of land. At the outset the flowers or grasses may become symbols in our thinking, not as "indicators" of some hidden presence behind the scenes, but as "representational" images in our visions of what our land may become.[29] Let us call them *transfiguring symbols*, as contrasted with *indicative symbols*, since by concentrating on the former we transform perception of what is an ambiguous situation into a clear picture of its future development. We make appreciation of the symbolic uses of language in religion more difficult than need be, if we stress indicative symbols to the neglect of transfiguring ones. If persuading someone to see the wisdom of a religious way of life is like sharing a joke,[30] what we need are not pointers to what is always hidden but ways of transforming the other's vision of what is already potentially present.

Of course, some among us may be more visionary than others. They may see fully what to us are barely possibilities. If they persuade us to join in their activities, we may come to see what they have discerned all along, such as a garden in a plot of weeds. Or we may share their sense of the possibilities, but reject their vision of it. To take a contemporary example, suppose their proposal is to turn the plot into a parking lot.[31] Then we may actively work to ensure that their dreams do not come true. In any case, we shall need transfiguring symbols, if we are to tell a convincing counter-story and win them over to our point of view.

Notice that our disagreement now is not over contradictory picture preferences in any purely subjective sense. Our disagreement is over policies based on conflicting visions of what is an ambiguous setting for present and future action. In this connection it may be relevant to study the history of the place and establish who has authority to impose a view of possible developments on others. At issue is a judgment concerning developments in which all are directly involved. Whose is the lesser vision and whose ambition should be supported are crucial questions. If, as I argue in Chapter Ten, truth most often is realized between stories, so that the ability to "pass over" from one viewpoint to the next is essential to sound judgment in religion, then it is vital that we understand the nature of the symbols used in our stories.[32] Through them our future takes shape.

As Gestalt psychologists remind us, talk of parts only makes sense against the background of assumptions concerning the nature of the whole. Thus before we debate whether there is an invisible agent "behind" the universe, we have to ask whether it makes sense to see the universe as a kind of screen. If the gardening symbol makes sense to us, must we not say that screen-talk enshrines far too static a conception of the universe? The reality of which we are parts is a whole nexus of actualities and possibilities such that, in realizing some, we exclude others. We may be deluded and see possibilities that are not present. But arguments on this score cannot be settled simply by reference to personal feelings. At stake are our relations with others and the principles and policies by which we reach some agreement concerning our common future. To this end we need the dynamic thrust that symbols give to religious thinking, in order to evoke the kind of faith that makes our dreams come true.

With these remarks our discussion of symbols and meaning in life takes up the theses developed in Chapter One. There we observed that the dynamics of religion is due to the interplay of tradition and hope. Here we have added that the juxtaposition of symbols of the future is what gives content to patterns of faith. In this connection it is noteworthy that even authors like Tillich and Ricoeur, who acknowledge changes in our conceptions of ourselves and our environment, tend to assume that somehow "the sacred" remains the same. If meaning is the outcome of a "cosmic discourse," the divine side of their conversation still tends to have but a single theme. If the discourse literally takes ages, this is due to the density of the other partner in the conversation, "man." He is why symbols are so opaque. Essentially, the cosmic message does not change.

I think rather that religious symbols are open-ended in order to allow for our contributions to the "conversation." Where moral policies and ultimate visions are in question, rather than technical formulae and scientific theories, we need room for improvisation and the development of personal perspectives. If we could recapture the spirit in which doctrines were formulated as "symbols of faith," and myths were danced out as dramas of sacred power,[33] we might acknowledge more readily than we do the positive value of myths and doctrines in the history of religions.

When the mood in religious life is mainly one of expectation, the focus in religious thinking is on "indicative" symbols. Transfiguring symbols by contrast suggest harmony, glory, rest, fulfillment. But the contrast is not absolute. For instance, a Buddha image in the context of meditative devotion *(puja)* may be used to transform our vision of life in this suffering world. But in time certain Buddhists, anticipating the "end" of history, may use this same image to indicate confidence in the coming of the future Buddha. Or a garden may symbolize both the permanent structure of the universe, for those who see it so, and the future setting in which we may find perfect peace.[34] Thus symbols may be used in both ways at once. Moreover, to a master of mystical vision talk of hope suggests a sense of separation that the master does not share. But, for others on the way, hopeful indicators may be all that they have.[35] Insofar as the masters shape the traditions, their transfiguring symbols are basic to all religious thinking.

With regard to mystical awareness especially, the talk in religion is of seeing clearly what we ordinarily look at rather differently.[36] Supposedly the seer sees things as they "really are." Or no "thing" is seen and all sense of the gap between seer and seen dissolves. Then seeing itself may become the transfiguring symbol. In this context, "seeing things as they really are" is not so much a factual statement as an affirmation of what is ultimately important. If our quest is only for permanent peace then, in order to realize our ends, we may focus on what is constant in our awareness and discount what is ephemeral. To support our judgment we may then argue that only what is permanent is "real," while what is transitory is illusory. But readers should not be misled into taking this to be a literal description of the everyday world. It invokes a superimposed vision of transcendence, a context which was readily recognized in classical debates on these topics.

When our concerns are ultimate and our language is about the limits of the human condition, shifting interests shape our choice of images just as much as at other times.[37] Our need to adjust our thinking is here as important as ever. The vitality of the major world religions is shown by their capacity for adjustment. What makes for fluidity in religious thinking at its best (which is what we are now considering) is that religion involves our creative energies, not just our instinct for survival. "Demythologizers" and "dehellenizers" have made this point when insisting that personal decisions and doctrinal reformulations are mandatory in religion.[38] They remind us that we do not have to mean what the ancients meant by talk of the sacred, in order to aspire, as they did, to the good life. Their conceptions of the ideal need not be ours. Indeed I contend that they should not be, if our faith is as vital as theirs. The relevant point for us is not their substantive conception of transcendence, in terms of gods or sacred cities, for example, but the process of realizing the higher order issues which pervade our daily business, without always being mentioned in ordinary conversation.[39]

Religious thinking is stimulated particularly when previous answers to ultimate questions become confusing. Confusion results from conflicts of loyalty between groups or over the demands of multiple roles for individuals, or for other reasons. A variety of symbols may express our sense of situation in the world. Then our problem will be to integrate these into some coherent pattern, such as we shall consider in the next chapter. Here I want to stress that, if the relevant symbols are of what we would become, rather than of what we have been, then they are likely to be the antithesis of those which characterize current circumstances. Thus in times of social upheaval we, like Augustine, shall focus on symbols of stability. In times of stagnation we are more likely to be moved by whatever upsets our equilibrium. In either case, our transcendent reference will not simply reinforce the cosmic status quo. Rather it will promote that vision on which we build our hopes, as we strive to leave behind us the ambiguities of our present life. In this connection we do well to remember that, among so-called primitive people, creator gods are seen to be not only preservers. They are also destroyers.

According to our definition, what we "see" in religion is primarily our "way" in life, including some vision of our own identity and the integrity with which we live this way. Religious perception includes perception of an identity consistent with the end in view. If the perceiver is a member of a tribe, for example, then his sense of self will almost certainly be linked inextricably with his perception of his tribe's future. If he is a member of a guild, his guild role will predominate, and so on.[40] Changes of identity from tribe to guild will reflect and be reflected in changes in thinking of the way. In the following chapters we shall consider the symbolic patterns of such thinking and the principles governing their transformations.

In this chapter I have insisted on the importance of symbols for traditional patterns of life and thought. I have stressed their transfiguring impact on our perception of everyday matters. I have suggested that visions of meaning and purpose in life come not necessarily by looking "away" from the world but by putting in perspective our present situations and roles. Here I have considered how symbols are developed. In the next chapter we must examine the relative importance of particular symbols, however developed, and those patterns which seem most apt to express our sense of continuity through change in religion.

CHAPTER THREE

Central Symbols and Patterns of Faith

OUR TASK in these opening chapters is to provide some way of characterizing the continuity through change which typifies the dynamics of religion. So far we have defined religions as ways of life. In particular, they are ways directed toward the realization of transcendent ends. Their elements of meaning are symbols, which are used to indicate our sense of direction or transfigure our sense of place. In this chapter I shall begin to propose a particular model for conceptualizing patterns of symbols, based on a contrast between central and auxiliary symbols. In the following chapter, I shall say more about the contexts in ways of life and stories of faith, in which such patterns occur. Throughout, I shall use the phenomenon of centering as a key to questions of identity through change.

The patterns found among religious symbol systems have recently been studied in a number of related ways. Among biblical scholars and anthropologists the natural setting of basic symbols is, as we have already noted, often thought to be a myth or a combination of myths and rituals.[1] Related to this emphasis on myth is the developing interest among theologians in the category of story—whether biography, autobiography, or current fiction.[2] Shifts in the significance of symbols are typically expressed in the stories that we tell of our lives, as in Sam Keen's account of his spiritual journey from Tennessee, in which Jesus' story begins to be subordinated to recollections of his relations with his own father.[3] Among philosophers of religion, especially those influenced by Max Black and Thomas Kuhn, the talk is rather of models or paradigms.[4] Throughout there is a growing realization that symbols belong in individual and communal contexts which have to be appreciated as wholes.[5] But there is as yet little made, even among structuralists, of the fact that, within these contexts, some symbols are more important than others, and some features of religious thought survive cultural transformations, while others do not.

What we find when we look into the history of religions is that a nucleus of images, such as that of God as Father and the Buddha as Teacher, is developed and retained at the center of a tradition, while other ideas and images are treated as marginal and expendable. In Chapter Eight we shall find the same conception of centers and margins in accounts of individual conversions. Related to this conception is the fact that some metaphors are regarded as basic or "radical" while others are not.[6] *Although religious language may be generally symbolic, therefore, we cannot conclude that in religion all symbols are equally significant.* There are symbols and symbols and, if we would understand the phenomenon of identity through change in patterns of religious thinking, we must develop our ability to notice which among our symbols are really important.

In what follows I propose to distinguish between primary and secondary symbols, when I wish to emphasize differences in their importance for the dynamics of religion. *In my usage a primary symbol is one which is central to the development of a particular religious tradition.* It is constitutive of the distinctive character of that tradition and is not lightly given up by believers or followers of that particular way of life. For example, in Christianity images of God as Father, Lord, Creator, Judge, Covenant Partner, and Redeemer are central. They recur from the first century of the Christian era to the present. Concepts of redemption, for instance, may change as ideas of a ransom to the devil are replaced by stories of forgiveness and reconciliation.[7] But anyone who thinks of God as the Creator but not Redeemer, or Redeemer but not Creator, is rightly said not to be thinking of God in a Christian way.[8] Similarly, in Buddhism, images of enlightenment remain central, while particular conceptions of how we may achieve enlightenment vary from century to century and country to country. In all major traditions, we may discern a nucleus of primary symbols in the collections of myths and rituals which constitute the first line of truth found in their scriptures or oral traditions. Even in such a secular movement as Marxism, we find in the writings of the young Marx images of freedom and alienation which are seminal for subsequent Marxist-Leninist and related strands of Communist thinking.[9]

A symbol such as fatherhood may be primary for one strand of a tradition and secondary for another. And a secondary symbol, such as that of the Messiah in early Judaism, may become primary in the growth of early Christianity. *What determines whether a symbol is primary or secondary is not the symbol as such but its place in the pattern of current life and thought.* There are few symbols, not even those of God as Father and Lord, which are so central to a tradition that we cannot find some thinker in that tradition who treats them as secondary. (Consider, for example, among recent Christians, the "death of God" theologians.). We have therefore to understand the primary or secondary status of symbols according to their places in a pattern, not vice versa. To do this I propose to distinguish also between *central* and *auxiliary* symbols. Those symbols that are more or less central to the formation of a pattern are generally primary. Those that are marginal are generally secondary or tertiary. In almost all traditions, among those symbols which are constantly kept in a primary position, I find one which consistently holds *the* central position. *I shall refer to this hereafter as the central symbol* of a tradition. Within its tradition it is never for long relegated to the margins of faithful thought and practice.

We have always to remember that whatever expresses and focuses the central hope in a tradition is defined by a developing faith. It epitomizes both continuity and change in a way of life. On the one hand, for instance, the negativities of existence are the same for all of us, and their meaning does not change all that much. We all have to confront death, taxes, a tendency to exaggerate our own importance, and so on. But, on the other hand, my death means something different to me at fifteen, at fifty, and at eighty-five. If I am to transcend the negativities of existence, to realize a finer hope and a deeper love, therefore, I need symbols which inspire me to make my own way at each stage of my life.[10] I need symbols which both give me a sense of continuity through change and enable me to adapt to changing circumstances and perceptions along the way.

Here, in the face of so many functionalist and sociologically based theories of religion which stress a yearning for unchanging order, we must also remember that we never have exactly the same faith as our fathers and mothers, or even as our friends.[11] Our symbols in religious thinking reflect this fact. Moreover, "father" and "mother" mean something different for the first child and the fourth, for the child become a parent and the parent become a grandparent. These nuances may seem insignificant to some. But if we fail to take account of such variations of meaning we shall never understand the dynamics of religion.

As we act on the vision communicated through particular images, we redefine our symbols in relation to our developing situation. We might, for example, assume the archetypal image of the Garden of Eden to portray the Paradise awaiting us at the end of a faithful life. But, as experience of gardens became British rather than Babylonian, the nature of our expectations would be modified. We might look less for paths beside reflecting pools and more for an active life of planting and planning. *The meaning of each symbol shifts as we act in terms of it and relate the history of our thinking to new and different frames of reference.* Thus symbols do not simply "participate" in essentially unchanging patterns of meaning. Rather their meanings change for us in a dynamic world. Symbols are part of the interactive process which is life. Not only do we use them to articulate our chosen ways but also we live through them, gaining in wisdom as we do. Seeing through the inadequacies of previously satisfactory symbol systems is one essential aspect of this process.

Some symbols, such as light and truth, seem to be of universal appeal. Others, for instance those derived from the habits of animals and fish in particular regions, seem to be of purely local significance.[12] But most are derived from roles and relationships, such as that of parent-child, whose meanings change with the culture. Thus the nucleic structure of a pattern of faith may remain constant and its set of primary symbols may recur in traditional patterns of thought. But the meanings conveyed through these forms will not invariably be the same.

The fact that shifts occur in our symbolism should be understood positively rather than negatively. For instance, the fact that "lord" could mean arbitrary tyrant, birthright proprietor, or revered master is part of what made it possible for worshipers in theistic traditions to turn from hating God to loving God. The range of possible variations of any given symbol is important to the vitality of those who live in terms of it. A tribe that is wedded to images of itself based on hunting, for example, may be much less able to make a forced transition into industrialized society than a tribe building on military metaphors. The organizational lines of the latter need not be disrupted by a change, say, from thinking of a war against pestilence to thinking of a war against poverty. The ability to rethink what it means to gain victory in war, and to share their new vision, would be a real test of and challenge to the faith of a tribe's "spiritual" leaders.

Until recently theologians have tended to assume that, although the world changes, God does not. Similarly Indian philosophers have supposed that what the rishis "see"—as contrasted with our illusions about the world—is always essentially the same. Consequently, in religious thought we have often acted as if at least one part of our frame of reference has been fixed. But even if that were the case, our theory of symbols requires us to recognize that the *meaning* of God or Brahman or Buddha for us is essentially variable. Consequently, when we speak of continuity in our patterns of symbols and of sharing the faith of our fathers, we must always be aware of the inherent fluidity of these patterns.

At any given time in religious history what counts as primary for a particular tradition may not be exactly what counted as primary a few generations earlier. What seemed weighty for Buddhists in Asoka's time, for example, would scarcely give us the measure of Mahayana Buddhism as it later flourished in the Indian northwest.[13] How John saw the Christ in relation to Caesar would certainly not lead us to deduce what we read in

Eusebius of Caesarea two centuries later. As the images of monks and emperors change for better or worse so their suitability for expressing religious truth also changes. Religious thinkers, particularly teachers and preachers, consciously or unconsciously reshape their thinking to take account of such changes. And to the extent that "dharmologists" and theologians conduct second-order seminars on such teaching and preaching, their critical reflections follow suit. This is not simply, as Luckmann for instance suggests, because of a need to meet the demands of the "consumers."[14] It is an expression of the fact that in all living traditions there is a range of options. There are no hard and fast sets of symbols alone suitable for articulating the spirit in which realization and self-fulfillment may be found.

Since units of meaning are typically not isolated symbols, but stories or segments of stories focusing on one or more symbols, we find in most affirmations of faith a mixture of primary, secondary, and even tertiary symbols. We cannot rule out the presence of marginal symbols in such contexts. But the main subject will be found in the thinking coordinated by the juxtaposition of primary symbols. Given these conceptions, *my thesis is that the identity of particular traditions may best be discerned in their selection of particular sets of primary symbols at their core, with one of these, the central symbol, providing the identifying reference for each way of life and pattern of faith.* Images of Creator, Lord, and Covenant, for instance, may be said to be primary throughout the history of Israel's faith, with the central focus on the Covenant or Law (Torah). For some "Creator" may be relatively marginal and "Wisdom" more central. But in patterns of faith typical in this tradition such terms as these will appear more regularly than, for example, "the Divine Man" or "the Heavenly Bridegroom."

We can now restate the theses of our first two chapters with reference to the function of the central symbol. *A central symbol is that in a tradition which enables its exponents to organize their perceptions and express their vision of their way in life toward the realization of some transcendent end.* As their identifying reference it is typically that which determines the relevance and relative importance of other symbols. It indicates the final court of appeal for judgments on new experiences in life. *The central symbol provides the nucleus around which other symbols are clustered to develop a particu-*

lar pattern of faith. The central symbol is what makes the master story of a given tradition a common story for all its diverse practitioners, despite their differing versions of it and personal developments of faith within the tradition. *The interactions between this symbol and the changing roster of primary and secondary symbols are what define the meaning of being Christian or Buddhist or whatever at a given moment in history.* The transformations which occur in the patterns made by the juxtapositions of different symbols around the central symbol are what characterize the dynamic developments in religion. Changing one's set of primary symbols about the central reference point amounts to a reformation. Changing one's central symbol in the pattern of one's faith amounts to radical conversion. These are the theses which we shall be "unpacking" for much of the rest of this book.

Examples of central symbols in my usage are Jesus the Christ, Gautama the Buddha, the Torah in Judaism, the Qur'an in Islam, the Veda in India, the Sage in China, Socrates the Lover of Wisdom, and Mao the True Comrade. I am less sure of some of these than others and, if my general thesis be accepted, leave to the members of each tradition the decision as to what in fact is central for them. Notice though that, whether the reference is to a person or to a set of rules or verses, in every instance what is mentioned is a concrete entity or set of entities available to public scrutiny. *The focal point of each tradition is an object observable by both faithful and faithless.* [15] What engages the emotions, concentrates attention, and invites reflection is not initially some esoteric entity whose very existence may be called in question. This public availability is important since, as we shall see when we consider the question of truth in religion, one role of the primary symbols, especially the central symbol, is to serve as an integrating agent in our estimates of the relative importance of all levels of perception. Fancy may embroider the stories of the child Jesus or the infant Gautama, of the revelations to Muhammad, or the reverence shown to Confucius. Chairman Mao may be said to have swum incredible distances when well on in years. Lao-tzu may be said to have left this earth in a manner reminiscent of Elijah. But at the core of each tradition is an actual human figure or text to which we may turn when asking what in this world affords us the possibility of a vision of something better. To serve as "elevating keys" between levels of awareness central symbols must at some point connect our everyday religious encounters with the brute facts of existence.[16]

A set of legal terms of relationship, of hymns of celebration, or anecdotes about exemplary living, becomes a central symbol, or the matrix for the development of a central symbol, when it becomes the means whereby those of the same faith realize something of their transcendent end. For example, if the goal be final freedom *(moksha)* then the verses of the Veda, especially those concerning the Atman or Self, must be found by devotees of Shiva and Vishnu to open up vistas of liberation when they are recited or used as foci for meditation. If Gautama is declared to be the Enlightened One then those who take refuge in him must have, in his presence, some sense of entry into Nirvana or feeling of Enlightenment.[17] If Jesus is confessed to be the Christ then those who follow him must have through his presence—whether physically in Galilee or spiritually through what are given as his words in the Gospels—some assurance that the Kingdom of God is at hand.[18]

Whether the goal be power in this world, recollection of wisdom lost in a previous world, or transport into fields of bliss in the next, *the sense of being on the way to its realization is intrinsic to the experience of the central symbol among the faithful.* At the same time those who disagree with the faithful have in common with them some experience of that which has such symbolic import in the traditions. *The centering points in religious thinking are not the end-states as such*—Nirvana, life as an Immortal, or whatever. *Nor are they the powers which epitomize those states or our means of achieving them—God, Brahman, "Virtue" (Te) and the like.* (In this we find a major difference between religious thinking and theology.) The central symbol is the occasion either for following the traditional way or departing from it. It is not an optional extra in the repertoire of either believers or unbelievers. Believers know that others deny what they see in or through this symbol; and unbelievers know that others consider them to be missing something of moment when they treat as incidental the symbols of faith cherished by those others.

Because they are symbols of transcendence, there is an element of indeterminacy in all the central symbols. This allows room for vital growth and diversification within the traditions. In actual experience the central symbols are isolated only in thought. Changes in their significance come slowly. But in principle it is possible, for instance, to imagine an Ethiopian Christ, a Latin Christ, a Hindu Christ, a Chinese Christ, and a Nordic Christ. When the same set of Gospel stories is juxtaposed with different cultural expectations of whatever fulfills life in this world, it is possible to derive a great range of experiences of transcendent joy.[19] That which is seen on the religious level through the story of Jesus is his identity as the Christ. With this perception comes assurance that the Christ stories of Judaism and early Christianity have some basis in reality. But how the impact of Christ on the life of his followers is to be described depends upon further elaboration of their faith. That this is the way is something of which they become convinced through seeing not just Jesus the man but Jesus the Christ. What this way means for them is something that they then only begin to understand.

The identification made by means of central symbols is in my view not so much that of holy persons or books but of a religious way of life. It involves discovery of oneself as well as of the Christ, the Buddha, or the Law. Such a discovery may be more a matter of gradual realization within the tradition of one's ancestors. Or it may come as a momentous and shattering experience. (We shall refer later to William James's comments on the difference).[20] But in either case it would be a mistake to single out the awesome feelings often associated with such an existential revelation as *the* distinctively religious feature of the occasion or to imagine that the perceiver in such situations remains untouched by or uninvolved in what is perceived.[21] If we describe such an experience as an encounter with "the sacred" or what is holy, we must also add that such an encounter has moral consequences for the believer which may be much more germane to the question of his or her continuing on "the way."[22] More vital than any such set of ideas is the spirit in which we approach the way, following those figures whom we associate with its central symbol. This point should become clearer when we consider the strengths of character or "virtues" identified with following the way (in Chapter Six).

An example of the inherent vagueness of a central symbol, even at the beginning of a tradition, is the figure of the Christ in the Pauline literature. The major incidents of the Gospel stories and a few sayings from the Lord are important to the message in the Epistles. But the significance of the Christ is presented rather by the juxtaposition of this figure with the primary symbols of Rabbinic Judaism and the Hellenistic milieu in which Paul preached. In particular we should note how Paul's conception of the Christ is shaped by his understanding of the Torah. His faith is dynamic and his thought dialectical in that he does not simply reiterate what he was taught about Jesus while in Damascus. Rather he modifies his expectations of Primal Man and the Messiah, in the light of the Jesus story, and pivots his interpretation of the Law around a new "eschatological timetable." The figure of Jesus takes on meanings previously associated with the Torah in Judaism and images of Wisdom and Power in the Hellenistic world, even though the manner of his death would seem to render him a religious outcast.[23]

At the same time, Paul's understanding of his Jewishness is radically refocused through his identification with the Christ. The Torah remains a primary symbol for him. But it is no longer the central one and it is no longer simply identified with the Mosaic code. The religious ideal of the Torah remains constitutive of his conception of life in Christ, even as it is transformed by a new understanding of the Way of Israel as the Way of Resurrection.[24] Pauline thought proceeds on the basis of the central Christian faith expressed in terms of such images as the Body, the Spirit and Justifying Grace.

If for the moment we accept the academic contrast between the Jesus of History and the Christ of Faith, we may say that Jesus is known to many as an historical figure, without being acknowledged by all to be the Christ. Moreover, what it means to call him the Christ has to be understood in terms of such other symbols as God as Father, the Spirit as Life-Giver and the Torah as the Will of God for Israel. Similarly, to say that Confucius is the Sage, or the Great Master Teacher, has to be understood in terms of the legendary Chinese dukes and emperors portrayed in the Book of History, according to the sense of family harmony in the Book of Rites, expressing the rhythms of Tao adumbrated in the Book of Changes, and so forth. Reverting to Ricoeur's conception of double intentionality, we may say that the second intentionality depends upon a shared sense of the way signified by the symbols clustered about the central one. *No central symbol can be lifted out of its context of other primary and related secondary symbols, and understood religiously, without some such network of wider meanings.* We do not make a religiously identifying reference to a "way" simply by pointing to the historical figure of Jesus or Confucius or Moses or Muhammad. For us to be able to point to the observable person is a necessary but not sufficient indication of the Christ, the Sage, or the Prophet.

We do not have to commit ourselves to a particular tradition in order to be able to appreciate its symbol system. But in order to understand its symbolic significance we do have to see things from the perspective of the faithful. A George Foot Moore, for example, may have understood Rabbinic Judaism better than many a devoted Jew. But in order to do so he had to enter into the spirit of the rabbis' love of Talmud and Torah. It was not enough just to study histories of rabbinic disputes in Babylon and Jerusalem. He had to convert his mind, if not his "heart," to their sense of being Israel as long as he wished to present Judaism to us as a religious tradition.[25] In my terms he did this by developing a feeling for what was central and what was marginal in the welter of material available to him. His principle of relevance would have to be his sensitivity to the centrality of Torah in Jewish life and thought. Similarly, religious rather than historical criticism of his work would have to be expressed on the symbolic level of perception, that is, of the Torah as the Will of God for Israel.

As we remarked in the last chapter, when consensus is strong within a community, the central reality articulated in terms of primary symbols is not questioned. It may be questionable, but in general no one thinks to question it, any more than scientists question their conceptions of order in the universe.[26] Thus Jesus is seen not *as* the Christ but *to be* the Christ. Gautama is seen not *as* the Buddha but *to be* the Buddha. The Torah *is* God's Will for us, and so on. In Islamic thought with respect to the Law, as in Christian thought with respect to the Logos, this kind of identification required theological resolution of the difficulties that resulted from seeming to associate anything creaturely with the full power of the Creator. To function as a central symbol the composite figure Jesus Christ or the Qur'an/Word of Allah had to be grounded in contemporary, historical experience. But because its efficacy is tied to the realization of the transcendent end, the meaning of such a central symbol could not be overly circumscribed by too close an identification with particular historical conditions. When such identifications occurred their religious significance had to be restricted. Thus, for example, Jesus' pacifism was said to apply only to his dealings with the Romans before his death.

In the history of religious thinking, again to use Ricoeur's terms, the "opacity" and "depth" of a central symbol are protected by gradual distancing from its earliest associations. Early Jewish Christian interpretations of the Christ give way to Hellenistic perceptions of the Lord. The Vedic hymns of the ancient seers are transposed by the addition of the brahmanic Upanishads, and so on. In classical times what generally happened was that the master story of a central symbol took on the aura of sacred truth. As such it came to be ritually differentiated from everyday, "profane" existence.[27] It became insulated from the vicissitudes of secular history. But then it required new points of contact with everyday life through the introduction of new secondary symbols. Often these were derived from the lives of saints and stories of their original experience of the major tradition. Through the classic rituals at centers of worship, the significance of the central symbols would be maintained as the identifying core of the tradition. Thus to Mecca every Muslim would come if he could and from Mecca the pilgrim *(hajji)* would take a renewed fervor for the Will of Allah. But as the journey changed from being one from Medina to Mecca to being one from, say, Jakarta to Mecca the significance of the journey would change. Then the possibility of a different central focus and a new identity would begin to emerge.

While the core of a tradition remains unquestioned, therefore, its meaning as articulated by reference to the central symbol is constantly changing. Our clues to these changes are the primary symbols, and the shifts among symbols from primary to secondary status, as new primary symbols are preferred. For example with regard to sacrifice, even when temples and daily sacrifices remain part of a contemporary way of life, their significance changes as other techniques of worship begin to be preferred. Before the destruction of the temple in Jerusalem, for instance, the synagogues were beginning to set the stage for the emergence of Christianity and Judaism as we know them. Even within the precincts of temples in India gurus guide their followers into adjacent ashrams, in which new expressions of devotion come to the fore. Thus temples might remain as social centers and their rituals satisfy the need to celebrate a birth or mourn a death. But their relationship to the realization of a transcendent end becomes increasingly problematical. As the original chants and taboos enshrined in the temple routines become marginal, a process of redefinition and religious transformation occurs which may be accelerated by the destruction of the temples. But the tradition will survive and flourish in other forms, because already its central symbol has become detached from too close an identification with these particular secondary practices. It becomes possible to debate, *within* a tradition, whether or not these particular practices express true faith.

The conception of meaning in religion which I am developing is inspired in part by Wittgenstein's "rope" metaphor for continuities and discontinuities in semantics.[28] Just as a rope may be a single entity comprised of many strands, no one of which runs its entire length, so *a traditional faith identified by reference to a central symbol is not definable in terms of any one set of auxiliary symbols.* At any given time we may talk of a pattern of faith which is seen in a particular concentration of symbols, some of which entered into previous patterns and some of which will enter into subsequent patterns. Or, to invoke another Wittgensteinian metaphor, that of family resemblances, between one version of a master story and another we may discern distinct similarities, without ever seeing exactly the same features in every member. To be telling the same story we do not have to be repeating the same points every time. To be expressing the same faith we do not have to mean, in our use of symbols and terms, exactly what everyone else has meant or will mean. As we have already remarked, even when the same symbolic clusters recur, what they mean from one generation to the next is different. And where they change, they may all be legitimately regarded as affirmations of the same faith. In living processes, identity is not uniformity.

Even when traditions have established canons of scriptures, writings which set the standards for all subsequent expressions of faith, the variety of patterns within them gives rise to legitimately different stories focused on their central symbols. We shall consider this fact more fully, with reference to the Christian tradition, or family of traditions, in Chapter Six. For the present what I want to stress is that, although the appearance of the same central symbol throughout a tradition provides us with an identifying reference for that way of life, it does not follow that the meaning of the faith expressed in that tradition is the same throughout its history. Indeed, I should argue that those who want to keep it exactly the same have in fact *lost* their faith. They are no longer able to express it in new but authentic forms, as did those who established their tradition.

The model which I propose for thinking about changing patterns in religion is that of a nucleus of primary symbols clustered about a traditional central symbol and interacting with changing cultural patterns in society at large. Over a period of time some of the primary symbols are replaced and new secondary symbols are incorporated into the faith. The symbols are derived from anecdotes, incidents and major figures in the culture and contribute in turn to the vitality and development of the culture (for example, Calvinism in Europe and Tokugawa religion in Japan).[29] Preachers and teachers of a way of life exercise their ingenuity and express the depth of their faith by retelling the old stories in ever new and engaging ways. The result is an oral or written tradition of exemplary biographical, legal, and moral tales which are selected for their symbolic significance in the tradition. Although they reflect the cultures from which they are drawn, it does not follow that their incorporation into the tradition is antireligious. Nor is their thrust necessarily to reinforce the status quo. Nathan's parable to David, to cite a famous example, used prevailing patterns of behavior and principles of common justice to establish a moral and religious point. It certainly did not endorse the image of an Oriental despot.[30] *The whole cycle of stories and symbols developed in the history of a tradition is what provides the context for religious meaning. It is the network of relationships among stories and symbols that gives content to a particular faith.* We may illustrate a pattern of faith by reference to Figure 1.

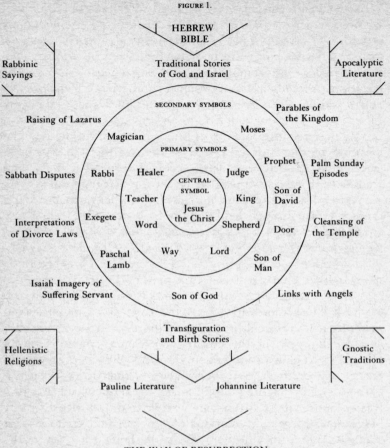

FIGURE 1.

HEBREW BIBLE

Rabbinic Sayings

Traditional Stories of God and Israel

Apocalyptic Literature

SECONDARY SYMBOLS

Raising of Lazarus

Parables of the Kingdom

Magician

Moses

PRIMARY SYMBOLS

Sabbath Disputes — Rabbi — Healer — Judge — Prophet — Palm Sunday Episodes

Teacher — CENTRAL SYMBOL — King — Son of David

Exegete — Word — Jesus the Christ — Shepherd — Door — Cleansing of the Temple

Interpretations of Divorce Laws

Paschal Lamb — Way — Lord — Son of Man

Isaiah Imagery of Suffering Servant

Son of God

Links with Angels

Transfiguration and Birth Stories

Hellenistic Religions

Gnostic Traditions

Pauline Literature   Johannine Literature

THE WAY OF RESURRECTION

When a central symbol is not a human figure, but a paradigmatic action or code, such as the Vedic sacrifice or Mosaic Law, then its elaboration is appropriately different. A clue to the kind of faith expressed is the role played by the religious leaders in the community. A sacrificial system naturally emphasizes priestly concerns, whereas a legal system becomes the responsibility of prophets, rabbis and ulama. The figures of Moses and Muhammad, for example, are both like and unlike Jesus in ways that are consonant with the fact that the first two are intimately related to promulgations of God's laws. They warn of judgment on those who disobey God, while the Christ is more directly concerned with the coming of God's Kingdom and the call to repentance. Yet these examples remind us that the roles may be interwoven in the lives of prophet-priests and priest-kings. Obedience to God's Will is still a mark of those who enter his Kingdom, which includes on its calendar a Day of Judgment.

The contrasts between patterns reflect differences of emphasis rather than irreconcilable oppositions. But these can lead to opposed perspectives, for instance concerning idols, which form the background to the religious dimension of subsequent conflicts, as between Muslims and Hindus in India or Protestants and Catholics in Europe. These differences remind us, incidentally, that the symbolic significance of a particular role or ritual, such as prophet or prayer, need not always be the same, even though these same types are used to express more than one pattern of faith. Similarities and differences among traditions may be brought out by a comparison of the inner core of different patterns of faith as, for example, in Figure 2.

Where the central symbol suggests that the way to realization of the end is through imitation of a particular figure, then the most suggestive auxiliary symbols tend to be those portraying complementary roles. Where the pattern is one of performance then the appropriate elaboration is through standard behavior, described in stories of obedience and disobedience, rules and promises, rewards and punishments. If the emphasis is on being rather than doing, as in stories of self-realization, then we may look for portrayals of ideal stages and characteristics, as in Hermann Hesse's *Siddhartha*. Depending upon the dynamics of a particular faith, as expressed by the interactions among its primary symbols, its traditional stories may highlight individual histories or de-emphasize personal traits, or they may dwell on a collective achievement, such as the Exodus or the Long March. In each case, emotions will be engaged and patterns of thought fostered which promote the path toward the particular end in view. Obedience to the Will of God, for example, is scarcely likely to be featured in stories of those who regard the gods as even more bound to the wheel of pleasure and pain than we are.

FIGURE 2.

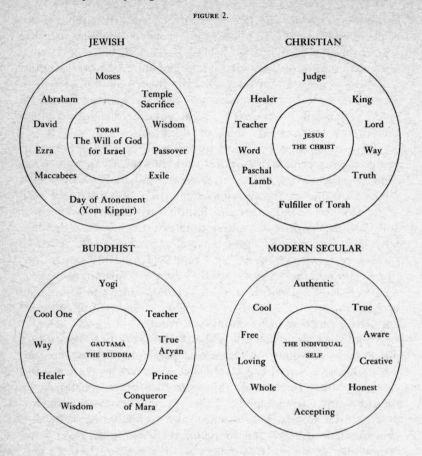

JEWISH

Moses
Abraham
Temple Sacrifice
David
Wisdom
TORAH
The Will of God
for Israel
Ezra
Passover
Maccabees
Exile
Day of Atonement
(Yom Kippur)

CHRISTIAN

Judge
Healer
King
Teacher
Lord
JESUS
THE CHRIST
Word
Way
Paschal
Lamb
Truth
Fulfiller of Torah

BUDDHIST

Yogi
Cool One
Teacher
Way
True
Aryan
GAUTAMA
THE BUDDHA
Healer
Prince
Conqueror
of Mara
Wisdom

MODERN SECULAR

Authentic
Cool
True
Free
Aware
THE INDIVIDUAL
SELF
Loving
Creative
Whole
Honest
Accepting

For them obedience to the gods may lead to worldly gifts in return. But true freedom will transcend the rituals of giving and receiving. *The significance of particular patterns can only be understood by reference to the intentionality of a given way, which is what the stories clustered about the central symbol are especially designed to express.*

When we speak of a pattern of faith we have also to remember that it is typically found in a still wider context, that of the prevailing culture of the people whose faith is in question. *What is "off center" is equally important to our understanding of a tradition at a particular time.* Indeed recent studies of myths, for example, suggest that the key to their interpretation rests on understanding the oppositions in life which myths help us to correlate. As parts of the culture, myths especially have enabled people to cope with the critical experiences of birth, puberty, marriage, and death.[31] In such contexts the paradigm propounded gains significance from the ways in which the associated religious figure faced death and healed the diseases and divisions among the people. If I pay less than the usual amount of attention to such contexts for religious life and thought in this book, it is because I wish to attend rather to patterns of faith in relatively modern times. I am interested primarily in the religious reasons for developing cycles of stories which show some promise of continuing to hold contemporary interest. Also, I have little to add to what already has been better said elsewhere on the social-anthropological aspects of our topic.[32]

The articulation of faith is a cultural act. The expressions used inevitably have overtones conveyed by our familiarity with their other uses, for example, in talk of Christ as Logos or of Dharma as Tao. Since a tradition enshrines cultural styles prevalent in the formative years of a faith, religious patterns of thought can very easily come into conflict with newer ideas. This happened, for instance, when Western Christian orthodoxy continued to use Aristotelian conceptions of motion at a time when European scientists had abandoned them.[33] The result was at least two centuries of theological confusion, during which questions of faith and problems of cultural evolution had to be disentangled. Confronted with such instances, we may be tempted to conclude that the answer for faith must be to "demythologize" and "dehellenize," without allowing any new cultural styles to inform our faith. But, according to our theory of religion, this prescription demands the impossible and rests on a mistake. For a tradition which cannot draw faith from the truth perceived by each new generation of scientists, historians, and other students of culture is dying. It is cutting itself off from one pole of that "cosmic discourse" which, according to Ricoeur, gives us the symbols that are essential to thought. Besides, unthinking faith honors neither God nor man.

Rather than a vain attempt to isolate the nucleus of a tradition from all cultural intrusions, therefore, our task must be to foster the ability to distinguish what is primary from what is secondary and to recognize new possibilities of symbolization in the challenges of contemporary styles of thought. Thus we may conclude that God was rightly thought of as the Prime or Unmoved Mover by Thomas Aquinas. But his intellectual heirs were wrong to retain this image as a primary symbol once it ceased to provide a means of perceiving religious truth. If we abandon the assumption that this conception of God was implicit in Christian thinking from the very beginning, we may become open to different expressions of faith, not because we have lost faith, but because the faith is ours as well as Paul's or Thomas's. There is a right way and wrong way of expressing faith in each cultural milieu. But what is right at one time may well be wrong in another context. Confusion on this point accounts for many misconceptions about the "problem" of relativism in religion.[34] To pursue this line of thought we must look more closely than we have so far at ways of life and stories of faith.

Summing up, I argued first that we must acknowledge in religious thinking a future orientation which requires fresh expressions of faith from each generation. Then I showed how this orientation can be seen in the way symbols are developed in religious traditions. Here I have pointed out the dynamic interplay between past and future found in each pattern of primary symbols. I have proposed a nucleic model for conceptualizing the phenomenon of identity through change, focusing on the respective central symbols in each major tradition. Embedded in slowly changing clusters of primary and secondary symbols, these provide continuous reference points in present experience, even as their meaning shifts with each development in the surrounding culture. Now we must look at the context of these changes in ways of life and stories of faith.

CHAPTER FOUR

Ways and Stories

WHETHER they are primary or secondary, central or auxiliary, symbols are not meaningful in a void. In the last chapter we indicated the kinds of patterns that they form in the dynamics of religion. These patterns change more or less radically through interaction with general cultural trends. Before looking in greater depth at such transformations we shall note in this chapter that these patterns are typically found in and developed through storytelling. I believe that we begin to grasp the spirit of a tradition when we come to know its stories. What happened during the first Passover or first Easter, how Krishna sported with the cowgirls, how Orpheus sang, or why Amaterasu was embarrassed, is the stuff of life among the traditions. We have little reason to suppose that things will be different for religion in the future. Ways of faith are rooted in and fostered by stories.[1]

Consequently, an analysis of faith is not just a study of isolated concepts or abstract ideas. *We cannot simply take terms from one tradition, look for their nearest equivalents in another tradition, and then suppose that by comparing them we have studied religion.* Our units of meaning are not single words or phrases or symbols which can be so readily compared. Indeed they are not even single sentences.[2] Who can know, for instance, what "the bishop is next to the queen" means without some sense of context? Is it chess, perhaps, or the seating arrangement for a state banquet? What determines that a word is a noun or a verb, for example, or that a symbol is primary or secondary is something that cannot be read off without reference to its connections with other units of meaning.[3] In religion these connections are typically found in stories of faith.

The category of "story" is rapidly being overworked in contemporary religious thought. To use it now is to invite the charge of catering to current enthusiasms rather than serious scholarship. But when we need categories applicable to more than one tradition, including some which de-emphasize abstract philosophizing, "story" seems the most helpful one available (better, for instance, than "games").[4] It is the most general and neutral term for whole classes of material found in the traditions ranging from myths, legends, and sagas through histories, biographies, and confessions to sermon illustrations, parables, allegories, and apocalyptic passages concerning the end of the world. It underlines the "narrative quality" of experience and the ways in which we tie together our sense of situation and hope of improvement.[5] It allows for both fact-oriented and fancy-filled accounts of ordinary and extraordinary events in religious life. It reminds us that reality includes possibilities as well as actualities, that truth is stranger than fiction and larger than our laboratory versions of it. It explains why in ancient times the faithful allowed their leaders to talk for so long on hot holy days, why poets became statesmen and kings listened to prophets.[6]

Even in antihistorical traditions stories are used to narrate journeys of the soul. Even in antireligious communities they are used to enliven reports of market trends and quota achievements. We do not have to agree with those who suggest that religion *is* story or theology *is* autobiography in order to appreciate the usefulness of this category. Especially in theology and the philosophy of religion we are not yet so free from arrogance with regard to the "real" meaning of doctrines that we can afford to ignore this clue to meaning in life.[7]

What identifies a narrative as religious is something which we must discuss in this chapter. At the very least we must say that a religious story is of a way from past to present experience which shapes our convictions concerning personal fulfillment in present and future. The past-present and future-present are brought home to us, and expressed by us, in the telling of old and new stories. Small wonder then that we so seldom resist the temptation to tell our own story, even though we are impatient for others to finish theirs. The narratives which link symbols in religiously significant ways have not only a past dimension but also a present focus and future orientation. Archaic traditions may no longer have a vital center from which to develop new story lines. They may have lost the nucleus around which old stories may be reformed. But living traditions include a challenge to new options for all sorts and conditions of men in the continuing master story of their central symbols.

According to my theory the symbol that best concentrates thought and action on its distinctive way toward the realization of some transcendent end becomes central in a particular religious tradition. Following the Christ is the way into the Kingdom of God. Taking refuge in the Buddha is the way to Nirvana. Keeping the Torah is the way to become truly Israel. Emulating Mao is the way to permanent revolution. The sense of direction informing the way is developed through the distinctive stories of the tradition which weave together its primary and secondary symbols into a pattern that is religiously meaningful to the believer. Thus stories of Noah, Abraham, Jacob, and the Covenant are told by and for those of their descendants who refuse to be assimilated by the surrounding community. Thus stories of Jesus' birth and death, of his preaching and healing activities, place him in relation to God and the prophets of Israel in ways which give meaning and hope to the lives of his disciples.[8] Faced with the ambiguity of "the meaning of meaning," when our concern is to express the intentionality of a particular tradition, we do so most easily by recalling its central story line. Told properly this "master story" conveys the spirit in which the tradition is lived.

In time, however, a master story hardens into a stereotyped portrayal of an ideal figure. In order to come alive for new generations it needs to be retold, especially in relation to stories of new secondary figures. Their lives touch the original, while making contact with our own. Where contact is not made, the religious interests and aspirations of a generation may focus on less traditional, even overtly antireligious patterns of faith. To illustrate this process and at the same time show how secondary symbols are developed through stories, I turn now to the biography of Norman Bethune.[9] A legend in his own time, he has become what I call a secondary symbol in the still-forming tradition of Maoism. His story serves to emphasize the fact that we may find religious significance in unconventional contexts. It will also lead us into the following discussion of the distinctive elements of more traditionally religious stories.

From a bare outline of Bethune's experiences we cannot discover all that he meant to those who worked with him. But we can see how, in the tradition centering on Mao, his story is a parable for others. The official version told by the Chinese may not reflect the less edifying incidents in either his life or the "permanent revolution." But where our purpose is to understand the ideal rather than the average practice of a people, the way his story is told is an important clue to their thinking.

Bethune's personal ambition was to become a surgeon. His vocation was transformed, however, by a brush with death from tuberculosis when he was thirty-six. Disillusioned and depressed, he came across a new technique in chest surgery, which saved him from a prolonged period of convalescence in upstate New York. He decided to become a thoracic surgeon himself, so that he could bring this new hope to thousands of others. In the early years of the Great Depression he moved to Montreal in order to work there under one of the leading surgeons of the day.[10]

So far we have a symbolic figure who survives personal tragedy and commits himself to the service of mankind through medicine. The next stage in Bethune's development came when he realized that he could not deal with his patients' medical problems without also attending to their economic conditions. Despite improving techniques, he discovered that for every surgical success there were a dozen new cases of tuberculosis spreading through the homes of his patients. Poorly housed and undernourished, they were reluctant to call a doctor for fear of the costs. Bethune took the lead in devising schemes for national health insurance. A physiological congress in Leningrad gave him the opportunity to see an alternative medical system for himself. He discovered that the Soviets were decades ahead of the Americans in public medicine. However, his memoranda on the subject made little impression on his medical colleagues and the government. Increasingly impatient with words in place of actions, he became not only a Fellow of the Royal College of Surgeons but also "Comrade Beth."[11]

When the Loyalist government came under attack from Franco's forces during the Spanish Civil War, Bethune decided to head the Canadian Medical Unit embarking for Madrid. There he was as impatient as ever with inefficient techniques and inhumane practices. Remembering his own convalescence, he demanded that each patient be treated as an individual and not just a case. He organized mobile blood donor clinics, saving thousands of lives which would otherwise have been lost in transit from the front to headquarters. As Hitler and Mussolini gave Franco the upper hand, while Britain, France, and America refused tangible support to the democratic side, Bethune's sponsors recalled him for a speaking tour of Canada. They hoped that his firsthand account of the situation in Spain would stir up public opinion enough to mobilize the politicians. But, while they were still talking in the West, the militarists struck in the East. The Japanese army invaded the Chinese mainland. Bethune decided that his services were needed there. Sponsored by the China Aid Council in New York, he left Vancouver for Hong Kong on January 2, 1938.

By November 13, 1939, Bethune was dead. But during the preceding months in China he had established a model hospital in the northwest, organized mobile medical units which cut Chinese casualties by seventy-five percent, and written *A Manual of Organization and Technic for Divisional Field Hospitals in Guerrilla War.* He lived long enough to help the ill-trained Chinese to become independent of foreign doctors. While he taught them the best techniques of international medicine, he served as a reminder to the Chinese that they were not alone in their struggle for independence. To Mao Tse-tung and his generals he was both a symbol and a source of vital expertise.

Ordinary militiamen were so inspired by the doctor's presence among them that they adopted "Bethune is here" as a battlecry.

When he was leaving the first model hospital to be built he was greeted with banners which proclaimed:

> Dr. Bethune, our teacher
> Dr. Bethune, our fellow fighter
> Dr. Bethune, our medical adviser
> Dr. Bethune, our doctor
> Dr. Bethune, our friend
> Dr. Bethune, our example
> Dr. Bethune, our comrade.[12]

Here, in the orbit of devotion to Comrade Mao, we have a clear cluster of secondary and tertiary symbols, used to convey what I call the Way of Revolution.

We may wonder how much of such rhetoric was based on sober appraisal of Bethune's achievements. Perhaps one anecdote will suffice to illustrate his impact on others. It is called the Story of the Stone and the Wounded. It begins with the fact that the bottom step was missing from a flight of stairs leading up into a Buddhist temple, which had been converted into a hospital. Leaping the gap, Bethune asked an attendant, "Do you mind jumping?" The other smiled and replied, "Not at all." "And the convalescing patients—do *they* mind jumping?" Bethune asked. The smile vanished. Together doctor and attendant moved a new stone into place. Out of this came a Bethune maxim: "Never leave a stone unturned in caring for the wounded."[13]

Without belaboring the obvious we can readily appreciate how this story communicates the Way of Revolution better than any number of dialectical homilies on the classless society. How Bethune himself saw the situation is shown by one of his last papers concerning the war. In it he asked:

> Is it possible that a few reactionary men, a small class of men, have persuaded a million men to attack and attempt to destroy another million men as poor as they? So that these rich may be richer still? . . . How did they persuade these poor men to come to China? By telling them the truth? . . . No, they told them that this brutal war was "The Destiny of the Race," it was for the "Glory of the Emperor," it was for the "Honor of the State." . . . Money, like an insatiable Moloch, demands its interest, its return, and will stop at nothing, not even the murder of millions to satisfy its greed. Behind

the army stand the militarists. Behind the militarists stand finance capital and the capitalists. Brothers in blood. . . . What do these enemies of the human race look like? Do they wear on their foreheads a sign so that they may be told? . . . No. On the contrary, they are the respectable ones. . . . They are pillars of the state, of the church, of society. . . . In their private lives they are kind and considerate. But . . . threaten a reduction on the profit of their money and they become ruthless as savages, brutal as madmen, remorseless as executioners. . . . Such an organization of human society as permits them to exist must be abolished. *These men make the wounds.*[14]

We shall look at the diary of a Japanese, not a militarist but a doctor like Bethune, in Chapter Nine.

At one point Bethune solicited the help of an Anglican missionary in running a blockade in order to obtain medical supplies. "You say you are here to serve God," he argued. "You want to save men's souls that they may have a future life in heaven. I want to save them for life on earth. Wouldn't you agree that no matter where along the road one of us might take leave of the other, at least the road we are traveling runs in the same direction? At least if you are true to the God you believe in, and I am true to what I believe in." Notice the future orientation in the pattern of argument. When the missionary hesitated on the grounds that she could not take part in war, he added, "I am not asking you to take part in war. I am asking you to do something that will save men's lives." She agreed to go and succeeded in bringing supplies through the enemy lines. When the Japanese destroyed her mission in reprisal, Bethune commented, "If she isn't an angel what does the word mean?"[15] Bethune himself died from septicemia because Chiang Kai-shek refused to allow supplies from America to get through to the Communists, even though at the time they were supposed to be making common cause against the Japanese. What proved to be a fatal wound would, with gloves and disinfectants, have been just a minor scratch during an emergency operation. In effect, Bethune died a martyr to his cause.

Bethune's story is religiously significant, whether or not it is religious. It exemplifies a way of life which enlarges the possibilities for individual and collective fulfillment. It helps to shape priorities with respect to personal choices in ambiguous situations. It includes a vision into which we can enter even if, like the missionary, we hesitate over his politics. Certainly in the Chinese Communist tradition his story is comparable to that of the lives of saints in the classical religions. If we fail to see it in this light, it may be that we are too used to thinking of religion and politics in watertight compartments, when in fact they flow into each other. We are accustomed to reading literary reviews, political commentaries, and church news in different sections of our papers, and to assuming that the religious news is in the church section.[16] We forget that the *Mahabharata* and the *Ramayana*, for instance, still provide both entertainment and moral homilies for artists and swamis in India.

We have to look at the themes, not the conventional images, if we want to appreciate the religious significance of stories. We have sometimes to forget the God-talk and mythical prototypes to discern new patterns of alienation and reconciliation, of creation and redemption, in the ways of our contemporaries. Through much of our culture we have to find religious significance in a collage of impressions rather than in any prearranged canon of texts. Thus among existentialist authors we may find ourselves plunged already into a "fallen" world in which there is little hint of redeeming relationships or transcendent hope.[17] Among orthodox Freudians, by contrast, we may find, in their use of the Oedipus myth, a ready replacement of the Book of Genesis but only the weakest prospect of a successful exodus into a new "promised land." Such sources become parts of contemporary expressions of faith without constituting a whole tradition. In the same way Bethune's story gives us part of a whole which is not yet complete with respect to the final judgment.

If we think of stories in terms of setting, plot, character, and tone or mood, then we may recognize that traditionalistic accounts of religious thinking have tended to assume that there is but one universal setting for all religious stories, the one established by the classical contrast between the sacred and the profane.[18] Caught in profane time, man is portrayed as striving to recreate the sacred order of God or the gods, whose time and space, while transcending ours, is nevertheless linked to ours in ritually acknowledged ways. The otherness of the divine milieu is pictured as man's lost home, whether it be the Paradise from which man was expelled or the highest heavens from which he has fallen.[19] As we have already remarked, in medieval times this otherness was abstractly expressed in terms of eternity and omnipresence and our transcendent end was identified with the Beatific Vision. Now we have to realize that that identification was just as much a result of reductionism in religious thinking —reducing religious significance to purely "spiritual" concerns —as is the reduction of God-talk to Ego-talk, in which the driving force in life is instinctual energy rather than the Holy Spirit. This is one lesson of the demystifying, demythologizing, desacralizing, dehellenizing movements in recent religious thought. They at length have said what Bethune said more succinctly, that the direction pointed by belief in God is toward liberation of God's creatures. To appreciate what this means in our time we may have to free ourselves from unchallenging pictures of man going to heaven. A geography which mentions heaven is not religious for that reason. It all depends on the sense of direction given in our story.

A religious story which sets its ending in an otherworldly context, for example, is religious only because it portrays *this* world as a place in which we cannot find peace. The alternative might be a story in which we are portrayed as having nowhere else to go.[20] Then our only hope for peace might seem to be to withdraw into an inner space opened up to us through drug-induced experiences or yoga.[21] *Whatever the sense of time or place adopted by the storyteller, it becomes religiously significant when it is perceived as something from which we must move or which must be transformed.* To the extent, for example, that Bethune was calling for a new heaven and a new earth his was a religious story.[22] The fact that its setting was secular, and consciously contrasted with a conventional Christian one, is less important than the fact that in that setting Bethune had a sense of direction which promised an end of man's inhumanity to man. His appeal to the missionary, notice, was a religious appeal which was heard on that level even though she did not share his faith.

Any attempt to define religious stories solely in terms of primitive dichotomies between "sacred" and "profane," or their medieval variations, is an example of giving one literary feature priority over the rest in the analysis of a genre. Even then it would be giving preeminence to one kind of setting among others. So-called primitive mythologies, which are worldly, or medieval philosophies, which are otherworldly, are made paradigmatic for *all* religious thinking only if we succumb to what I have called the fallacy of archaism. This is a variant on the genetic fallacy, which assumes that an account of origins or of abstract first principles is of itself sufficient to give the full meaning of all subsequent developments in a tradition.[23] The opposite mistake might be called the modernist fallacy, which tempts us to dismiss all classical patterns as irrelevant to our understanding of present conditions.

What is in fact relevant to a religious criticism of story settings is some appraisal of the dynamics of the situation in which we begin to realize the need for and promise of transcendence. Whether the present situation is perceived to be a chaotic version of the heavenly cosmos, a purgatorial antechamber to some heavenly mansion, or the battleground of the fight to bring heaven on earth, what is significant religiously is that the story of the present is set against the horizon of our expectations, *whatever* that horizon may be. Thus if we can imagine an otherworldly state to be a real possibility for us then it will enter into our religious story. If not it won't. *What is required is that the frame of reference be universal relative to our culture's conception of the universe at any given time.*

As has been well established in discussions of the New Testament, the settings for its stories were not invented by the first evangelists. They simply articulated their faith in the terms which came naturally to them and their audiences. If their message is to speak to us in a differently conceived setting, we may have to rephrase quite radically what that message was.[24] It does not follow that we learn nothing from what they perceived to be the truth of their condition. Obviously the setting an author gives a story determines the range of expectations allowable for his characters and, as we saw with Flew in relation to Wisdom and the garden story, how another resets a story can help to make the characters look more or less ridiculous. Camus' setting for the myth of Sisyphus, for example, hardly invites a call to social revolution. By contrast, Graham Greene in *The Heart of the Matter* allows Scobie an existential choice between Gnostic and Catholic forms of spirituality. What is not a realistic option for him is to bring justice to an African town. But eternal peace *is* a live option, and on this fact hinges the drama of his eventual suicide.

A fully developed religious criticism of stories will indeed comprehend archaic conceptions of the cosmos along with classical ideas of time and eternity and contemporary assumptions about evolution and immortality. But it should offer critiques of spiritualistic, as well as materialistic, kinds of reductionism and appraise fairly both worldly and otherworldly settings for religious stories. It can do so, however, only on the basis of an undogmatic appreciation of the range of settings possible for stories which are religiously significant.

As Stephen Crites has pointed out, stories reflect the tensed quality of temporal existence in a way that is missing from discussions of timeless categories. Also, stories enable us to focus such concerns as love and death.[25] Dramatic decisions may not be the order of our every day. But when we come to visualize what it means for us to live and die, we enter personally into the characters and contexts of other lives in other times. Crites illustrates his thesis by discussing the story of Jacob wrestling with the angel in Genesis 32. To appreciate the religious significance of Jacob's transformation into "Israel" we have to take what may originally have been a folk tale and read it in a wider context. Some legendary ancestor's encounter with a water sprite may then be used to dramatize the tale of Jacob's mounting tension before his reunion with Esau. Now the horizon of meaning reaches all the way back to the beginnings of the cosmos and ahead to the story of Moses and the Promised Land. Thus Genesis 32 becomes part of Israel's master story and Jacob's wrestling one of its symbols, as Bethune's biography has become part of mainland China's master story and his doctoring one of its symbols.

By "nesting" the folk tale in the saga of Israel the biblical narrator suggests an identity of Creator, Wrestler, and tribal deity which underscores the ensuing promise for the future. What comes out of it is a sense of a "way" in relation to God and man which is not that of Esau or the Egyptian pharaohs. It is the story of *Israel*, and we should miss its symbolism if we were to confine our attention to the "original" story taken in isolation. It is the character of Jacob and that of his antagonist which are decisive for the religious significance of this story.

If we were to make any narrative features dominant in religious thinking they would be plot and character rather than setting. *In my view to be religiously complete a story must have a plot which brings its central figures to "salvation" or healing or wholeness. It must communicate some affirmation of identity with integrity, some hope of personal fulfillment or self-realization, which enables its characters to transcend the negativities of existence.* In what sense this may be so we shall consider further in the next two chapters, especially with reference to transcendence and character. But here we shall begin our elaboration of these ideas especially concerning plot.

Whereas detective stories end with the solution to a crime, love stories end tragically, or with living happily ever after, and psychological case histories end (hopefully) with some kind of therapeutic resolution of conflicts,[26] religious stories as a genre must end with some sense of transcendence, if not within the confines of the story then as a result of the storytelling. As we have already noted, hearing the story, the faithful should feel closer to heaven, more loving toward their neighbors, firmer in their commitment to keep the Law, freer from the distractions of their engrossed egos, more inspired to give their lives to party or country, or to whatever the ideal conclusion may be. In short, *typically religious stories are in some sense dramas of redemption.* We may possibly forgo myths of creation, as in some versions of early Buddhism, and leave last judgments open. But we cannot do without talk of finding yourself by losing yourself (or finding the Self by losing yourself), of dying to the "old" man and rising to the new, of leaving the shadows of the cave for the sunshine of transcendent truth. An account of time and place which brings neither into meaningful juxtaposition with our evolving sense of self has lost the relevant "double intentionality" of which Ricoeur speaks. If we adopt Northrop Frye's suggestive use of the four seasons, rather than a linear pattern derived from biblical eschatology, we have still to look for spring, summer, and autumn to complete the religious cycle.[27] A winter's tale alone is not enough to constitute a tradition.

When we analyze particular patterns of action in religious stories we may distinguish among a variety of ways of life such as what I call the Way of Resurrection, the Way of Renunciation, and the Way of Revolution.[28] Which plot informs our understanding of meaning in life depends upon the way we speak of the primary symbols of the faith. Thus Bethune's story fosters the Way of Revolution. Jacob's story may become part of the Way of Resurrection, and so on. The master story in each case is that based on the central symbol of a tradition. Thus, if we follow the Christ, for example, we shall draw inspiration from stories of God's covenants with the Hebrew patriarchs. We shall accept the prophets' insistence that Israel's survival and revival depend upon divine rather than human initiative. And the setting for our thoughts will include apocalyptic expectations of a suprahistorical climax, vindicating the one for whom all hope seemed to be lost in terms of this world's ordinary ambitions.[29] By contrast, among Stoics Socrates may symbolize the Way of Renunciation, forgoing physical survival for the eternal consistency of that wisdom and truth with which he became identified through his career as a teacher. He lives his truth and dies for it in such a way that that part of his life which defines his integrity cannot be destroyed by the manner of his death. Both Jesus and Socrates symbolize the transcendence of life over death and teach victory through suffering, rather than escape from suffering, but according to distinctively different ways.

Once more labels are less important than the general conception of religious courses of action defined by particular symbolic patterns. The identity of each tradition is determined, in my view, by the shared intention to realize, eventually if not immediately, that end-state already realized in the completed master story of the central symbol, such as the vision of the Risen Christ in Heaven, the Buddha in Parinirvana or the Chinese Sage among the Immortals. As we shall see, what that story means to each generation has to be determined by that generation. But *it may be said to express the same faith as it did for preceding generations if the ending intended in each retelling of the master story expresses the way of life associated with the central symbol.* That the faith is the same can only be determined, for reasons to be considered later, with hindsight by the faithful community.[30] Here I would stress that religious faith is a movement whose "trajectory" is plotted by the primary symbols clustered about the central symbol.[31]

Again, *the central symbol provides us with an identifying reference and what is identified is the way, its tradition, and its hope.*

How important the theme of death and new life is to a tradition depends upon its master story. In the same way, how essential God-talk is depends upon the ideal of redemption climaxing the story. For the Way of Resurrection, a transcendent Creator distinct from all creatures is essential. Since they cannot save themselves, according to the drama of redemption, their only hope lies in the power of another. For the Way of Renunciation, by contrast, the life-enhancing power of the spirit must be seen to be immanent in us all. For the Way of Revolution what is sacred is the community to which all else is sacrificed. In order to determine which is our way, or whether we have left the way, it is not enough, however, just to mention the central symbols or chant the approved party slogans. In times of debased verbal currency these may be left unmentioned precisely in order to further the movement. It is the reality intended, not the terminology as such, which decides the identity of a tradition. Of course there can be no intention formed without some use of terms. Religious critics can always point to symbols and stories as indicators of the way in which a given individual or group may be moving. But insofar as the master story is their story also, a story which is still being told, the critic cannot prejudge its outcome. We can characterize the way by reference to the stories. We can be less sure of the actual faith of specific individuals on the way.[32]

On the other hand, changes in terminology and symbolism cannot be completely arbitrary. In the spectrum of stories old and new we must be able to discern some strands of continuity of setting, plot, character, and tone. There must be some comparability among episodes and congruency of events, if the way is to have integrity. Given that the ways in question are redemptive processes, which reflect the conditions of those in need of redemption, there still must be some discernible continuity in the patterns of faith clustered about the central symbol. Granted that, as the Buddhists say, considerable "skill in means" may be used to bring men to enlightenment, the goal is, nevertheless, enlightenment in some sense consistent with what Gautama realized under the Bodhi Tree. Just when a story has been so transformed as to constitute a departure from the faith is something which we shall discuss in a later chapter. Our task now is to understand the kind of complex in which continuity through change is found in religious life and thought.

Some religious stories emphasize character rather than plot. In theological parlance I have been focusing on soteriology (theories of salvation) rather than Christology (theories of the nature of Christ). But anecdotes about Zen masters, for instance, convey something of the quality of enlightenment *(satori)* rather than tell of stirring exploits or seeming reversals of fortune. The *character* of the Buddha, the Prophet, the Christ, may be what the story-teller chooses to emphasize. But even so the central figures are known as those who have completed the paths along which we too might go. Who a leader is cannot be divorced from what he has done or what has happened to him. We listen to a Bethune's words more readily, for instance, knowing something of his deeds. A particular narrative may feature one element more than others, as we remarked above. But the tradition includes all.

We shall look again at the spirit which shines through the lives of central religious figures, when we consider what is involved in talk of transcendence. Already we can acknowledge that these figures provide us with exemplary images of the style of life which may be encountered on the way in question. *The Sage, the Prophet, the Guru are religiously significant for us insofar as they are what we would become.* They are paradigms of the religious possibilities open to us in life. In the dramas of redemption described by theistic, humanistic, naturalistic, and monistic authors, they are our symbols of victory over evil, vindication after rejection, inspiration in moments of doubt. Taken alone they are too remote. But in conjunction with other figures on the way they indicate something of the character needed to win through to the end. Whether we say that plot arises out of character or character is formed by action we see in their collected stories the kind of resolution which may carry us through changing circumstances and ambiguous situations, if we choose to follow them.[33]

Concerning tone I would briefly draw attention to the Hindu distinctions among the ways of contemplation, action, and devotion *(jñana, karma,* and *bhakti marga).* In all traditions with any appreciable history we find some who are cool, contemplative, seemingly dispassionate, pregnant in silence. We find others instigating a flurry of political movements, writing pamphlets, leading marches, training cadres of activists, finding truth in "praxis." And we find still others winning us with their poetry, enchanting us with songs of devotion, drawing us erotically into union with beloved Wisdom, dancing us out of our depressions and into the ecstasy of requited passion. Western preachers have assumed that such ways must be mutually exclusive. Hindus have tended to regard our differences as illusory and all ways at bottom the same. Most traditions have had the wisdom to allow all ways of self-transcendence, recognizing that to banish a Gandhi permanently to an ashram, for instance, would be as futile as trying to banish music from Quaker meetings for worship.[34]

Mood or tone may initially be the most important factor in drawing us one way rather than another. Some of us, like Bethune, are put off by inaction. Others feel crowded by the imperative tone of prophetic calls to mission and threats of impending judgment. The way of meditation has generally been preferred by a select few whose mood is disrupted by chanting and demonstrative crowds. In general the tone for a tradition is set by its central figure. But each of us adds his or her overtones to the ways that we follow. Some may try all paths at different stages of their lives.

Mention of Hindu talk of illusion reminds us, finally, that most stories are fantasies. Whereas monists tend to regard our individual differences as illusory, personalists have tended to assume that what is illusory is any sense of ultimate merging with God. Under the influence of Freud or Feuerbach, we are likely to think that the illusory power is that of repressed sexual energy or the magic of death—now you see me, now you don't—which both separates and unites us as living beings. In religious thought we are only just beginning to regard our imaginative powers positively and to recognize that not all stories are wild fabrications.[35] Especially in the philosophy of religion, positivists since Hume have so ironed out the symbolic thrust of our language that we have constantly to remind ourselves of the truth in the varieties of fiction found in religious traditions. Where the truth lies in religious storytelling is a question to which we shall return in Chapter Ten.

To this point we have asserted that a way of life becomes religious when we superimpose some vision of its end on the scene in which we presently find ourselves. This vision is articulated through symbols grouped to highlight a master story of redemption in one of a number of possible ways. We have seen that the meaning of the story changes for us as new auxiliary symbols are used to bring its message home to us. Its plot, climaxing in the realization of some transcendent end, is crucial to its religious character. Its setting may be far from conventional. But it must reach to the horizon of whatever reality we comprehend. The character of the exemplary figures in a tradition is closely connected with the theme of its master story. They set the tone for the story and suggest the mood in which others make its way their own. Now in order to understand more fully what makes a way religious we need to consider further the nature of its transcendent end. This is the subject of the next chapter.

CHAPTER FIVE

Transcendent Ends

TRANSCENDENCE is a notion which we find easier to use than to define.[1] The phrase "transcendent end" underlines the fact that what interests us, in the dynamics of religion, is the nature of the *transcending process* rather than the nature of some transcendent entity.[2] Some traditionalists define religion quite simply as our duty to God and our neighbor. In that case, arriving at a precise concept of God becomes very important. I shall give briefly my own concept later in this chapter. But first we must recall that not all traditions are oriented toward faith in some transcendent being. If they mention divine power at all, they may conceive of this as immanent rather than transcendent. Yet even the most secular story of redemption suggests an end which requires movement from conditions of despair to conditions of hope. *There is a promise of transcendence in the outcome of the drama, even when the setting is this-worldly and the plot mentions only human characters.*

What often leads to talk at cross-purposes on the subject of transcendence is the fact that "transcendence" is a relative concept. What is a transcending move for one may not seem so to another. What is a transcendent state at one stage in a life story need not seem so later on. The conception of stages on life's way helps us to understand why this is so. On this subject, I agree with those who find Abraham Maslow's conception of a hierarchy of basic needs to be relevant.[3] It helps us to understand why satisfaction today can generate discontent tomorrow. Once fed, we seek shelter. Once sheltered, we seek wealth or prestige.[4] Of course, earlier demands recur. But once our source of supply is assured we move up the scale to meet other deficiencies. Then satisfying needs no longer preoccupies us. We are free at last to realize our identity in whatever ways best express our mastery of life.

Maslow's conception cannot be mechanically applied, for instance, to yogis who renounce wealth and sex. (The point for them is that they *could* gratify such desires if they wished.) But the fact of differing aspirations of people at different points on the scale helps to explain why what seems urgent to some seems of marginal concern to others. Revolutionary cries for redistribution of wealth, for example, not surprisingly fall on deaf ears among the bourgeoisie. The latter are not so wealthy themselves that they are free to take up radical causes. But they have sufficient wealth to meet their own needs and are now concentrating on other concerns, such as the right to vote. What revolutionaries deplore as heartless greed, or preoccupation with trivia, on the part of those who fail to support them may be due, rather, to the latters' preoccupation with different "deficiency motivations." *Everyone's* vision is colored by his or her needs. Consequently, the best hope in moving others to share our concerns is to induce them to share our circumstances. Promote the dissident and he soon becomes an apologist for the promotional system. What disparate groups have in common is the desire to progress to some "higher" or "better" situation in life.

According to Maslow's scheme, we move from egotistical to altruistic forms of self-realization only when our basic needs cease to worry us. Bethune's story fits the pattern. As a doctor, once he had recovered his health, he had all the status and security that he desired. His experience of personal fulfillment, in the midst of the fighting in China, fits what Maslow says of the "peak" experiences of self-actualizing people. They act out of their abundance rather than their need. Their love is self-giving *(agape)* rather than self-seeking *(eros)*. Insofar as they no longer act out of a sense of deficiency their lives are governed by a different spirit. Transition to this kind of life is portrayed as the final stage in religious success stories. Consequently, the kind of self- or ego-transcendence known at this level tends to be identified with *the* transcendent end-state sought in all religion. Maslow is vague, to say the least, about peak experiences. He claims that all of us have them. The "saints" differ from us only in the degree to which they live out of such motivations during their lives.[5]

The example of Bethune reminds us, however, that personal fulfillment is not just an individual affair. It raises the question of universality with reference to Maslow's ideal. As a psychologist, Maslow naturally confined his attention to individual development. But might not his hierarchy of needs have a parallel on the social side, in a hierarchy of concerns? If, as I shall suggest, freedom is the central ideal in current conceptions of goodness, can we countenance a conception which allows some to be free while others are not? Furthermore, if we look more for "horizontal," rather than "vertical," transcendence, must we not include in this some demand for social evolution? These are questions being asked by contemporary philosophers and theologians who emphasize anew the communal nature of our transcendent ends.[6] Against a purely psychological model for theories of transcendence, they raise the issue of its inclusiveness. In principle, Maslow's "peak experience" as the prototype for religious transcendence allows for the Bethunes of this world. In practice, however, his mistrust of the institutional dimension in religion makes his an incomplete conception on which to found a theory of religion.

We can illustrate another problem, both for hierarchical theories and ideals of social progress, by playing on the word "peak." Imagine someone walking in the hills. At the top of each rise the walker sees another crest in the distance. Suppose this is all on one side of a mountain range and the walker never actually sees or reaches the summit. Knowing what he or she does of mountain ranges generally, the walker may simply assume that one peak is higher than all the rest. Even if this is right, are *we* right in assuming that the object of the exercise is to reach the summit? Are we correct in assuming that, for every "way" there is an "end," and that, among ends, one is in some sense ultimate? In short, what does our recognition of relativism do to the entire conception of transcendent ends? If we follow those who fasten on the image of play as a model here, must we not suppose that going for a walk is an end in itself?

A first answer to these questions is that we are creatures of history. What we have been discussing primarily are historical traditions in which, as a matter of fact, various transcendent ends have been proposed. Whether or not we accept their assumptions concerning their uniqueness and absoluteness, we must initially "pass over" to these points of view if we would understand them from within. For the time being, then, we shall continue to discuss these traditions on their own terms. In Chapters Nine and Ten, however, we shall have to reconsider our tacit acceptance of the traditional framework.

Also, as individuals we are, in Heidegger's phrase, "thrown" into existence.[7] We do not begin with a total blank. Rather we start, more often than not, in the middle of some master story and share the expectations of our social group. Our views will differ initially according to the stories to which we have been introduced. If at the center of our pattern of hope is the True Comrade, for example, then our idea of a "happy ending" will differ from those whose center is the True Individual or the Buddha. We may be so deeply drawn into a particular story that we do not regard relativism as a live option. In Chapter Eight we shall look at an individual, on the other hand, who begins without any traditional central symbol. Her preoccupation is with the patterning process itself. Until she brings some conscious order to it she has no freedom, either to participate in its development or to renounce it.

The phenomenon of thrownness applies also to our future. Whether we like it or not, we are increasingly thrown together in this world. There may be an ebb and flow to our interest in Asian traditions, or in our own roots, but in religion these never were entirely separate. They may have been separable in our immediate past, but no more. It may be, in fact, that working through the story of relativism, in the context of an industrialized society, is the common fate of all the traditions in the current era.[8] In any case, if indeed the dynamics of religion involves the interplay of traditional wisdom and transcendent hope, then the cloth with which we cut our patterns of faith is not entirely a matter of choice.

A second answer is that we have to distinguish between the relativity of particular conceptions of the end and the dynamics of a way of life as such. Theologians have always recognized that the reality of God is not contained by their conceptions of God. In this chapter we shall remark that the intentionality of the transcendent end outruns particular images of it. In this lies a clue to which we shall return in Chapter Ten concerning the importance of silence. But here I wish to take up a suggestion made in Chapter Two regarding the importance of transfiguring symbols.

If we regard all our symbols as merely pointers toward an uncertain future, governed by an unknown god or driven by some mysterious physical force, then indeed we have nothing to say to absolute relativists. But if in fact we share through our stories a sense of their ending, even now, then we shall not take seriously any thoroughgoing denial of that present experience. In that experience are included already the seeds of the future. They are not fully realized. But neither do they spring from the void. They are in fact the very ideals and aspirations on which we are reflecting now. In short, there are only so many live options available to us in our present circumstances. As we give them more or less attention, we ourselves are contributing to the determination of which will be the dominant patterns in the future.

What is absolute, in this view, is not any entity on the map of ideas, to which we can conveniently refer at all times. Central symbols may change. Each individual ego must die. The world of today would scarcely be recognizable even by our forebears of a few hundred years ago. *What is absolute is the transcending process itself.* God, the consistently life-enhancing power in this process, is not some master manipulator in the sky. God is not some inner demon pulling the psychic strings of our "collective unconscious." Rather God is the transfiguring presence in our life-support systems, including our symbol systems.[9]

It is still a question whether such a God "exists." Tillich, for example, spoke of "the God above 'God,'" the Spirit of the new life seen in Christ.[10] But he despaired of persuading Anglo-Saxons to mean by the word "Spirit" what, in German, he meant by *"Geist"*. Also, in philosophy, the word "exists" carries such an overload of technical problems that we do better without it. Among many of my students, "Does God exist?" is not a live question. Some take an affirmative answer for granted and cannot imagine themselves into a contrary frame of reference. Others are unsure what the question means and are not very interested in finding out. But the question "Do you experience the presence or absence of life-enhancing power in your life?" *is* interesting. Conceptions of this presence vary according to our master stories.[11] If it is like the garden story, in Chapter Two, then it might make sense to wonder about the presence of a gardener. If it is like the jungle story, it will not. But then we may wonder about "the Tao."

What is finally important here is not the naming of names, as such, or finding a spot for "god" in our pattern of faith. Rather the question is: what bridge do we have between present and future hope? Do we leap into the future on our own? Do we join hands with our comrades? Do we rely on our instinct for survival, or superior technology? Each of the traditions has its answer to this question, narrated in its master story by reference to its primary symbols. How *we* shall answer depends on what, from the traditions, we carry over into our lives and on what we base our hopes for the future. We may see already present in transfiguring symbols a foundation on which to build our promises. Our way in the present is not entirely blind. If we do walk in the hills, we are not entirely without landmarks. Whether we then decide to go for a walk or to make the ascent to the top, or simply to sit and admire the view, there are options and prospects from which to choose. One step toward making an informed decision here is to ask others who have walked before us what the prospects are along the paths that they took.

For people like Bethune (and Bonhoeffer, among Christians), the thrust of transcending processes is "horizontal" rather than "vertical." They look to a this-worldly future for a new society in which all can participate. *In general, an indication of the kind of transcendence sought is given in answers to the question: what do we hope for, for those whom we love?* In Bethune's case the answer included increasing self-reliance and freedom from exploitation. A comparable answer could be given for Mahatma Gandhi, Martin Luther King, or Malcolm X.

In preceding chapters we have already remarked that typical ends among the traditions are Heaven for Christians and Muslims, Nirvana and ultimate freedom for Buddhists and Hindus, the Classless Society for Marxists, the True Israel for Jews, Immortality and harmony with the Tao for classical Chinese.[12] The images that we favor tell us more about the quality of life to which we aspire than about any particular picture of Paradise. Indeed, as a glance at religious art quickly establishes, our imaginations are much more fertile concerning the nature of hell than of heaven. Eager young converts may dream of themselves in the arms of celestial nymphs. But their teachers soon undermine such visions.[13] In this respect, religion is again not unlike politics. Marcuse's critique of "one-dimensional" man, for example, relies mainly on negation in evoking a sense of our many possible dimensions.[14]

None of the major traditions provides its adherents with a complete blueprint of the end. Even those which decree very specific patterns of conduct for those on the way stress submission to the will of God, whatever that might bring, rather than high hopes for personal bliss. *Their intentions to follow the way outrun the specifics of any particular story ending.* Accordingly, the stories of the central figures leave us with a sense of unfinished business. The Christ commissions his followers to go out into all the world. The Buddha seeks the enlightenment of all beings, to the ends of time. Those who identify with the Prophet or Sage do so at the point of his active mission, more often than with his period of rest.

Lack of specificity in symbols of the end invites participation in the shaping of the end. In this connection, we must remember that such symbols as the Kingdom of God are of a commonwealth of creatures, not of individual ecstasy.[15] Each creature in turn has a creative part to play. Once more a political analogy is helpful. In a democratic community, for example, what democracy means is subject to constant redefinition. The United States has a written Constitution. But it has to be continually reinterpreted by the Supreme Court and reaffirmed by each citizen. The original signatories to the Declaration of Independence are not the final interpreters of their own work.[16] The democratic "way" is not something static, which can be unambiguously defined for all future generations without involving them in its development. Landmark judicial decisions, presidential speeches, and fresh protest movements among minority groups, all contribute to the articulation of a tradition which, ideally, is directed toward the universal promise of life, liberty, and the pursuit of happiness.[17] Those who think that the written "constitutions" or scriptures of the traditions place them on a different footing in this respect are laboring under an anachronistic doctrine of revelation. In practice these also require constant reinterpretation.[18]

When I refer to an "end-state" rather than "the End" I do so to remind us that, according to some, the end is already present. Pictorially they say that the Paradise to be regained is the Garden of Eden. More abstractly they speak of the *presence* of Eternity. In much Hindu thought, for example, ultimate bliss is portrayed as an extraordinary state of consciousness rather than as some supernatural place, to which we might go at journey's end. Reacting against cruder conceptions, some theologians identify Christ's Second Coming with the giving of the Holy Spirit. Citing texts to the effect that the Kingdom of Heaven is "within us," they see its presence in the self-giving love already felt in the Church. (In technical terms, theirs is a "realized," rather than a "futuristic" eschatology or doctrine of the end.) They consider that distracting visions of the future merely tempt us to postpone living in the present for what may amount to no more than pious hopes.[19]

To some extent such theologians are right. The end *is* always already present. For, as Mahatma Gandhi reminded us, *our ends cannot be realized by self-defeating means.*[20] Life is organic. Our processing means must be congruent with our processive ends. We cannot lie our way into true relationships. If our end is freedom, we cannot abolish all freedoms in the process of becoming free. Our being free at the last is only possible if we begin to exercise that freedom now. At the same time, however, a taste of freedom now is not the same as the "perfect freedom" promised at the end of the way. To be out of Pharoah's clutches in Egypt and across the Red Sea is not yet to be in Israel.

On the one hand, therefore, the end is part of present experience. But, on the other hand, affirmations of the end express a future hope. While there is life there is growth. Each new phase, except perhaps death, may be welcomed for itself. But it cannot plausibly be regarded as unchanging. Being loved and loving, or enlightened and enlightening, are both present blessings and future aspirations. The ambiguity of the phrase "the end" catches this point. Insofar as love and enlightenment characterize life at the end of the "way," this end cannot adequately be pictured *either* as a place removed from where we are now *or* as completely coterminous with it.

In the last chapter we noted that the religious significance of a movement may be indicated by the universality of its scope.[21] Insofar as a feminist's concern is with liberating both men and women, for example, then, on a spectrum of concerns, that is closer to what is ultimate than the concerns of one who assumes that "men" means both sexes, while tacitly subordinating women and children. By contrast, *the Third Reich was an inadequate symbol, even though the Nazis' methods were consistent with their ends. For by eliminating some from their ideal state, they dehumanized all.*

What counts here is the intention defining the meaning of an action. Thus if our conception of reality is strictly secular, but our goal is to bring freedom to all, then our movement is religiously significant. This is why I regard most forms of Marxism as quasi-religious. Of course, if we regard this world as just one of many in an infinite series, then the religious range of our thinking *must* be otherworldly. Worldly *or* otherworldly, such thinking may be false. Nevertheless, our *intention* will be religiously significant if it encompasses the realization of perfect freedom or bliss for all.

Our intentions are expressed in actions which may serve various purposes along the way, some "religious" and some not. For example, both Bethune and the missionary intended to help the Chinese to work out their own salvation, though they disagreed concerning what this meant. But their immediate purpose was to bring relief to the wounded and this was consistent with both their goals. Some Chinese also saw a romantic interest in their cooperative activities. Who knows what their dominant motives were? If we distinguish among intentions, purposes, motives, and goals, then *the intentionality which counts for religious thinking is that which is directed to the realization of whatever transcendent end is proposed.*

As with the disagreement between Bethune and the missionary, religious disputes typically focus on ultimate ends or means toward such ends. Is this the Messiah or do we look for another? Does wisdom come from books or despite books? Can we tolerate a state which interferes with the churches' preaching of salvation? Can we tolerate a church which deflects people from alleviating the misery of the poor? As we answer such questions, transcendent ends may not be uppermost in our minds. But reference to some common cause is the basis on which we must reach agreement concerning our courses of action. Even in religious disputes over scriptural interpretation, the issue is not simply past meaning but present integrity and future identity.

In one form or another the traditions portray realization of a transcendent end as living the good life. In religious thinking such an end is accorded ultimate value. In this connection *we must recognize a paradigm shift in prevailing conceptions of goodness and criteria of the good life away from order in the direction of freedom.* The reward for a virtuous life used to be thought of as the kind of peace that would be imposed by a heavenly magistrate. He would bring "law and order" to wayward citizens, led astray by their unruly passions.[22] But more recently we have been invited to realize life in a sort of universal Esalen Institute, where all previously repressed passions have been declared to be beautiful. The challenge, whether from individualistic existentialists or collectivistic revolutionaries, is to become free members of a free society. Whether mystical or mundane, the distinctive movements of our times are for one sort of liberation or another. Fear of economic recession may retard their progress, but they are now a seminal part of our history.

An indication of the changing outlook is our attitude to ritual. We use rituals to give structure to potentially destructive situations. Ritual acts can be our assurance of being understood. (We feel most misunderstood when our intentions are misconstrued.) Prayer is one move toward understanding and being understood. Confession is one move toward liberation, whether in the confessional or the commune. Liturgy is a reenacting of the liberating process or a celebration of salvation in a staged setting. Music, drama, song, and dance draw us into rhythms of existence which give us joy and consolation.[23] Comrades and communicants program performances in which they reaffirm solidarity in their cause.

Yet regimented ritual acts are distasteful to many of us. Lovers who follow set routines do not long remain lovers. Precisely when we feel insecure we fasten on signs of seeming indifference and demand performances which are more than mere performances. We change the setting, rewrite the lyrics, translate the mantras. Or we break away completely and withdraw to the ghetto or the desert.[24] It seems that in religion, as in politics, we need slogans and half-truths to goad us into action.[25] Yet the successful are those who use these, while dissociating themselves from rival gurus and politicians. We want to be free spirits while acknowledging only the existence of embodied spirits. We are ambivalent about inherited rituals, yet try to *guarantee* spontaneity.[26]

The paradigm shift is not a matter of total displacement. Christian freedom and love, for example, have always been linked to images of judgment on "the Last Day." Where there is judgment there is also an idea of social order, though not necessarily one that reflects current hierarchies.[27] In Indian philosophy also we find compassion paired with wisdom, release *(móksha)* with social structure *(dharma)*. In Hindu mythology the force destructive of all incarnations is recognized to be the same as the force which is the mother of us all. Freedom is not anarchy.[28]

Myths of the End have never simply portrayed the End as a repetition of the Beginning. Also, far from rationalizing present power structures, they have been covert, or not so covert, challenges to established authorities.[29] In this connection again we must bear in mind that the first Christians made no special demands on the credulity of their contemporaries, when they spoke of their Father in Heaven. In those days, everyone had a father or a mother in heaven and the question was: whose parent is winning? When there was war on earth there was also thought to be war in heaven. The difference was that life on earth was like life in the provinces: there is a time-lag until the action in the capital has its effect on the local town. If you know what has happened at the center of action, you can anticipate what will soon be happening at home. Thus good news in heaven today is good news for earth tomorrow. This does not make the present bad news on the home front any less bad. But it does give grounds for hope.[30]

The reality of God that counts in all this is that which bridges the gap between present experience and future hope. In the traditions the presence of such power is affirmed by the master stories of the central symbols. The authoritative symbolic figures, as we remarked in Chapter Two, *are* what we would become. That the Christ feels forsaken on the Cross or the Buddha suffers the onslaughts of Mara, the Evil One, is not the last word in each story. In it each realizes his humanity. But the final word of the faithful is that in and through such suffering comes transcendent peace.[31] In this connection, as mentioned above, *I define divine being as unambiguously life-enhancing power.* The question whether or not "God exists" thus becomes: are we aware of any presence which is *unambiguously* life-enhancing? In response to this question, all the traditional and contemporary symbols of transcendence suggest an affirmative answer: there is a dimension of reality which is not just that of the symbols as such.[32] It is that which gives them power and makes peace possible through their effect on us.

Our own answer to this question depends primarily on what we mean by "life." It makes a difference whether we mean the life of the soul, the energizing of a complex mechanism, the maturation of an organism, or something else. With regard to the end, especially, mechanistic images foster an ideal of equilibrium. Organic images suggest developing stages and dreams of progress. (Compare Freud and Marx).[33] Soul-talk leads to rejection of materialistic "Western" culture, and so on. Running through these concepts are questions concerning our personal identity. Again it makes a difference whether we think in terms of Ego and Non-Ego, membership in some elite, or the Self of the Universe. In classical religious thought, the relationship of God to the world is compared to that of mind and body. Often, the concepts used are too static to do justice to the dynamics of religion.[34]

Also crucial for our answer is how we regard death. In the last chapter we saw that myths of creation serve mainly as introductions to myths of redemption. The interesting myths of redemption are those telling of boundary situations in which our worldly aspirations seem to be frustrated. Again we recall the example of Norman Bethune. Stories of the death of Socrates, or Mao's struggle for "revolutionary immortality," are central to their traditions.[35] Gods are not supposed to die or, if they do die, they are supposed to rise again. When rebirth is thought to be just the prelude to another death, gods lose their ultimate importance.

If we cease to believe in the gift of new life guaranteed by a transcendent Redeemer, we turn to other strategies for some sort of survival of death. Thus some look to the divine possibilities in "Nature." Others embrace nationalistic or communistic symbols of hope, according to which the group lives on. Here individual death is not a major problem. As Indian traditions attest, it can be regarded as simply a transitional phase. But a meaningful death is still uncertain. Where transcendence means "passing over" to other selves and other viewpoints, even the question of personal significance is relativized.[36] More important to living faith than specific images of immortality is some ground for hope in "impossible possibilities."[37] In passing, it is worth noting that, through the figures of Abraham and Isaac, Kierkegaard's hope was for this world, despite his faith in God as Transcendent Other.[38] In this he shared the modern assumption that hidden life-forces come to fruition in present social relationships rather than the classical view that the divine becomes human, in order that the human may eventually become divine.

We must at this point acknowledge that end-thinking is in disfavor in some quarters of the academic establishment. Some would-be scientists of language and behavior, especially, want to abolish all vestiges of "teleology" from their systems. Partly, I believe, their position represents a continuing backlash against Aristotelianism in philosophy and theology. Partly, what they do, in practice, is to slip one particular end—equilibrium, for instance—into their schema from the start, without noticing its hold over their thinking. However, it requires a whole book to argue this point.[39] Suffice it to say here that the work being done on legitimation theory, "futurology," and the theology of hope is ample evidence that the issue is still open.[40] In the dynamics of religion, what is obviously true for the majority is that realization of its highest hopes is still a project for the future. What gives structure to each way into that future is the subject of our next chapter.

Finally, in this chapter, we must note that traditionally there have been sound religious reasons why our perception of our end and its way is filtered through symbols. Those who claim to have encountered absolute power in the raw have only with difficulty retained their sanity.[41] On the negative side, such an encounter includes a judgment on our previous behavior. The perception of absolute value includes an inkling of how far we have yet to go before we may realize such worth in ourselves. On the positive side, moments of ecstatic vision of the end lift our ambition to worthier aspirations than before. But maturing love requires freedom for partners to grow tall in their own space. Their story is not one of uninterrupted union.[42] In all the traditions, the presence of such love is a sign of hope.

We began this chapter by stressing transcendence as process and noting confusions in terminology. There is a horizontal rather than vertical thrust to recent thinking on our subject. Modern aspirants to the good life use freedom rather than order as their main criterion of goodness. Their aspirations are religiously significant if universal in scope and if their means of self-realization are consistent with their ends. Important here is the spirit in which we face death. The positive symbolism in the traditional master stories includes a promise for the future as well as their judgment on the present. What counts is the intentionality of each way rather than its specific images of the end.

If our emphasis on freedom is correct, the openness of religious symbol systems, including their vagueness concerning the future, is necessary to their function. An inflexible pattern of expectations would stultify the spirit in which our ends are realized. Rather than fear proliferation of conflicting schemes for the good life, we should welcome the variety of ends proposed. We learn as much about ourselves from the ends that we reject as from those that we affirm. The central symbol of our master story indicates the horizon of our highest hopes. Whether or not we ever fully realize our end, that story gives us a sense of its presence along the way.

A vague ideal is not a sufficient guide in everyday life, however. We rely on other factors to shape our changing patterns of faith.

In particular, since the spirit on the way must be congruent with that in which we realize our transcendent end, its character is basic to the story of the way. In the next chapter, we shall consider the kinds of principles which inform this character.

CHAPTER SIX

Constitutive Principles and Transformations Within Traditions

BECAUSE of the elusiveness of religious claims about transcendent ends attention within the traditions tends to center rather on means. In many master stories the focus is more on the quality of life leading to the end than on details of the ultimate vision. There have to be such visions and they have to be more than dull repetitions of traditional motifs. But it is the way in which such visions set the horizons of faith, not their specific predictions, that is important for the dynamics of religion. In the last chapter we noticed how some use the emphasis on present experience to argue that, in principle, the end is already wholly realized. This emphasis also encourages one side of a debate in religious ethics. Against those who justify means by reference to ends (a "teleological" ethic) it favors those who insist that we should do our duty for duty's sake (a "deontological" ethic).[1] If controlled thinking is a mark of good thinking, then the best thinking in a tradition is likely to be on the realities of life along the way, rather than on speculations about its end.

Already in the last chapter, concerning the intentionality of religious actions, we remarked on the close connection between means and ends in religious processes. Now we must consider the convictions and strengths of character which enable us to carry out such actions in the spirit of the traditions to which we may belong. We must take note of the constitutive principles by which we choose the means to our ends in changing times and circumstances. Of course, as we have remarked with reference to our central symbols, our conceptions of ends are modified by new insights into what are appropriate means. The dichotomy between means and ends must not be overdrawn. But in our accounts of the dynamics of religion it is important to understand what gives shape to the spirit in which we judge ways and means.

What I am calling constitutive principles are virtues in the classical sense. They are, if you will, spiritual powers which define the ethos in which end-states are realized. We may neglect to think of virtues in this connection because, in our compartmentalized studies, they are properly dealt with under "ethics." But, when our subject is religious thinking, it is a mistake to concentrate on doctrine to the exclusion of ethical reflection. For both apply to a way of life.[2] Before they became doctrines in the Christian tradition, for example, creation and redemption were themes in stories of the Way. They were dramatic motifs on which particular policies were based. They were expressions of a sense of priorities regarding our obligations in life and expectations concerning its outcome. Doctrines taken out of context lack the intentionality which determines their significance for faith. By contrast, faith itself has been considered one of the virtues and religious thinking concerning faith has often stressed the duty, not just the right or the will, to believe. When we are looking for conceptual links to ultimate values and religious ends, we do well to consider the strengths of character which are necessary to their realization.

If we characterize ultimate values and end-states in terms of freedom and order, happiness and blessedness, then *virtuous lives are everywhere in religion regarded as the precondition* for their achievement. This is as true of Chinese and Indian traditions as of the covenantal communities of Judaism, Christianity, and Islam. When we include such contemplative strengths as single-mindedness and insight on our list of virtues then the powers to which we refer are not just preconditions. Their exercise is part of the actual process whereby religious promises are fulfilled. In religious life and thought *the bridging moves whereby breaks are healed are in the first instance paradigmatic acts of inspired characters, not myths or doctrines or ideologies as such.* We do not turn to just any narratives in times of crisis. We look to stories of powerful lives told sometimes in the form of myths or legends but also in the form of gospels or martyrologies. Our bridges are built in life as well as in thought, and in religious thinking the virtues epitomize this fact.

Constitutive principles or major virtues in traditional patterns of faith are, for example, love and justice in Christianity, wisdom and compassion in Buddhism, social order *(dharma)* and freedom *(moksha)* in Hindu traditions, benevolence *(jen)* and good manners *(li)* in Confucianism, and equality and fraternity in revolutionary communalism. There can be several such principles whose arrangements vary in the traditions. For instance, Indian thinking traditionally includes wealth and sex *(artha* and *kama)* as well as social obligation and liberating insight.[3] Considering the propensity among social scientists for analyzing religion in terms of dissonance, fear of disorder, and the like, it is noteworthy that these constitutive principles are positive. They are springs of action, not just expressions of reaction, as seen in the lives of the central figures of a tradition. They are not always virtues in the conventional sense. The heroes in the *Mahabharata,* for instance, realize *artha* by gambling, cheating, and generally behaving like medieval "gentlemen." But as such they have character and are able to win out over adversity in the end.

No doubt much behavior in religion as elsewhere is due to aversive conditioning. But when we want to consider authentic religious developments and intrinsic motivations we have to look through the functions of religious institutions and exercises among the rank and file to the idealized behavior of their religious heroes. In this connection, since Kierkegaard if not before, existential psychologists have recognized that religious motives are the obverse of apathy and despair.[4] Fear as such does not generate faith. Suffering does not necessarily translate into ecstasy. Only through the stories of exemplary figures in the traditions do we perceive a quality of life which makes us dissatisfied with our present performance and hope for something better. For although the figures begin where we are, identified with the insecure and alienated, the redemptive processes working through their life stories give us some assurance of a more positive ending in joy, peace, freedom, and bliss. We should not let the caricature of all this in "the power of positive thinking" distract us from acknowledging their kernel of truth. If we would understand the dynamics of religion we must understand the pull as well as the push of religious motivation.

In ethical theory it is helpful to differentiate principles from norms, rules, laws, maxims, and prescriptions. Often we find such terms used interchangeably. But when we single out principles our point is that rules may be changed, exceptions made and conflicts resolved, by suspending the application of one rule in favor of another. But *principles abide. They are constitutive of a community* as such.[5] Thus the true Israelite lives by the righteousness of God. The true Buddhist realizes the teaching of the Buddha. The tribesman on a hunt respects the taboos of his group, and so on.[6] In the history of religions what we have to add is that the principles underlying the prescribed pattern of conduct and the personal qualities necessary to follow that pattern meet in the figure of the central symbol; or, where that symbol is a code, in the central figure in the master story. *Code and character intersect to reveal the power and intentionality of the way in the climax of this exemplary life.*[7]

We have already remarked that the spirit of the Christ, the Sage, the Prophet, or the Chairman, expressed in his words and deeds, gives a tradition its continuing identity.[8] His vision of the end becomes normative for those who come after. His is the example to imitate or emulate. The principles by which he lived and which he articulated in his teaching receive his personal imprint before they become part of a community's canon of faith and practice. Thus such principles as love and justice which are the springs of right actions—the *archés*—in a tradition are not simply abstract propositions propounded by some armchair social critic. They are known to be true in the lives of the saints. As such they are definitive for decisions concerning roles played and policies adopted by their followers. In religion *it is the principled life*—the loving, hoping, righteous, humorous, profound life —*which participates in the power of the end-state.* Thus, on the one hand, the doctrines and codes are less impersonal than they might seem out of context and, on the other hand, the central identity has more character and structure to it than we might otherwise suppose. *Personal and impersonal truth both receive definitive expression in the exemplary life found at the center of a pattern of faith.* Where no actual life exists in our cultural history, there is not yet a religious tradition.[9]

As New Testament scholars have pointed out, early Christian expectations concerning the Kingdom of God were articulated in terms of the life of Jesus. The messenger of the coming Kingdom himself became part of the Message. His life establishes a role, sonship, and policies, love for God and man, which control the expectations and aspirations of his followers. The same process occurs with figures like Confucius and Mao and, to a lesser extent, Moses and Muhammad (e.g., in the Hadith or traditions concerning the latter). If, in what follows, we look more closely at Christian conceptions of love and justifying faith and the changing roles and policies associated with these principles we shall, I think, find transformations within a traditional pattern of thinking which are not atypical of comparable transformations in other traditions. In this chapter, I shall concentrate on the Christian examples with which I am most familiar. But I believe that the lessons to be learned from them have wider applications in the interpretation of religious thinking.

Our contention has been that meaning in religion changes when the central symbol is reinterpreted according to new primary symbols of the faith. As long as the same central referent is used in thinking of the way, we say that the faith is the same. The ongoing intention, which outruns specific visions of the end and outlasts changing cosmological and ontological presuppositions, gives the tradition an identity which is discernible through the varieties of expression and shifts of emphasis typical of a living process. Now we shall give some content to these ideas by considering contrasting affirmations of Jesus the Christ which lead to quite different conceptions of what it means to be a Christian. We shall look for these in the policies adopted and ideas emphasized, concerning paradigmatic roles and relationships, by the faithful in the history of the Christian tradition.

Let us begin by considering sonship in relation to kingship. The Israelite tradition of kingship stressed responsibility rather than privilege.[10] But images of Oriental potentates and Roman emperors tended to introduce different connotations, such that sonship typically meant subordination to the kingly father. Hence difficulties arose in patristic thought over doctrines of the Trinity. Patterns of subordination were expressed in the institution of episcopacy and the authoritarian policies which enabled the catholic churches to assert their supremacy over others. The logic of this line of development led to what is called caesaropapism.

By the twelfth century of the Christian era, Christian laymen could literally believe that their entry to heaven was jeopardized by the appearance on the scene of more than one pope. The dependencies were such that they were afraid of being declared illegitimate sons who could be eternally disinherited. By contrast, as kingship became a secondary symbol and sonship related to professional concerns, Reformation preachers could write of the freedom of the Christian man in ways which gave precedence to conscience over the claims of ecclesiastical courts.[11] The ethos had changed. The fate of the sons no longer hinged on their sponsorship by their earthly "father in God." Yet they were still within the framework of Christian traditions and expectations concerning entry into heaven.

Developing ideals of sonship were paralleled by changing ideas of love. This is not surprising since true sons are supposed to love their fathers. It is instructive, therefore, to look at some recent theologies of love.[12] Karl Barth, for example, accepted a sharp distinction between self-giving love *(agape)* and "eros," understood as self-seeking desire.[13] According to Barth, even when the desire is for possession of perfect beauty and goodness, its orientation is the antithesis of true Christian love. The whole point of the Christian master story is that God loves human beings in their impotence and error. The dynamics of faith are to be seen, not in the drive toward completion on the part of empty selves, but rather in the fullness of life *given* to them out of the overflowing mercy of their Heavenly Father.

The framework for Barth's thinking is a Calvinistic emphasis on the glory of God. It makes the divine so transcendent that even such institutions as the church are perceived to be subject to the corrupting power of sin. The basis of hope for sinners cannot be in themselves. Earthly sons are prodigal sons, whose only future depends on confession of their need. Faith demands trust in the transcendent spirit revealed in Christ, not with a view to subsequent rewards, but as an expression of thanksgiving for release from the nightmare strivings of Eros. The symbol of the Christ, especially identified with the symbol of the empty Cross, is the expression of that Agape which runs through the entire story of the Way of Resurrection. How this story finally ends for particular individuals remains an open question. But it is to be determined by reference to God's love, not by reference to some speculatively conceived "eternal decree," according to which some are predestined to salvation and the rest to damnation.[14]

Ironically, however, such Christian accounts of love are cut from the same Platonic cloth as the views which they are meant to repudiate. In both cases one pole of the love relationship is treated as virtually an object—man for Agape and God for Eros —and, whether condescending or ascending, the essential movement is unilinear. The direction of transcendence is vertical rather than horizontal, skyward to eternity rather than ahead to novelty. The Good, God, is imagined to be like the sun, the unmoved source of energy, beside which all earthly passions are base. Existence is perceived hierarchically and the appropriate policies are paternalistic. The supposedly good news for Christians is that they are basically unlovely, have nothing of their own to contribute to the covenantal relationship, and are fortunate to be offered a share in arbitrary glory. Indicative of such hierarchical thinking is the attitude to women, seen as mothers but not lovers, as objects of veneration not equal partners.

In its classical Augustinian forms, Christian ideas of the good life are shaped by an obsession with goodness as order. Lust is wrong because disordering. Peace can come only from purer motives, from single-minded acceptance of what God has done for us in Christ and from higher order pursuits of more aesthetic objects. The underlying theory of being is not that of the Cartesian kind of mind-body dualism but the older conception of a chain of being in which each species is assigned its proper role and place.[15] The only real disagreement is over whether the initial movement is from the top down or the bottom up. Even that, if we follow William James on conversion, may be more a matter of conscious awareness than actual impulse.[16] Either way, the dis-ease at the bottom is supposedly due to whatever in the chain of being is most distant from the source—that is, the body or the wicked will.

A basic change in the meaning of being a Christian follows from a different view of love. If we link sonship with brotherhood, for example, and assert that followers of Christ are joint heirs to the Kingdom, then the appropriate policies will express friendship rather than filial obedience. Already we have seen what comradely concern could mean for Norman Bethune. Now, if we follow Tillich rather than Barth, we shall assert that Christ-like love is a compound of self-giving, self-seeking, and other elements.[17] Also, if we accept a portrait of the Christ as the Man for Others, who lets us be ourselves rather than dictates God's will to us, then we may see in Jesus a symbol of liberation. His will be the policies of a man "come of age" whose maturity is affirmed by the power motivating his love.[18]

Adopting patterns of brotherhood and sisterhood while centering our faith on the Christ and following the principle of love, we would be as Christian in our way as Barth was in his. But *what our shared faith would mean to us would be different, legitimately different, in that it had the same central symbol and the same aspiration to live in a community where God's will is done.* It would represent a new way of being "in communion." This is not to say that Barth's view was unchristian. But *any suggestion that only one path with one set of signposts and stories is the right way would be mistaken.* In addition to John's route of self-giving love, there is Augustine's love for God *(Amor Dei)* and the mutuality of Buber's I-You.[19]

What it means to be Christian changes, accordingly, with the way traditional Christian stories are developed and different kinds of love are emphasized. If the love is paternalistic, the accent falls on expressions of free giving or grace—the fortuitousness of the Virgin Birth, the self-giving at the Last Supper, and similar incidents. If the theme is more erotic, the accent falls on the beauty of holiness and divine glory, as expressed by heavenly choirs, the pageant of Palm Sunday, and so on. If, by contrast, we would identify love with friendship we could relate to

Jesus the comrade of outcasts, the one crucified with outlaws. Looking at the full sweep of the tradition we see, of course, that each accent has its moments—the grace, the glory, and the humanity of God. Even Karl Barth came to emphasize the humanity of God, once he had established divine transcendence to his satisfaction. The Good News is not delivered in a monotone.[20]

Already within the New Testament we find a diversity of emphases. Such diversity occurs on central points in the story of redemption, not just on marginal issues. Most notable in this regard was the divergence between James and Paul concerning the relationship between what we do and what God does for us in the process of salvation. Must we work out our own salvation? Or do we simply have faith in God's redemptive act in Christ? Specific "works" were understood by reference to the Mosaic Law. We saw earlier that the Law remained as a primary symbol in Paul's thinking. He still had his love for Torah. But as far as our salvation is concerned, he insisted that the demands of the code have been met by Jesus. By fulfilling the Law, Jesus brought a new spirit of love into the community of God's people. Paul's policy hinges on our acceptance of this spirit, identified as that of the Risen Christ.[21]

According to Paul, the intention of the Torah is now expressed in Christian deeds which are a consequence, not a cause, of the nearing End. Throughout, the power and wisdom enabling Christians to realize who they are is said to be divine, not human, yet incarnated by Jesus in a specific historical movement. The sense of this movement directed policies toward other Jews, to early Christian anarchists, and toward the Roman authorities. We notice here that the thrust of Pauline thought is toward the future not the past, not even the recent past of Jesus in Galilee.

In general, specifically Christian roles and policies are most often found in sermons, where generations of preachers adapt their favorite texts to their own times. Images of a gracious lord are chosen to reinforce paternalistic policies. Stories of ascetic self-denial are used to fire the desire for heavenly glory. Anecdotes of exemplary conduct are cited to arouse concern for humanity at large, and so on.[22] As these narratives combine to shape Christian history, we find in this one tradition quite distinctive streams of faith—Antiochene, Alexandrian, Cappadocian,

Augustinian, Thomistic, Lutheran, Calvinist, Anabaptist, and the rest.

The question of faith and works did not again become a major issue in the Western churches until Augustine's dispute with the Pelagians concerning grace and free will. The terms of the debate were not Pauline. But the principles of love and justice were meant to be the same. Augustine wrote as a bishop, determined to uphold the Catholic practice of infant baptism.[23] The Way of Resurrection is meant for them too, even before they can act on their own behalf. Their salvation must depend on grace through faith.

The majority of the church did not share Augustine's single-mindedness. Later theologians preferred the view that faith expressed in works should count for something on the Day of Judgment. Consequently, by the time of the Reformation it was from ecclesiastical, Christian codes that Luther and others demanded liberation in the name of Christ. The patterns of faith changed again. Justification of the sinner before God was understood in terms of Hebraic righteousness rather than Latin justice. For Luther too the future Day of Judgment was more important than past precedent. His idioms were those of his own day, especially with reference to individual conscience. But the pattern of his faith did not change until the Papacy ceased to be a primary symbol in his conception of Christ and the Church. Only then did he become convinced that he must initiate a fundamental revision of the tradition.[24]

If we leap across the centuries to look at a theologian like Tillich we find these familiar themes developed in yet another frame of reference. For Tillich the images of the Day of Judgment have become marginal. The significance of Christian symbols is stated in terms of existential psychology. Justification by grace through faith now means having the courage to be ourselves in spite of our ambiguous expressions of love and confused dreams of the future. How to accept our unacceptability in our own eyes, as well as in the eyes of others, was crucial, especially for those like himself who were still proud to be Germans. Because he had lived through the trauma of World War I, the great hopes for Christian socialism between the wars, and the cynicism and organized brutality of Hitler's Reich, Tillich could express not only faith in freedom through grace but also the sense of vulnerability which typifies much modern thinking. Of course his account of human finitude is a reconception of old themes. But the suspicion that the gods don't live here any more is relatively new. Perceiving the interplay between divine and demonic forces in our human search for love and justice, Tillich's last word is affirmative, if not for the past, at least for the future.[25]

If we measure Tillich's theology against medieval notions of eternity and omnipotence we shall miss the spirit of his thought. Of course, he may not always have been consistent either in life or in thought. But if we would understand his meaning we must see how he took what he considered to be the best in German classical idealism and applied this to Pauline and Augustinian themes in the Christian tradition. To the extent that his discussion remained centered on the Christ and that new symbols of absurdity, acceptability, and the like are incorporated into his portrayals of the Way of Resurrection, we must call his thinking Christian.[26] It is by reference to *these* criteria that we must answer the question: in what sense is his faith identical with that of Tertullian rather than Tagore? Where the center shifts and the way becomes unfocused we may call it non-Christian. But this conclusion has to be argued not by pointing to doctrines taken out of context but after appreciating Tillich's thought in relation to his times. Otherwise we may achieve verbal victories over his works in translation. But we shall not be engaging him on the religious level.

Changes of meaning within a pattern of faith need not lead to what Antony Flew has dubbed "the death by a thousand qualifications." Not all elaborations of a tradition are secondary elaborations designed to avoid embarrassment. A shift of emphasis which makes some symbols secondary that once were primary, such as those regarding God's power over individual lives, may be more true to the intentionality of the tradition than misapplied liturgical exaggerations.[27] In my view, every claim that God is love *must* be qualified at least as many times as there are generations making this claim.

Atheistic critics like Flew tend to freeze the development of doctrine at a point where it is most open to attack. They disallow for others changes in patterns of thought which they allow for themselves.[28] No doubt, for example, it suits critics of Catholicism to concentrate on Vatican I and ignore Vatican II. But such critics should not be taken seriously.

The claim that God is love becomes empty of Christian content only when Christians cease to relate it to stories of Jesus and to express themselves through new symbols, such as sisterhood or the idea that God is black. When their policies and sermons of the End recapture the spirit of love, in one of the senses warranted by the biblical tradition, no critic is entitled to dismiss their thinking as unchristian. Indeed, a perceptive critic will recognize their paradigm shifts and still be able to discern their family resemblances. The earliest Christians may not have anticipated all the actions of their spiritual heirs. Certainly our excursus into their history has been all too brief. But, nevertheless, it should be enough to indicate how a tradition lives, how it adopts new images, new policies and new strategies, without necessarily losing its identity along the way.

What we have been discussing are series of changes within a particular tradition. With reference to our earlier diagrams the changing nuclei of primary symbols in three periods may be portrayed as in Figure 3.

For each of these patterns distinctive kinds of love and expressions of right relationship with God will be found in the attendant stories, hymns, and prayers in which the symbols are used. What the family resemblances are can be determined by reference to such symbols as King, Lord, and Word.

These rough diagrams suffice to emphasize a point concerning clusters of symbols. *The nucleus in each case is the overall pattern, and it would be a mistake to suppose that there is an essential core running through all three,* consisting of Lord, Way, Truth, Life. For the kind of Lord, the meaning of Truth, the tone of the Way, vary by juxtaposition with the other symbols and the stories in which they are elaborated. A lord who is a messiah-rabbi is quite a different kind of lord from a suffering servant and friend of sinners. The fact that each of the predicated pairs is found in the New Testament is important in that that is the source for most primary Christian symbols. What governs their significance, however, is their relative placing. For example, if the image of the Suffering Servant remains dormant for a time, it cannot be

FIGURE 3.

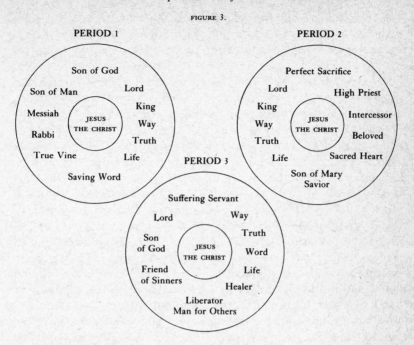

PERIOD 1

Son of God
Son of Man   Lord
Messiah   King
        JESUS   Way
        THE CHRIST
Rabbi   Truth
True Vine   Life
        Saving Word

PERIOD 2

        Perfect Sacrifice
    Lord   High Priest
    King
    Way   JESUS   Intercessor
              THE CHRIST
    Truth   Beloved
        Life   Sacred Heart
          Son of Mary
            Savior

PERIOD 3

        Suffering Servant
    Lord   Way
    Son   Truth
    of God JESUS
            THE CHRIST Word
    Friend   Life
    of Sinners
              Healer
        Liberator
        Man for Others

considered a major element in the statement of Christian principles during that period of religious history.

Within a tradition most symbols can be reactivated if circumstances warrant their recall. *Transformations of thought typically occur not by jettisoning parts of the tradition altogether but through shifts of emphasis.* If only as parts of earlier patterns which contributed to the tradition, the more archaic symbols still play a role in contemporary religious life. Generally, changes are only gradual, as new cultural contexts suggest new meaning for stories grown too familiar. A plague, a famine, or an enemy invasion may throw reflective men back onto images of healing, sustenance, or military success, which in other times have lost their appeal. Thus we hear more of the Prince of Peace in time of war and more of the Word and the Light in times of intellectual confusion, not because religious apologists are arbitrary but because the Way is their way also, with expressions to match their particular concerns.

It is difficult to determine if and when any completely new idea appears in the history of religious thought. We suggested that classical Christian stories were biased in favor of paternalistic rather than fraternalistic views of love. The rituals in the cathedrals tended to reflect the style of the courts, even though the sacred histories always offered an alternative set of images against which to measure the reigning princes and prelates. By Anselm's time, for example, talk of atonement evoked images of an infinite debt, such as a serf experienced in relation to the lord of the manor and the lord of the manor experienced in relation to his prince. The cultural influence of these relations was consistent with the vertical orientation of devotional treatises on the beauty of holiness and romances of the soul in the genre of Augustine's *Confessions*. We might regard the emergence of the fraternal orders as something quite novel in this context and in a sense they were. But they had their warrants in the spirit of earlier millenarian movements and the fraternalism of the churches in the catacombs.[29] Likewise the serf had his prototype in the history of the Hebrews. Themes which had been de-emphasized remained as precedents for later preachers, who presented what seemed new as really a return to earlier and "purer" patterns of faith, just as the Hebrew prophets had before them.

Looking from a distance, however, we can discern distinctive styles of faith emerging, for instance in Eastern Orthodoxy. We can trace the evolution of particular policies with respect to infant baptism, the eucharist, and the like.[30] How successful the adaptation of a particular cultural ideal may have been is a moot point. If we had a simple yardstick of faith in the Bible we might quickly determine how Christian a particular expression of love has been. But our argument has been that the Jesus stories legitimately lead to various expressions of love. As long as the nucleus of the story told is consistent with the master story of the Christ, that is, the pattern of redemption according to the Way of Resurrection, there is no reason to anathematize the storyteller.

The yardsticks used by many church dogmaticians have been too simplistic. After delineating *a* Christian point of view they have presumed to know what *the* Christian point of view must be for others.[31] This is not to say that any and every viewpoint can be twisted to pose as Christian. What counts, we have said, is the intentionality running through the stories told, that is, the quality of faith and hope and love. But, in practice, any one of several points of view might count as Christian depending upon what "way" is being proposed in the present juxtaposition of traditional images. Indeed, we shall see when we consider the question of truth that we are more likely to find our way if several points of view have been expressed. We are not entitled to judge our contemporaries, whose patterns of faith are still emerging. But we can judge previous generations, as later generations can judge us.

What we have seen with reference to the Christian tradition has parallels in the history of other traditions also. But we shall not find the identity of these others if we look only at original sources and external pressures, that is, at the body minus the spirit. We cannot analyze the faith of Gandhi, for instance, simply in terms of his family relationships, his experiences with the British in South Africa, and his deviations from traditional interpretations of the Sanskrit text of the *Bhagavad Gita*. We have to give these factors their due. But we have also to see how he applied the ideal of *moksha* to a political as well as a personal end. If we identify the nucleus of Hindu traditions with the kind of self-knowledge expressed in the Veda, then we have to recognize that his intentions were Hindu, even when they ran counter to the thinking of local brahmans and orthodox nationalists. Similarly, with respect to Marxist interpretations of Buddhist compassion in Sri Lanka, nonviolent expositions of holy war *(jihad)* in Islam and Zionist renditions of righteousness in Israel, we may or may not judge them to have sufficient family likenesses to count as legitimate expressions of their respective traditions. But unless we judge them in terms of their primary symbols and ultimate intentionality, we shall not be giving a religious estimate of their development.

However cursorily, I have tried in this chapter to look at the dynamics of religion within a tradition in terms of its constitutive principles and attendant policies, while continuing to use the model of primary and secondary symbols as a means of identifying a living faith. I have concentrated on examples from our own Western Christian history, especially concerning love and right relationships between man and God. But we might equally have looked at Buddhist developments in the lives of Indian, Chinese, and Japanese masters or at patterns of righteousness in Israel, from the period of kingship through the rabbinic movement to contemporary orthodox, conservative, and reformed expressions of Judaism. In each case we should discern real transformations within the traditions, not just variations on a single theme, whenever important primary symbols in the formative tradition became dormant and new meanings were found in old stories. Just what the difference is between this kind of transformation and changes which spell the end of a faith will become clearer after the next chapter.

Because we have stressed process and change in religious ways of life we make it difficult to account for stability and continuity.[32] Since previous theories of religion have tended to focus on abiding structures and substantive referents I do not think that this is a weakness that should unduly worry us. If religious truth is dialectical, we may confidently leave it to the reader to find the way between extremes. The challenge in accounting for religious thinking is that its "substance" is the spirit, the character, the distinctive personality traits and qualities of ecstatic experience which, while not disembodied or located elsewhere than in the overt processes which give them expression, is, nevertheless, only finally perceptible as we enter into the master story of each "way." Our contention has been that the kind of vision in which its intentionality is perceived is superimposed on our ordinary ways of looking at institutions and events. We see through these the spirit in which they are given shape. But there is always the danger that we are reading into such processes meanings which are not there. How we are to correct our impressions of current movements in religion is a problem to which we shall return in the last chapter.

The thesis of this book is that religion must be understood as much by reference to future orientations as to past traditions. Meanings change not wrongly and deplorably but rightly and laudably in each new context of faith. In this chapter I have indicated how this is so with regard to particular symbolic patterns in the Christian tradition. At the same time I have shown how the dynamics of faith, hope, and love need not be thought to be devoid of form. Despite the variety found in theology and liturgy we can discern the family resemblances to the constitutive structure of the master story as this is presented by each new generation of preachers. Critics who dismiss all "Christian deviations" as signs of loss of faith are, quite simply, missing the heart of the matter.

CHAPTER SEVEN

Transformations from Traditions

So FAR we have discussed meaning in religion in terms of symbols, stories, end-states, and virtues. We have considered changes of meaning within a tradition when its central symbol continues to serve as an identifying reference for new patterns of faith. Now we shall consider similar patterns of meaning in which the central reference is changed or lost altogether. We shall not consider individual conversion as such since that is the topic of the next chapter. But we must remember that what is separated for the sake of analysis generally runs together in our experience. As we look at changing thinking in the growth of new traditions, transitions from one established tradition to another, and transformations in which the way articulated can no longer be said to be religious, we shall inevitably touch on personal loss of faith. In order to give some specific focus to our reflections we shall look particularly at some Jewish reactions to the Nazi Holocaust and some contemporary Christian responses to secularization. These reactions and responses will point us in the direction of conversion experiences and demonic stories which we shall be discussing in Chapters Eight and Nine.

Transformations from a tradition occur when the central symbol in a system effectually ceases to be the same. The process may be sudden or gradual, and the last to realize what has happened may be those making the transition. For example, the earliest Christians undoubtedly thought of themselves primarily as Jews. At a time when the main patterns of Rabbinic Judaism were forming around the Torah it was an open question whether the Christians, like the Essenes, would develop into just another marginal sect. In that case what it meant to be Jewish might vary from sect to sect but the common intention would be to become the true Israel worshiping in Jerusalem, at least on high holy days. The common aspiration would be to be righteous in terms of the Torah, as we see in Paul. The fact that others may see more clearly than we do the direction in which we are moving will prove an important control on too subjectivist accounts, when we discuss truth in religion. Also, while our sources are too uncertain to allow a firm judgment, it seems plausible to suppose that the Pauline churches might not have departed from the mainstream of Judaism so rapidly without the impetus of the fall of the Temple in Jerusalem. If this is so, it suggests that a combination of "internal" and "external" changes forced the new community to go its separate way.[1] Those who were first called Christians by others now accepted the name and accepted martyrdom rather than renounce what it meant to them.[2]

Although Paul can hardly be thought typical of the first apostles of Christianity, he is an important figure for our understanding of transformations in life and thought. He illustrates what happens when one symbol replaces another as the central point in religious experience. Once he focuses on the Christ, in reflecting on the Will of God for Israel, he has begun to think as a Christian. Then he understands Jesus' Spirit as the new Torah which supersedes the Mosaic code. The significance of keeping the code changes accordingly. What it means to be a faithful member of the community now hinges on questions of table fellowship and the like. Circumcision and sabbath observances become optional to one for whom such an attitude would once have been unthinkable.[3] Paul still thinks as a Jewish Christian, keeping the holy days in Jerusalem when he can and regarding the Church as the New Israel. What were primary symbols for Saul as a Pharisee remain primary symbols for Paul as an Apostle. But the meaning of Israel and its Covenant has changed for him. In the light of the resurrection experience on the road to Damascus he sees them in a new way. In later generations those who share his resurrection faith but not his Jewish background can relegate Israel and the Mosaic code to the status of secondary symbols. By then the new tradition had been formed by the common stories of the life, death, and released Spirit of the Christ in a way that was no longer distinctively Jewish.

A glance at Muhammad's first pronouncements as a prophet indicates a similar kind of development. The angel Gabriel was appearing not only in his visions but also in those of Nestorians and other Christians scattered throughout the Middle East. Not until the prophet had become a statesman in Medina was he forced to acknowledge his difference from the Jewish traditions identified with Abraham and Moses.[4] At the same time his sense of community from the beginning extended beyond the limits of established Jewish and Christian communities. He gave lower priority to the Will of God expressed in books than to the Voice of God heard by his chosen Messenger. The core of a new tradition in a new community existed before anyone thought to identify it as such. Indeed Muhammad regarded his as the original community extending back to Adam, from which Jews and Christians had diverged. The strand of meaning reappearing in his rendition of the Qur'an or God's Word was, from his point of view, the central one all along. For its articulation Jewish and Christian symbols remain important. But now their meaning is associated with the experience of pilgrimage to Mecca, the purified ritual around the Ka'aba, and a new vision of the coming Day of Judgment.

It is easier to map the emergence of new traditions among strongly communal faiths. If we look at Gautama's Aryan path, for instance, we find that we are generally looking at him through the eyes of the Sangha, his monastic community of spiritual heirs. But in his own time he appeared as one holy man among many who attracted disciples by their prowess in yoga. Countless forgotten gurus before him traced the patterns which he explored. Thousands since have extrapolated from his teaching their own sense of what it means to achieve enlightenment. Rules for living in ashrams and forms of *puja* practiced before images tend to conform to common standards of style and discipline. Where anonymous and legendary individuals, rather than historic leaders, constitute the major figures in the formation of a tradition, we can be less certain of the specific changes which led to its development. Nevertheless, we can see definite family resemblances, for instance, in Shaiva and Vaishnava commentaries on the Hindu Veda or in changing views on animal sacrifice in the worship of the Mother.

We can readily appreciate how, in theory, it is possible to transfer from one tradition to another by reference to our model for patterns of faith. If, for example, we cluster such primary symbols as the Way, the Truth, the Light, the Physician, the Compassionate One about both Jesus the Christ and Gautama the Buddha, then seekers after truth who are aware of both sets of stories will naturally begin to compare them. As they make these stories their own they will either articulate them from the perspective of the Way of Resurrection, the Way of Enlightenment, or some other, perhaps syncretistic system. Suppose they read a life of Shinran and realize that here is a story of "justification by grace" earlier than Luther's, without some of Luther's more objectionable theses. From this they may be led to investigate the Way of Enlightenment further, to the point where their vision is transfigured by the symbol of the Buddha much more than by the symbol of the Christ. Or, moving in the other direction, a Shin Buddhist in Japan may be led by the industrialization of his country to ponder the impact of secularization on his culture. He may find Christian thinkers much more insightful on this issue than leaders of his own tradition. From this he may be drawn into centering his concerns on the Christ story. In this instance we have imagined someone who is action-oriented, whereas before we imagined people whose mood was devotional. In fact those who are contemplatives have most frequently crossed over from the mystical strand in one tradition to similar strands elsewhere.[5]

People tend to follow the way practiced by the dominant community of which they are members. Thus unless there is a Buddhist temple nearby our Christians interested in Shinran are not likely to join a major Buddhist sect. Instead they are likely to incorporate Buddhist ideas into their conceptions of grace and to see their Christianity differently as a result.[6] A possible example of this, for which I lack adequate empirical data, is the incorporation by Hindus and others of such Christian humanist institutions as hospitals and schools. My impression is that the impetus for their establishment came largely from Christian missions. These had relatively little impact in terms of numbers of converts. But they had enormous influence on medical care and educational standards. We might object that these reflect secular rather than religious influences, the cultural effect of Christians as Westerners rather than the religious result of a different faith. Apart from the fact that this objection introduces a questionable contrast between "secular" and "religious,"[7] it is noteworthy that the hospitals and schools were generally missionary foundations, whereas the secular concern was with trade and law enforcement. Even indigenous foundations, such as those associated with the Ramakrishna Maths and Missions, appear to be examples of appropriating what was best in the Christian presence while setting aside the rest.

My point here hinges on how we understand a religious presence. The missionaries with whom I talked in India seemed to take seriously such secular measurements as statistics on new baptisms and church attendance. On this view Christianity is making headway in India when more Hindus begin to call themselves Christians. But the distinction between intrinsic and extrinsic religious values leads us to suppose that when this happened under the British Raj the reasons had more to do with the Hindu quest for status *(artha)* and a desire to be like the sahib. What I have in mind instead is a structuring vision concerning welfare, especially among outcastes, which contrasts with the kind of view fostered by stories of the self in terms of rebirth and fate *(karma)*. The Christian structure—the "Word made flesh" in hospitals and schools—has, in my terms, occasionally been superimposed on the Vedic structure—the Self in the Wheel of Rebirth (the Atman in *samsara*)—without those accepting the Christian vision in this respect ceasing to be orthodox Hindus. If I am right, what we have here is an example of interaction on the religious level which is expressed on cultural and other levels as well. Conventional Hindu thinking concerning sickness and education is shaped by Christian and humanist thinking in a way which modifies the Hindu view of life. Unless we shared the missionaries' narrower and more worldly concept of success, we might well regard this interaction as a sign of the *vitality* of both Christian and Hindu traditions.

Defining religion as a personal way of life informed by traditional sets of symbols and concentrating on a shared vision of some transcendent end, we may describe *a person in transition* between traditions as *one who draws symbols from more than one tradition, or from outside any of the given traditions, and is not yet part of a community with a centering vision which he or she shares.* Transitional thinking also would be characterized as thinking which employs a variety of symbols and stories without concentrating on any one religious pattern of faith.

Bethune provides us with an example of transitional life and thought between the time of his cure and his departure for Spain. From his parents he retained the symbols of service and responsibility which informed his thinking about medicine, but without sharing their Protestant ideology of stewardship. Until his return from Leningrad he had his role as doctor and policies of healing to keep him going. But he lacked any universally applied framework for his thinking and any cause greater than his own satisfaction, in which to achieve self-realization. These he found in Marxism and they led him finally to China. The personal moves were all his own. But the symbol-system informing his thinking was given by, and held in common with, countless others.

The bridging work between traditions appears to have been done for Bethune by his continuing role as a doctor and interim policies based on ideals of service. His old reasons for adopting these were no longer valid but they were sufficiently ends in themselves to give him some sense of meaning in life. The Communist vision, when superimposed on these, gave his life a more transcendent reference. From this he derived a principle of integration, for instance when deciding whether or not to stay in Spain. As long as priorities were not called into question, he had enough cultural momentum, so to speak, to lead an active life without reference to deeper levels of meaning and truth. In the absence of historical evidence we may surmise that the pattern was similar for Jesus, Muhammad, Confucius, and Gautama (I have in mind their respective roles as carpenter, merchant, court tutor, and crown prince).

The interplay between internal and external pressures is not one that we can confidently map for individuals. We may follow Lévi-Strauss and other theorists concerning general cultural transformations, especially in relatively less complex societies. But among the classical civilizations and those who look for more than cargo from the sky, we can only point to distinctive features without presuming to know all the ins and outs of a religious situation.

Consider, for example, contemporary Jewish reactions to the Nazi Holocaust. On the one hand there are some who say that the Jewish traditions are unchanged by this experience.[8] It was just another example of the problem of evil. That it was utterly evil cannot be doubted. But its significance for the faithful is not in principle different from that of the sufferings of Job. Within the Bible and postbiblical Talmudic literature are reflections on experiences no less terrible for the people involved. The Exile, the destruction of the Temple, the slaughter by Antiochus Epiphanes, and pogroms through the ages, all provide symbols and stories which, seen in the light of the Torah, serve to express the righteousness of God and the election of Israel. It is contrary to faith to give Hitler a "posthumous victory" by bringing Belsen and Treblinka into the tradition. Where classical Judaic symbol structures are intact, there is no reason for admitting the Holocaust into the Holy of Holies.[9] In a forced choice between the eternal truth, identified through the Mosaic code, and loss of faith, after Auschwitz, the historic role of the Jews is to bear witness to the former. With Elie Wiesel we should respect the dead with our silence, not by calling stridently for new definitions of Jewish identity.

But the forced choice is a false choice. It arbitrarily limits the alternatives, as writers like Emil Fackenheim have shown.[10] He too tries to remain faithful to the witnessing role. But he recognizes that, since the Holocaust, the righteousness of God has been called into question in a new way. For the survivor generation "the Voice of the Red Sea" is almost drowned out by "the Voice of Auschwitz." As the Passover happened to us so did the Holocaust. Facile appeals to the saving events recorded in sacred history will not hide the fact of so many millions forsaken, not only by their fellow men but seemingly by their God. Neither our silence nor our speaking as such is true to their memory. Nor can we be true to their tradition if we fail to realize that it was because of that tradition that they were murdered. Only as we share their hope, saying "next year in Jerusalem," and translate this into a meaningful memorial to them, can we deny the last word to the fascistic murderers in our times. For many, like Fackenheim, the expression of this fidelity is an aroused Zionism, in which the survival of the State of Israel is both a literal necessity and a symbolic demand.

By contrast with Fackenheim, a more "radical" thinker like Richard Rubenstein no longer acknowledges the intellectual force of the Talmudic literature in its own terms.[11] He too wishes to affirm the identity of the community expressed through its myths and rituals. He too sees the need for the survival of the State of Israel. But in his thinking the Holocaust appears to have replaced the Exodus as the pivotal event in Jewish history. He juxtaposes traditional symbols with psychological ones to find meaning in life.[12] There can be no pretense here of business as usual in the yeshivas. Events have overtaken them and turned their interpretations upside down.[13]

Against the authority of "establishment Judaism" Rubenstein sets the authority of his own experience.[14] This is the experience of a vulnerable individual whose mortality will not be "passed over" by any transcendent deity. No traditional reading of the Way of Israel is plausible in the evident absence or nonexistence of a supernatural saving force. Instead the whole story of love and death is symptomatic of the interactions among Id, Ego, and Superego of which Freud wrote. He has taught us to see through the breaking of the pleasure-principle against the reality of our limitations. The primary and secondary symbols of Jewish thought, including Pauline thought, are therefore best understood as elements in a Way of Sublimation. We need no longer accept our unacceptability before God, as Tillich still argued. Rather we must accept the inevitability of our finitude, bowels and all.

We can see, then, how the Holocaust's significance changes according to its juxtaposition with different patterns of faith. In our first example the Holocaust is at most a secondary symbol. For Fackenheim it is clearly a primary symbol, so much so that the pattern of faith is more elliptical than circular.[15] Whereas for Neusner and others the master story is that of Jacob's wrestling and its sequel, in which Job is the key to Auschwitz rather than vice versa, for Fackenheim the mystery of this new evil threatens to make nonsense of earlier patterns of meaning. There can be no explanation of man's inhumanity to man which takes the measure of the enormity of what happened in the death camps. By beginning and ending his reflections in the midrashic mode Fackenheim shows his intention to be traditionally Jewish. The Holocaust does not destroy his faith but reminds him and us that faith exists in fear and trembling. No neat patterns of thought can iron out the ambiguities of life. But because this is so the intention to keep the faith is not always sufficient to keep it within traditional frameworks. External pressures may over-whelm the individual, as we often see in Elie Wiesel's stories.

When the Holocaust becomes not just a basic symbol but the central focus for reflections on the Jewish tradition, we have not just a transformation within the tradition but a change of faith. In Rubenstein's early writing we have an eloquent example of its negative impact. It elicits the Nietzschean thought not only that God is dead, but that we have killed him. And if it is a symbol which transfigures our vision of the end, that end tends to be thought of as eternal nothingness. In his later writing Ruben-stein understands psychoanalytically the image of God as infanti-cide. Our ambivalence concerning the Commanding Voice can then be understood to be part of our growing up. We must learn to see ourselves in a world in which the real furies are within us. By this time the Oedipus story has replaced Genesis as a key and a therapeutic plot dominates the reading of events. The Holo-caust remains as a symbol of death. But beside Thanatos, Death, we must put Eros, Love, if we would understand what kind of wrestling match we are in. Here the Holocaust is a bridge experi-ence. At the center of one tradition it was disruptive. Aligned according to a more psychoanalytical vision of the human condi-tion, it expresses the shadow side of primordial energy. Taken alone, it is as opaque as Fackenheim insists. But in this new context it takes on a meaning which promises life for the children through the death of the parents.[16]

Without following either Fackenheim or Rubenstein we can learn from them how the Holocaust experience remains an obstacle to any traditional pattern of Jewish thinking. Faith simply cannot wash away such brute facts in the stream of consciousness. The force of faith may carry us around them or roll a few boulders along in its flood. But it cannot dissolve them. For this reason it may be a misnomer to call the Holocaust a religious symbol. As we shall see with reference to Hiroshima in Chapter Nine, the negative impact of such an experience may disrupt the stability of any pattern of faith. Our reactions to it may be so strong that we end up with a different faith concentrated on a different center.

Fackenheim and Rubenstein bear witness to the dynamics of religion and to an integrity of thought which refuses to cope with painful experiences by repressing them. For the philosopher this is a matter of intellectual honesty.[17] For the psycho-social historian of ideas it is a therapeutic necessity. Their concern may seem obsessive to those in the mainstream of the tradition, for whom the Holocaust represents a challenge to renewed appreciation of the old stories of faith. But for all who enter into the experience of modern European Jews the Holocaust cannot be a matter of indifference.

For members of a living tradition like Judaism, such events as the founding of the State of Israel call for expressions of new faith. They evoke patterns which may be more or less traditional but in any case cannot simply remain unchanged. To the extent that the Torah is seen to be the Will of God for contemporary Jews, the new generation will not be assimilated into other cultures. To the extent that this symbol recedes to the margins of consciousness, we may wonder how long Jewish images will remain potent expressions of their identity. Like his brother Paul, Rubenstein may still wrestle with what it means to be a Jew after his conversion. But for his students the Torah may not remain a live symbol.

In a wider context what is distinctively modern about Rubenstein's thinking is not so much his neo-Freudian terminology as his emphasis on the authority of his own experience. We see the same kind of thinking at work in the earlier writing of Paul van Buren and Sam Keen. The former still acknowledges the centrality of the Jesus story for his autobiographical reflections. But the symbolism of Jesus' freedom for others destroys the symbolism of God as the Absolute (if it even makes sense). In van Buren's *The Secular Meaning of the Gospel* we again have an almost elliptical pattern, where the twin foci are the Christ and the author as exponent of a secular philosophy. In Keen's *To a Dancing God* the center is the author's autobiography, to which the Christ is related as a primary symbol (or a secondary symbol in conjunction with Keen's father as primary). In general terms, the central symbol is the Individual Self and priority is given to authentic self-realization. The Self is both a very specific, finite, bodily existence in our time and an exemplar of the creative and recreative rhythms of the evolution of the species. Keen's humanistic story is informed by psychoanalytic images also. For others who share similar backgrounds, he offers the outlines of a Way of Education with an optional curriculum and student-centered course material.[18]

Concentration on oneself as the authoritative center of experience may seem to spell the end of all tradition and, according to our definition, a complete departure from religious faith. However, as Keen's story of the man with aphasia shows, some sort of memory is necessary to self-realization. In fact, there is no reason why the individual should not appropriate symbols from all the traditions now available in our culture. This is what William C. Shepherd suggests when he advocates "polysymbolic religiosity" and conscious eclecticism.[19] In a spirit of free play, the individual remains open to any avenue which currently holds out a promise of ecstasy. This is a *principled* position, directed toward the realization of some sort of transcendent end-state, in which the exclusivist ethos of sectarian traditions is repudiated. Such a proposal raises the question whether we must always have a continuing or common center in order to be religious. A religiously motivated liberation movement today might want to include liberation from the image of centering. In Chapter Nine we shall reexamine our assumptions on this point with reference to the formation of patterns of faith.

As Shepherd notes in another paper, the fragmenting effect of the principle of individual choice is largely offset by the convergence of cultures remarked on by both Marshall McLuhan and Teilhard de Chardin.[20] The varieties of religious expression encountered in California and elsewhere tend to be variations on a finite number of themes.[21] An individual who listens to Cat Stevens records, reads Hermann Hesse, and smokes the occasional joint of marijuana or experiments with premarital sex may indeed be "doing her own thing." So far as she is conscious of religious choices as such, she may see herself as rejecting the Protestant straightjacket of her parents' faith. She may never have heard of Norman O. Brown, Robert Bellah, or Theodore Roszak. But behind her is a growing tradition of lyrics, stories, symbolic styles of dress and gesture, complete with commentaries by approved authors. Her mix may be her own. But she is far from unique. Rather, as I see it, she is living out that paradigm shift in values from order to freedom on which we commented earlier. It would be a mistake to ignore the religious dimensions of her vision of self and treat her departure from parental norms as a purely psychological aberration. Indeed, in Shepherd's view she would be *religiously* wrong to renounce what fits her experience in favor of what fits theirs.

The authority of individual experience over communal norms is typical of the mystical strand in all traditions. The figure of the "wandering rhinoceros"—the individual seeker after enlightenment—is a familiar one especially on the Indian scene. R. C. Zaehner and others have recognized similarities in varieties of mysticism while arguing that there is a difference in kind between their sacred and profane forms.[22] Among the many issues raised we comment on only two. One is the question whether "chemical ecstasy" offers only an ersatz enlightenment.[23] The other is whether polysymbolic religiosity is, in Kierkegaard's sense, an aesthetic rather than a religious passion. We cannot, of course, answer for every individual. Indeed Kierkegaard warns us not to be deceived by appearances concerning who is unique and who is not. But he also reminds us of the principle stressed in Chapter Four: that the passage to faith is through moral discipline. This does not mean conventional mores but action based on universalizable maxims.[24] With regard to ecstasy then the question is not so much how it is induced. (The physiological side-effects of ascetic exercises in the past may not have been so different from the action of drugs as Zaehner supposed.)[25] The question is whether the experience becomes pivotal in a disciplined life and whether, if this is so, "natural" means to its realization may not be healthier. We cannot assess the experience in isolation from its existential context. Here too lies the answer concerning aesthetics. There may well be an aesthetic component in some forms of faith, especially those motivated by Eros or Desire. But this does not preclude the possibility of their having religious significance as well.

What concerns us in this chapter is not so much the religious status of private beliefs as the changes in thinking which accompany moves away from traditions. Among contemporary movements it is apparent that the central symbols of major world religions may function as primary symbols in new expressions of faith. There may not seem to be much resemblance between the figure of Muhammad in the Nation of Islam among American blacks and the Muhammad portrayed in Arabic traditions (Hadith). Jesus Christ Superstar may not be quite what Saint Matthew had in mind. Zen Master Hakuin might find a "chocolate-coated Buddha" hard to stomach. But, however variously perceived the symbols of traditional faiths may be, they are ineradicable elements in our common cultural context. Whether we blame superficial surveys of world religions in introductory college courses, or the impact of America's military adventures in Southeast Asia, the fact is that, at least in our "counter-culture," these symbols are still transfiguring. Thus it is possible for someone on the margins of our intellectual establishment, such as Malcolm X in Boston, to discover the figure of Muhammad and end his life as an orthodox follower of an historical tradition. At the same time it is possible for someone to move from an historic faith in the other direction, toward an eclectic appreciation of the host of inspiring figures whom David Miller plausibly sees as reincarnations of classical gods and goddesses.[26]

Viewing such movements religious critics of contemporary culture are in danger of emphasizing what may be of major importance for a sociology or psychology of religion, but is of secondary significance in the dynamics of religion. For the latter we must look to the redemptive processes that are at work in whatever ideal lives are central to our stories of identity and integrity. Until very recently, these might have included stories of American presidents and romanticized versions of the New Promised Land.[27] Instead of focusing on the secularity of churches we need to ask what ends are envisioned in the major literature of our generation. What is at issue, religiously speaking, is the intentionality of a Tillich or a Rubenstein or a Keen. In the lives of their echoers, what is religiously important is the presence or absence of constitutive principles in their self-selected stories of faith. *Where there are no coordinating symbols and no visions transfiguring everyday lives we must say that there is no religion.* Persons in that condition have either lost their way or not yet found it and their thinking reflects their confusion. They may then be psychologically incapable of tolerating the ambiguities of existence and opt for authoritarian social systems. They may even continue to attend religious services for extrinsic reasons. They may regard death as a defeat. In any case, they will exemplify the twilight zones of religious experiences. They do not provide us with paradigms of life through which a sense of worth and transcending purpose may be revealed.

Referring to Tillich's three kinds of anxiety (death, moral condemnation, and intellectual emptiness), we should say of those who lose their religious identity in one tradition and find nothing to replace it that they are indeed empty. There is no spiritual power in the depths of their lives to carry them through a crisis. There is no process of self-realization that brings them a sense of personal fulfillment. However Tillich's analysis was too idealistic in that he gave inner direction priority over external pressures. The lesson of the Holocaust, as we find it, for example, in Wiesel's *Night,* is that meaninglessness may be a byproduct of fate and death.[28] Tillich himself never suggested more than that in certain periods and places one type of anxiety predominates. He took the existentialistic authors of before and after World War II to be expressing above all a sense of meaninglessness rather than guilt or dread of death. But since then we have thought more of our collective responsibility for the state of our environment and the poverty of our neighbors. We know enough of thought control to see that faith, hope, and love—or wisdom, compassion, and courage—are shaped by what happens *to* us, as well as by what we ourselves do in moments of decision.

Elie Wiesel tells the story of a succession of patriarchs, the outline of which is something like the following. The first patriarch remembers God's promise to come to his people in time of persecution, provided that the right rituals are performed in the right place. When trouble comes the patriarch retires to that place in the forest, follows the prescription, and all becomes well. In time, the troubles arise again. The next patriarch remembers only part of the prescribed routine. But he too goes to the place in the forest and intercedes with heaven on behalf of the people. Again God saves his people. But they again forget him in their prosperity and, when the troubles return, the next patriarch remembers only the place in the forest. Again his intention is accepted by God. The cycle is repeated. The patriarch after him remembers only that there was a place. This too is enough. There remains the barest pattern of a faith. But still it brings salvation to those who were otherwise lost.[29]

But what if the first patriarch had been killed and no one else knew the sequence? Or what if they had all forgotten that they were Jews? They could not then have had the same intention to be sons of Israel. Whatever else, the Torah could in no sense be called the central symbol of their tradition. They might even have forgotten, in their hour of need, that there was another dimension to their destiny. They might have passed by the place in the forest without recognizing it for what it was. For whatever reasons they would have become people of no religious faith.[30]

By contrast, in the Holocaust and the founding of the State of Israel, we have examples of a people with a continuing sense of tradition, now concentrating their thinking on new symbols. Among some of them it would still be possible for the symbol of the Torah to die the "death by a thousand qualifications" and for the community to become simply a secular state. But others like Fackenheim would believe that they were on the negative tack of an Hegelian dialectic of history, out of which might come new symbols of hope. The meaning of the Torah then would not be empty. But its thrust would be in the direction of active participation on their part in the shaping of events. Where they might differ from Marxist dialecticians would not be that they were idealists and the latter materialists (a *dialectical* materialist is not so far from an immanental idealist). It would be in their conceptions of the power which realizes the future.[31] Both could be humanistic in emphasis. But those who retained their Jewish identity would still have as their master story a Passover narrative which was as much promise as memory.

An example of a humanistic vision without transcendent reference is *The Plague* by Camus. In a minimal sense there is some kind of transcendence in the affirmation of I-You relationships over I-It.[32] But the only absolute is the plague itself and any vision of an end transcending the level of everyday observation is systematically debunked. The moment when Tarrou and Rieux swim in unison under the stars, for example, which T. S. Eliot might have presented as a transfiguring vision based on the symbolism of the elements, Camus treats simply as an interlude. There is no hint of the Always You (Eternal Thou) which Buber sees through every I-You encounter. What makes such a story nonreligious is this resolute rejection of any vision of transcendence. The presence or absence of clerical figures in the story is irrelevant. What is relevant is an ethos in which religious thinking is either entirely absent or presented as darkness and not light.

Whitehead remarked somewhere that philosophies of life are never refuted. They simply die away. Death in this context means dispersal. The various centers of concern dry up. The relationships between one part of a symbol system and another are broken. The river becomes a stagnant pool eventually to be transformed into a meadow. The process need not happen all at once. What brings decay first may be different on different occasions. But the upshot is, in the metaphor of the Isopanishad, that the eater of food becomes food for others. Old central symbols become new primary and secondary symbols. Living believers become dead witnesses. Living faiths become dead traditions. Where once there was an identifiable pattern of life and thought now there is nothing binding. The religion has gone out of the temple. We may see shades of the old faith haunting the streets. But the power and the glory will be forgotten and the names on the doors will be changed. The emptiness becomes a silence which allows new voices to be heard. Or, to shift metaphors, the final symbol may be a wasteland under a mushroom cloud. However we describe the situation, we shall have to say that the transformation is complete at the moment when we can no longer identify a consistent pattern of development which has a single continuing nucleus. This may be an occasion for relief or for increased anxiety. Either way, it is what happens when traditions cease to be transformed by fresh hope.

CHAPTER EIGHT

Individual Transformations

THE DYNAMIC interplay of past tradition and future orientation is characteristic also of individual transformations in religion. The past guides our behavior through habits formed over the years. The future exists for us as our potential. Possible roles and future selves form patterns in present thinking which may or may not be harmoniously integrated. Where we lack a centering focus or sense of identity our experience is of the self divided against itself. In addition, we feel separated from others. Without at least the outlines of a master story, we cannot realize personal wholeness ("salvation" means health or wholeness). Self-realization in this respect depends on individual affirmation and interaction with others in our community. But it also depends on developing some cause, or identification, with a wider world or Self, a deeper, more inspiring Whole. These are the points which we shall elaborate and illustrate in this chapter. As we do so, we shall begin to pay attention to another aspect in the process of transformation. That is the importance of "objective" truth, the realism as well as the optimism in our future orientations.

The process of coming to an integrative pattern of faith in individual lives is usually called conversion. Accounts of conversion too often betray a Protestant stereotype. They focus on moments of conscious decision, in which previous convictions are dramatically reversed. They tend to minimize the more characteristically Catholic tradition of gradual sanctification through habituating exercises of virtue. Even William James succumbs to this stereotype in his classic account of conversion in *The Varieties of Religious Experience*. However, if we read his remarks there in conjunction with his general lectures on psychology, we find a concept of centers and margins in individual experience which meshes with what we saw earlier concerning patterns of faith and transformations in and across traditions.

James begins with the experience of the divided self. He finds it in all the major traditions. He interprets this experience according to a conception of a multiplicity of selves, which is akin to Hume's in Western philosophy and to Buddhist doctrines of No Self (Anatta). (Nowadays we tend to speak of roles rather than of selves in this way.) I shall summarize James's conceptions here with particular reference to his concepts of the potential religious self and the process of conversion. Then, for an example from a more contemporary milieu and an outlook closer to Jung's in psychology, I shall turn to Margaret Atwood's most widely acclaimed novel *Surfacing*. It gives us one young woman's quest for identity and integrity in a "post-Christian" setting that lacks any consciously affirmed master story. Then I shall turn briefly to observations about prisoners subjected to thought-reform. Atwood's heroine and such prisoners exemplify the interplay of inner and outer pressures which provoke individual transformations in religion. What makes for lasting transformations, and how our examples differ from stories of more traditionally religious conversions, are questions to which we shall turn at the end of the chapter. But first we need the theoretical framework suggested by James's pragmatic analysis of our topic.

What distinguishes James from the British empiricists, whom he otherwise tends to follow in philosophical psychology, is his emphasis on the continuity of experience. He spoke of this as a "stream of thought" (he would as easily have said "stream of feeling" if he could have avoided misinterpretations). In this stream a multiplicity of selves or roles attaches to a variety of objects and relationships.[1] What characterizes the flow is the succession of our interests in now this and now that, always on the basis of a distinction between "me" and "not-me." The former is "the empirical self" which is the object of self-knowledge and psychological study. The latter is the world, which is unique for everyone since the "me" from which it is differentiated is always different.

The nucleus of each "me" is the bodily existence felt to be present at any given time. Among my memories what counts as "me" are those now present to consciousness which resemble the felt objects for which I now care as expressing me and mine.[2] That is to say, I have a selective memory which recalls whatever fits my intentions concerning my future roles and relationships. (James speaks of "thinking of" rather than intention. There is no separate entry for "Intention" in the Index to *The Principles of Psychology*.) In its widest sense, says James, a man's self is the total of all that he can call his own—wife, children, ancestors, friends, reputation, deeds, house, yacht, bank account, and so on.[3] As these diminish he dies a little. As these grow he becomes "somebody." Here we have the authentic voice of European materialism, transplanted to America.

For James the constituents of the self at any given time can conveniently be grouped under three headings—the bodily, the social, and the spiritual. Each of these in turn could be analyzed into further clusters so that we could say, for instance, that "a man has as many social selves as there are individuals who recognize him."[4] His selves or roles vary according to whether we think of him in the midst of his family, at work, at play, reading, or singing. His "bodily me" is his set of material objects, including physical attributes and physical environment. His "spiritual me" is his portion of wit, charm, intelligence, and the like. His "social me" is his set of interpersonal relationships, including past and future relationships, that is, not just with present acquaintances but also with predecessors and potential future admirers, detractors, and judges.

Since for James there is no substantial self, what counts as "the real me" depends upon which self I act on in moments of conflict. For example, to a soldier it is important to be thought a hero. In battle his honor is at stake and, therefore, he will stand and fight. By contrast an honorable citizen accosted by a thief does not consider himself, and is not considered, a coward if he runs away. Each is being true to his "real" self.

Psychologically this "real" self may be a potential rather than an actual set of attributes and relationships. Also, we may attain as much satisfaction from renouncing as from realizing this "self." This, James suggests, may be a reason why some follow what I call the Way of Renunciation, whereas others follow the Way of Revolution. "How pleasant," James remarks, "is the day when we give up striving to be young,—or slender! Thank God! we say, *those* illusions are gone." In this experience he sees the key to justification by faith since, in the history of evangelical preaching, it comes as a follow-up to convictions of sin and despair of self. The pleasure is in the renunciation of "salvation by works." The relief at ceasing an attempt to be moral paragons is at least as great as any satisfaction that we might feel in becoming saints.[5]

It is important to notice that the touchstone of religion for James is our potential social self. (He is not as individualistic as many assume.) This self may or may not include a God-relationship but, in any case, it includes an ideal order of existence which is active in our imaginations.[6] Due to his father's interest in mysticism and his wife's interest in psychical phenomena, James became open to the thought that our universe includes a host of agencies extending well beyond the range of our "normal" waking experience.[7] In this wider psychic context, the point of religious importance for him is our need for corroboration and consolation of our "real" self. Here we see the pragmatic thrust of his thinking, the emphasis on results rather than causes, pointing toward conclusions later spelled out in his more philosophical writing on religion.

For those of us whose basic needs are met, our problem in life, as James remarks, is that we can imagine many more possible selves than we can ever hope to actualize. Even if we rotate roles, some of our dreams are mutually exclusive. It gives me pleasure, perhaps, to see myself as both an ascetic secluded in Tibet and a bon-vivant making the rounds of nightspots off Broadway. But "the thing is simply impossible."[8] I have to choose, as James had to choose between becoming an artist or a scientist.

But recognizing that I have to choose is only the first step in an uncertain process. For, in backing one self as my real self, I may make a mistake. I may be disappointed and I may be called misguided by others. In this latter case especially, what is decisive is who those others are. For if I am a spiritual aristocrat I can live with the condemnation of the mob, provided that I believe that my choice would be approved by members of my own social set. Moreover, these peers need not actually exist. Provided that I believe that *posterity* would approve, if ever it were to hear of my exploits, then the thought of these possible future judges can outweigh the verdict of my present detractors. In this context the ultimate possible judge is God or the "communion of the saints."[9] I can solve my problem by deciding on the course of action of which I think they would approve.

Instead of picturing a thing called an Ego battling with a thing called an Id and working up a Superego, via a set of identifications in the context of family rivalries, James portrays "ego strength" as a matter of habitual reinforcement of one set of identities over others. In this process we may be formally religious or not. We may imagine astral associations or limit our relationships to the members of a single tribe. We may attain a permanent sense of self gradually and without difficulty or only after great conflict. We may be conscious of our choices, or conditioned by forces of which we are only dimly aware. Whatever the factors, the basic process is the same. "To be converted, to be regenerated, to gain assurance," says James, "are so many phrases which denote the process, gradual or sudden, by which a self hitherto divided, and consciously wrong, inferior and unhappy, becomes unified and consciously right, superior and happy, in consequence of its firmer hold of religious realities."[10] This definition applies whether or not the convert believes his moves to have been inspired by God.

James recognized that in a secular world many would attribute their individual transformation to subconscious urges rather than to supernatural sources. To him such attributions were irrelevant since *results rather than origins are the key to religious behavior.* Individuals may differ in the degrees to which they refer their decisions to some ideal tribunal. But, according to James, social progress consists in appealing to ever "higher" courts of opinion for judgment on our real selves. Those who deny thoughts of an ultimate judge may simply be deceiving themselves. "Probably no man can make sacrifices for 'right' without to some degree personifying the principle of right for which sacrifice is made, and expecting thanks for it."[11] Here we see that intersecting of code and character on which we commented in Chapter Six. Whether thoughts of an ultimate judge are always inspiring is a question to which we return in Chapter Ten.

In the stream of thoughts, which is our experience of existence, some currents run deeper than others. James is true to Hume's legacy in thinking that the strongest currents are those built up by force of habit.[12] We may imagine ourselves playing an almost infinite number of roles. But many of these form only fleeting aspirations. The center of our energies will be the system of ideas associated with our choice of "real" self. In terms of this choice many other choices, as noted above, will be *practically* unreal. They exist only on the margins of consciousness.

But the center of interest changes and we may find ourselves torn between two equally attractive possibilities. We may grow literally hot or cold at the thought of becoming involved in the realization of one vision of ourselves rather than another. Then what counts is the view from the "hot spots" in the field of felt associations. This is the perspective from which aim is taken in our movement from one self to another.[13] Since we are constantly on the move, and easily exhausted by a succession of existential choices, after our initial impulse toward one goal rather than another we tend to let ourselves move automatically. Hence habit, says James, is "the enormous flywheel of society, its most precious conservative agent."[14] This is as true for those who practice yoga as for those who attend church. It is evident in the physical idiosyncrasies of voice and gesture, which we adopt in early adulthood, and in the patterns of thought on which most of us settle during our college or early professional years. Consequently, even when the plot changes and new symbols are preferred in religious thinking, the character and tone of our religious life do not markedly change. An earnest Methodist today can become an earnest Catholic tomorrow, and so on.

According to James, following Starbuck, what happens in the case of a "sudden" conversion is that an habitual drift, which was running counter to the direction of our conscious wishes, bursts to the surface of our self-awareness. James was too suspicious of the extravagance of psychoanalytic theorists to listen to their more elaborate accounts of subconscious forces. (Atwood will give us a more complex image of surfacing.) In any case, whether gradual or sudden, for James *a convert is one whose ideal social self now takes the central place until "religious aims form the habitual center of his energy."*[15]

Psychology cannot tell us why we tip the scales in favor of one course of action rather than another. But it can give us a general account of the kinds of personal processes to be found in our "mental system." Relying on "the hackneyed symbolism of a mechanical equilibrium" James describes the habitual course of our development. He accounts for changes of direction in terms of an "explosion" of some violent emotion—love, jealousy, guilt, fear, remorse, anger, hope, or ecstasy. These are not symptoms of Oedipal conflicts but simply normal parts of adolescent development. Traditional religions have always recognized and channeled such changes in socially approved ways.[16]

James does not explain how his account fits with the fact that, in religious literature, the classical conversion stories are not of adolescents but of middle-aged adults. But he does insist that there are different "higher and lower limits of possibility set to each personal life." We cannot generalize about any given individual's experience. But we may call ourselves "saved" when we "touch upon our own upper limit and live in our own highest center of energy."[17] (A genius is one who has a "high" upper limit and "wide" field of consciousness.) For all of us the margins of consciousness are indeterminate. The potential range of our "subliminal lives" greatly exceeds the bounds of ordinary expectations. Not only have we to be hospitable here to insights gained from altered states of consciousness. We have also to recognize the links between physiological conditions and psychological states. In this connection James refers approvingly to the findings of Binet, Janet, Breuer, and Freud.[18]

Throughout, the metaphor of centers and margins of conscious energy systems, coupled with the metaphor of hot and cold desires, constitutes James's most descriptive idiom. With these he depicts our growing sense of personal identity. Personal salvation then is that transformation enabling us to integrate our stream of thoughtful feeling on the basis of an ideal social self which takes center stage.

On the psychological level, this pattern fits what, on the cultural level, we have earlier described as a model for the dynamics of religion.

If we develop James's descriptions of individual changes on the basis of more recent work in developmental psychology we shall look to other terms than habit and choice in explaining patterns of behavior. Following Maslow we may suggest that, if "basic needs" *are* taken care of, our conceptions of self may become less egotistical than James supposed. A yogi may become indifferent to habitual centers and margins. Following Jung we may suppose that, as career expectations are met, other aspects of the potential self will begin to surface, which were repressed during the drive toward early achievements. Following Kohlberg we may suppose that there are degrees of maturity in moral and religious development, such that the roles and rules of early life are superseded.[19] With all three we are suggesting that, beyond the normal adolescent crises, lies a search for integrity or wholeness in later adult life which is fundamental to religious stories of salvation or redemption.

Whether we speak of bringing the various facets of our personality into some "mandala" of symbolic forms or of centering on one set of roles to the exclusion of others, the end-state is said to be that of a unified self interacting creatively with a changing environment. If we picture this end-state as ultimate freedom we might want to regard the completion of the process of redemption as a realization of "No Self." But, in any case, the quality of the experience will be said to be such that its attainment defines the meaning of ultimate value in the story of our lives.

In *The Varieties of Religious Experience* James assumes a typical pattern of religious experiences and then adduces an array of incidents to illustrate it. He never follows a single life story through. Nowadays our autobiographical literature is likely to be less overtly religious and less confident of a unified ending. In place of James's expansive self with wife, yacht, and fluctuating prestige, we are likely to encounter a single parent struggling to survive. Indeed, in a survey of Canadian literature, for example, Margaret Atwood finds the typical end envisoned to be one of sheer survival. The primary symbol for most heroes and heroines tends to be not that of a genius but that of a victim.

According to Atwood, a victim's strategies may conform to one of four "basic positions." The first represses the feeling of being victimized by attacking some supposedly inferior group. The second recognizes that we are all victims of circumstances but identifies the victimizing power as some vast abstraction, such as Fate, Biology, Class Warfare, or the Will of God, which is too much for us to overcome. The third position is reached if you "acknowledge the fact that you are a victim but refuse to accept the assumption that the role is inevitable." If you then succeed in repudiating the victim role you achieve *position four*, which is that of the ex-victim or creative non-victim.[20]

Repudiation of the victim role is hardly a conversion experience in James's sense. It leaves us rather where James begins, with the realization that we have to take responsibility for our own destiny. But in doing so it builds on insights in psychology which fill in some of the gaps concerning subconscious forces left in James's pattern. Atwood's four "positions" indicate some of the hidden agendas which wreak havoc in our lives. James by himself paints too optimistic a picture for our times. He leaves us without sufficient recognition of the extent to which our conscious thoughts are rationalizations. In short, if psychoanalysts err on the side of reading into their patients' stories plots which are not there, James errs in the opposite direction, taking their statements at almost face value. What Atwood and others help us to do is to probe the depths, while keeping in mind the need to surface if we are to survive as integrated selves. Atwood carries her theoretical scheme into her own novel, *Surfacing*, and it is through its story that we shall explore a "post-Christian" vision of life.

The "heroine" of *Surfacing* is an unnamed young commercial artist from the city who returns to the island cottage where she used to summer with her parents.[21] Her widower father has retired to the island alone. Now he is reported missing. With her lover Joe and another couple, David and Anna, the heroine has come to search for her father. During this search Atwood takes us into the woman's thinking, not only about her father, but also about her present divided roles and relationships. How she comes to some sort of self-realization is what interests us now.

In effect Atwood gives us a series of stories within a story, each one expressing the woman's sense of her "real self" during a given period in her life. What makes the novel hard to follow at first is the fact that the plots of earlier stories keep intruding on the heroine's accounts of present problems. Earlier characters are superimposed on her perception of present figures. Like the heroine readers are never quite sure where they are. All can only hope for some liberating insight by working through the distractions of past stories in order to face the present and the future with some composure.

We soon realize that the real struggle is not to find the father —that he is dead seems probable from the beginning—but to bring to the surface memories and past aspirations which keep haunting the heroine in the present. Atwood uses the image of diving in the lake for the father's body in order to express the symbolic journey which the heroine must complete in order to regain her sanity. In accordance with Ricoeur's concept of double intentionality, there is both the physical search for a physically missing body and a "spiritual" search whose object is not at all clear. Not until the heroine comes to terms with her past can she make any emotional commitments for the future. She drifts on the surface of a relationship with Joe, while the deep currents of her life swirl about scarcely acknowledged memories of a previous love.

Primarily Joe represents the possibility of a genuine relationship for the heroine in the future. At present he merely satisfies her physical needs and is the antithesis of her father. The latter was a rationalistic scientist, orderly, explaining and classifying nature, cerebral, seemingly self-confident and self-sufficient. By contrast Joe is an unsuccessful artist, inarticulate, physically present but locked in a nightmare dream life of his own. He is not inauthentic like David and Anna, who deceive themselves about their infidelities and artistic aspirations. There is hope of a future with him. But he must cease to regard love-making as a symbol of victory over the "weaker" sex, in the manner of people in "position one."

The heroine too deceives herself and us when we first meet her. We find her thinking mostly of her divorced husband and abandoned child. Scenes with him keep displacing from the center of attention scenes with Joe and the search for the father. The trauma of the broken relationship leaves her unable to feel anything for Joe. She has lost her way in the city and has lost her guides in the country. Instead of being married and living happily ever after, according to the master story of her childhood, she is in the midst of a plot for which she was unprepared. Alone and vulnerable she scans memories of past incidents for clues to her present predicament. But her memory is unreliable.

At one point, for example, she tells herself that she always felt safe in her own room, even at night. "That's a lie," her own voice says to her out loud. She ponders this and admits it was so, concluding:

> I have to be more careful about my memories. I have to be sure they're my own and not the memories of other people telling me what I felt, how I acted, what I said: if the events are wrong the feelings I remember about them will be wrong too, I'll start inventing them and there will be no way of correcting it, the ones who could help are gone. I run quickly over my version of it, my life, checking it like an alibi: it fits, it's all there till the time I left. Then static, like a jumped track, for a moment I've lost it, wiped clean; my exact age even, I shut my eyes, what is it? To have the past but not the present, that means you're going senile.[22]

The suggestion of a definitive "version" of one's life accords with our conception of meaning in life expressed in master stories. The suggestion that the *feelings* are invented to fit the facts reminds us of James's insistence that the stream of thought and feeling is one. The heroine refuses to panic. She forces herself to find firm reference points in the familiar surroundings. Then she goes out on the lake to resume the search for her father.

Formal religion is no help to her. She discarded the story of the dead Jesus in the sky when she first heard it in the schoolyard. He is a symbol of an alien, French Catholic culture. She is a modern young woman relying on her own experience, not by choice but because she knows no other truth to live by. The household gods are the ones that she has to reconcile. As she remarks concerning her atheistic upbringing:

> If you tell your children God doesn't exist they will be forced to believe you are the god, but what happens when they find out you are human after all, you have to grow old and die? Resurrection is like

plants, Jesus Christ is risen today they sang at Sunday School, celebrating the daffodils; but people are not onions, as (father) so reasonably pointed out, they stay under.[23]

But her father's Way of Mathematical Reason was equally unreal to her. His were only gods of the head. They did not reach the crucial nooks and crannies of her being. Her mother had been no help either since she was "no judge of the normal," and to be normal was what the growing daughter desperately wanted. The mother's innocence of the facts of life for a girl in the city had closed her off as a source of help. The heroine feels herself to be a head out of touch with its body. But the family album offers no clue as to how she had let herself be "cut in two."[24]

In James's idiom the divided self in this story seems to be the bodily me on the one hand and the spiritual and social mes on the other. Realizing that she is divided is the beginning of the heroine's struggle to survive. As she revisits the scenes of her childhood she realizes her near-fatal bifurcation. The "American civilization" which she shares with her companions is an elaborate war-game, in which the "realists" are the killers and those who have feelings are the first casualties. But the village school was just as cruel. Redemption does not lie in a return to childhood vandalism but in acceptance of adult, physical being.[25] Bethune's frame of reference for the question of war is not hers. Keen's answer more nearly meets her situation.

The symbol of survival is the woman's own child. But at first it is a negative symbol, not revealing but obscuring. We find out why when we are told that the husband memories are distorted. The admission comes only gradually, through flashes of insight which seem barely acknowledged. She had not had a baby, but an abortion, arranged for her by a former lover. The story of the abandoned child has been a myth used to anesthetize the pain of their separation.

After diving deeper than usual in the lake, the heroine sees what may have been her drowned father. She superimposes on this the image of a fetus in a bottle of fluid. Only then does she confess to herself that this too was a distorted memory. She realizes that she had been an accomplice, agreeing to the killing of her non-child. She had never seen it. They had not even been in a hospital. It had all happened in an illegal clinic.

> A house it was, shabby front room with magazines and purple runner on the hall floor, vines and blossoms, the smell of lemon polish, furtive doors and whispers, they wanted you out fast. Pretense of the non-nurse, her armpits acid, face powdered with solicitude. Stumble along the hall, from flower to flower, her criminal hand on my elbow, other arm against the wall. Ring on my finger. It was all real enough, it was enough reality for ever, I couldn't accept it, that mutilation, ruin I'd made, I needed a different version. I pieced it together the best way I could flattening it, scrapbook, collage, pasting over the wrong parts. A faked album, the memories fraudulent as passports; but a paper house was better than none and I could almost live in it. I'd lived in it until now.[26]

But her "husband" had not been there. He was at home for his real children's birthday party. They had never been married. Instead he had proposed the abortion and the affair was over, at least for him. *His reality had shattered hers.*

Breaking surface the woman feels the power of life again in her body. Stripping away civilization, her clothing, her inherited house and garden, she uses Joe to become pregnant again, making love to him in the woods. She rejects David and Anna's "geometrical" idea of sex, with its false professions of love, to seek wholeness in the wordless truth of animal relationships. It is possible with Joe because he says so little. But the lure of an animal way of life draws her back into the woods. Her companions are "Americans," predators who may kill this animal too. She has finished with pretense and prefers to be alone. "From any rational point of view," she admits to herself, "I am absurd; but there are no longer rational points of view."[27]

After her companions leave, she makes an offering to the forgotten spirits of the island and lies naked in the water. She feels like the mother of a god, more element than animal. "I lean against a tree. I am a tree leaning." But then she realizes that she is not an animal or a tree but a "place" in which these may grow. With this she begins to break to the surface again, after her dive into the depths of her origins. She has come to terms with the past, including her past as an accomplice of killers. She finds that the cottage is no longer haunted. She no longer regards her parents' deaths as desertion. When Joe returns for her in the boat she realizes that she may not succeed, but she can try to relate to him as a human being. She can let go the past by trusting him. For the first time she considers the future. If she goes with him now it will be her own decision. "So much for the gods and their static demands. . . . History is over, we take place in a season . . . to take that risk, to offer life and remain alive, open yourself like this and become whole."[28]

For Atwood's people to end with the possibility of a genuine individual choice is a triumph. Her heroine is a twentieth century figure in that she is unsure of her roles and completely cut off from family relationships. She rejects the only tribunal available to her, that of David and Anna, because their relationship is false. She has no assurance of a potential social self of which some ideal judge might approve. She is her own prosecutor, defender, judge, and jury. As in all such situations, her judgments are unreliable. That she transcends this situation at all is due to her "regression" to a less artificial level of existence, if only for a time. As a survivor she carries earlier claims to life in her refusal to play the war-game. She has finally to trust her own body and, through that, the relationship with Joe. But there is no guarantee that this trust will be vindicated by events.

The suggestion is that when she finally sees her parents and former lover as human beings, not gods, then she is ready to be a human being herself. She has traded in her "versions" of her life story for the ambiguities of existence. But she has no positive vision of what she wants to be or how she will survive in the city. Her conception of personal freedom is mainly negative. Her "way" is not religious in any traditional sense. It has only vestiges of archaic patterns of faith and forms of worship. Like Rubenstein and Keen, she gives no credence to transcendent sky gods. They are seen as projections of earthly fathers. But she discovers life-enhancing powers in the depths of her own psyche. Self-transcendence comes by diving down. The war within is the one that she must win.

In this instance "winning" means letting go, allowing the rhythms of nature to speak through us, taking memory down enough layers to purge our consciousness of false expectations.

Feminist critics of this novel have questioned Atwood's "solution" of having another child. The Jungian archetypes of femininity may prove just as fraudulent as the uncheckable memories.[29] What is authentic, however, is the heroine's recognition that all points of view are relative and that she must take responsibility for her own choice of roles. *It is not the role as such but the way in which she decides on her course of action that determines her salvation.*

Here what is important is not just her subjectivity, however, but the way in which she acknowledges factors beyond her control. She really had illusions which had to be shattered. She could no longer project onto her first lover her schoolgirl image of a perfect husband, because that conflicted with his image of himself. She could disregard this discrepancy for a time. But the abortion was a reality which she could not disregard. She also knows that she will have to come to terms with Joe's image of himself. The fact that it is only half formed makes for possibilities of mutual relationship which they can realize together. Habit has not destroyed hope. At the center of her concern is the true Individual Self. But its primary role is one of relationship and its principal virtue is openness and trust. As these elements of her identity come to the surface she begins to achieve the kind of integrity or wholeness which promises redemption.

Surfacing takes us to the edge of the "plausibility structures" of James's world. Its people still think in terms of family units and professional careers, if only negatively. Their experiences do not falsify his assumptions about the divided self and our egotistical pursuit of happiness. The precarious values are personal values of integrity and mutual respect. The father fails as a god not because he expressed such values but because he failed to meet their demands. In the end his job as a naturalist was seen to be contributing to our exploitation of the wilderness. Implied is a demand to respect other than human forms of life too and to repudiate our collective egotism. But there is no turning back on the rationalistic critique of traditional faiths. His scientism may be one-sided and therefore an insufficient guide to wholeness by itself. But it still informs the head in the dialectical development of head and body. The "hackneyed symbolism of a mechanical equilibrium" still lurks in the background.

Literally to become a mother is the key to survival for this father's daughter, although her own story proves that to be a parent is no longer a lifework. Her grasp of self is so fragile that she can afford to attempt only one step at a time. Indeed, like Keen she sees that living two steps ahead of oneself is self-defeating. David and Anna, who represent what happens to a relationship in which mutual respect is missing, also illustrate the inadequacy of living two steps ahead of oneself. Their illusions about the future are worse than hers about the past. Their rejection of parental norms and their pretensions as artists change nothing in the structuring of their existence. They are neither reformers nor revolutionaries but sterile mutants in a decaying system of values, reduced to "scoring" against each other in the game of sex as war.

When we compare this life story with the autobiographies of urban revolutionaries we see immediately the differences that social and economic conditions can make to a character's outlook and aspirations. Atwood's woman speaks for countless nameless individuals lost in suburbs where a culture of violence is hidden by a repressive veneer of law and order.[30] Her demand is for personal freedom and self-realization in which the natural world becomes the symbol of renewal. Wholeness means reuniting minds and bodies to become authentic individuals. By contrast, most recent revolutionaries in our society seem to come from large families in urban ghettos. There the violence is overt and the quest for freedom communal. The experience is not of a "divided self" but of self against society. The precarious value is justice and the way is the Way of Revolution, not the Way of Reintegration. The vision tends to be anarchistic.[31]

At the opposite pole of the social spectrum to the individual lost in the metropolis is the member of a communal group.[32] In revolutionary, communistic societies the boundary situation for discussions of his conversion is that involving thought reform or "brainwashing." On this subject there is still much to be learned concerning human responses under stress. But there are at least three points relevant to our topic.

The *first* point is that patterns of faith adopted due to thought reform are not truly chosen by the individual. They are contrived with an eye to conformity with the collective will. In this connection it is noteworthy that traditional techniques of evangelical conversion and of political thought-reform are similar. In both, the individual must want what the group wants and yet not appear to be conforming under pressure.[33] But the end in view is not to become free to find oneself in relationships of one's own choosing. The end is an imposed order prescribed by others.[34] We lack adequate psychological studies of those who apply such techniques. But it seems probable that their character and tone are as authoritarian as those of the regime that they have replaced. Theirs is an order of rules, not principles. It cannot tolerate the ambiguities of individual deviations.[35] Consequently the values transmitted are likely to be extrinsic rather than intrinsic and the conversion effected to be only "skin deep."

The *second* point is that the shallowness of an imposed outlook is indicated by a subject's probable "deconversion" on return to his original milieu. A prisoner of war, for example, may have been placed in a cell with those who seemed to be a group of fellow prisoners. In reality they are agents who play upon his fears and reinforce his doubts, until he accepts a new story about himself and his previous relationships. They testify to the plausibility of his new story line by accepting as "fact" only what fits its picture of events, often the reverse of previous views. In time the prisoner may willingly embrace the new story. But once he is back in his old environment, his new outlook begins to crumble. In the ambiguities of the "normal" world he is unlikely to maintain a faith that was implanted in an abnormally unambiguous situation. Unless he has been completely converted, he will not share the vision underlying the new story; without such vision he will lack the resolve to follow through with his second-hand ideology.[36]

Those who have the best chance of surviving the techniques of thought-reform are those who disregard the opinions of their new "peer" groups. Dedicated communists, or traditional religious believers in life after death, for example, expect persecution in a corrupt world. They look for vindication before a different tribunal. Their hope is actually confirmed by the present experience of persecution.[37]

As we saw in Chapter Two, a genuine "picture preference" exists precisely because several possible pictures of a situation are plausible. The picture given the political prisoner, by contrast, is only artificially plausible. He had no choice in its selection. In an uncontrolled environment, facts are facts regardless of who presents them. Coming to a judgment on them involves principles of relevance and analysis of arguments. But for the prisoner the judging process is short-circuited. All the "facts" presented to support the new story are given equal weight (in the same way as supposedly revealed propositions in a Bible interpreted by fundamentalists). There is no need to exercise powers of discernment and discrimination concerning evidence. Consequently the means to the end are self-defeating. They do not produce a self-involving participant in a way of life which is congruent with the end proposed.

More naturalistic, scientifically based interpretations of conversion differ from traditional religious accounts in that the former make clear the psychosomatic pressures on believers. This is the *third* point for us to notice. There is no doubt that a change of venue affects our judgment. We acknowledge this when we enshrine the possibility of such a change in our jury system of justice. What research adds to our understanding of the judging process is the realization that physical debilitation can lead to the collapse of almost anyone's convictions. Physiologically speaking everyone has a breaking-point. Moreover, the horizon of judgment changes when our physical being is attacked. Someone in intense pain is less able to concentrate on questions other than those pertaining to the relief of suffering. Ramakrishna with throat cancer, or Freud, may have sufficient self-control to be able to carry on with other concerns. But most of us lack the fortitude to set personal anguish aside. Or someone whose lands are threatened—for instance, in Israel or Lebanon—is hardly about to discuss dispassionately the future of the region. The wisdom of Solomon is not unconnected with the riches of Solomon: a judge without job security is less likely to be a just judge. This emphasis on physiological and material conditions of faith, among other things, raises the question of "pie in the sky" religion.

Classical faiths typically include the conviction that man does not live by bread alone. But there is a difference between holding this conviction on a full stomach and using it as an excuse not to feed the poor. That they should or should not be fed is itself a moral conviction, a question of more than "bread." In this connection we note again that Marxists, for example, are not simply materialists. Their cry is for justice in the distribution of goods and not merely for more goods. Their disagreements with others are cultural and raise questions concerning public policy. But their critique of religion as ideology brings home to us the extent to which self-realization may be thwarted by, rather than fostered by, religious faith.

In Atwood's story, for example, the heroine can assure herself of some kind of home and sustenance. Given that, the question is whether she will affirm an identity with other animals in the bush or return to a far from satisfactory situation in the city. Conditions force her hand to the extent that she realizes that she cannot survive a winter in the wilderness and may in any case go mad. But for her that is an option which *could* be preferred. Whatever she does, she will henceforth choose her fate and so move to "position four." In doing so she transcends her previous state. This example reminds us of the "internal" processes necessary to the discovery of meaning and truth in religion. Marxists and others remind us of the external pressures which are equally a fact of life. In the next chapter we shall look further at the dynamics of inner processes and external events. In the final chapter we shall look at the process of weighing their consequences for our future.

We began this chapter with a look at William James's model of the self in terms of which he described conversion. We found that this model uses the image of centering and the ideal of integration in the interpretation of individual transformations in religion. It also reminds us that religious judgment involves our understanding of a potential social self who may be judged by a "higher" tribunal than that of our immediate contemporaries. When we turned to Atwood's story for insight into a "post-Christian outlook" we found a character whose integrity is undermined by unresolved conflicts in her past. She is a modern "heroine," one of the crowd in her own private world rather than a major protagonist in world history. But her suffering is real, and her struggle to take responsibility for her life is symbolic of the effects of city-living on more and more of our contemporaries.

Atwood's heroine looks for life from the earth. A more conventionally religious story, which combines her individual focus with more revolutionary passions, is *The Autobiography of Malcolm X.*[38] In Malcolm's development from mascot, through homeboy, to hustler and prisoner, we again see the multiplicity of selves to which James draws attention, but in a Boston far removed from that of James's boyhood. Unlike the conversions of brainwashed prisoners, Malcolm's becoming Malcolm X is authentic in that it marks an integral stage in his development. His expulsion by the followers of Elijah Muhammad and assassination before he could consolidate his leadership of black militants make him a prime symbol of our totalitarian times. In his final repudiation of racism and conversion to orthodox Islam, we have a counter-example to Hitler and others of limited vision. Despite the many major differences between them, Malcolm's *Autobiography* and Atwood's *Surfacing* both speak to a world in which individual transformations require us to take responsibility in an environment which seems positively to undermine it. By contrast with James's ethos of affluent egotism, theirs are much more desperate attempts at self-realization. Where Atwood's story is of inner constraints, Malcolm's is of violent disruptions from without. Both individuals move to transcend their original situations by finding an identity with integrity which holds some promise of individual and communal freedom in the future.

Common to conventionally religious stories and the more contemporary outlooks expressed by existentialists and revolutionaries is the theme of transcendence through the quest for human freedom. What is rejected by so-called moderns is not our need for change but patterns of change imposed by otherworldly and spiritualizing forms of faith. What spelled freedom *from* the world for medieval monks sounds more like escapism to naturalistic materialists. But the latters' quest for freedom also runs into imposed realities which limit the options genuinely open to them. Malcolm did not live long enough to articulate his own vision of Muslim orthodoxy in a way that would mesh with the penultimate concerns of his people. But his own story shows that it was the perspective of that world religion which enabled him to overcome the spiritually crippling effects of his earlier devotion to Elijah Muhammad. His integrity stems from an assertion of identity based on principle, not just expediency, which is related to life-enhancing or divine power in such a way as to make inequalities of opportunity and racial divisions secondary in the final version of his master story.

The transformations of the divided self considered in this chapter may or may not lead to physical survival. What they underline is the human need to face ambiguous situations in a way that brings genuine hope. What each one hopes for depends upon the horizon of his or her expectations, as viewed from the perspective of a developing master story. That story may be a conscious reaffirmation of a classic tradition or a more or less unconscious individual recapitulation of the story of evolution. In either case, *it becomes important that the story be true*, based on sound memories of how things have been and on realistic aspirations concerning what they may become. *Centering alone is not enough*. It can collapse into shallow egotism or nihilism. In James's view the religions of deliverance are those of the "twice-born." They are the ones who come through the experience of evil to a state of unified assurance which is both happy and right. To appreciate the force of this conclusion, however, and to understand truth in religion we must first look at demonic stories and the possibility of decentralization. These are the topics of the next chapter.

CHAPTER NINE

Demonic Stories
and Decentralization

ATWOOD's set of stories within a story reminds us that narrative
may be used to hide as well as to reveal a situation which gives
us pain. Fantasy may concoct versions of events which enable us
to cope for a time, but then prevent us from facing reality in
constructive ways. In *After Auschwitz*, for example, Richard
Rubenstein points to the inadequate accounts of their defeat in
World War I as a partial explanation for why so many Germans
eagerly turned to the Nazi mythology. That mythology seemed
to offer a promise of life and prosperity to a depressed people. But
living by its "truths" the Germans brought destruction on all of
Europe. Of course, they did not act alone, and in our generation
the names of the British Prime Minister, Chamberlain, and the
place where he publicly backed away from a confrontation with
Hitler, Munich, have become symbols of appeasement at any
price. In Tillich's use of the terms, whatever promises life but
delivers death, whatever announces peace but leads to war, whatever means of communicating truth spreads falsehood, is not
divine but demonic.[1] In the case of the Nazi myths and others like
them, we have meaningful forms which could be life-enhancing
contributing instead to dehumanization and death.

Religious thinking would be easy if it were simply a matter of recounting stories clearly labeled "divine" and "demonic." But the concept of the demonic is of something which *could* be used in affirmative action being turned to negative ends. And the negativity is not simply a matter of use. If we think of parental love, for example, none of us would say to a mother or father, "Do not love your children." Yet if that becomes possessive and a substitute for other forms of relationship it can be life-denying. The situation becomes even more complex when what I may need to hear from you may be the opposite of what you need to hear from me. Suppose, for example, that I have terminal cancer and need to be told this in order to leave my affairs in order and make my peace with the world. But you cannot bear to tell me. Or suppose that my only child has just contracted cancer and, while I am absorbing this news, it is your job to tell me that I am being laid off from work. We can escalate the level of ambiguity in our story of life to the point where we cannot distinguish good news from bad.

Atwood's story indicates that the process of self-realization includes living through a series of stories, some more fanciful than others, which may be psychologically "true" but historically false. In this chapter we shall look at a narrative which is historically true but could be psychologically crippling, if taken as a master story. It is a story of the atomic bombing of Hiroshima. I choose it because it helps us to raise a question about the form of religious stories. These, we have been assuming, are typically redemptive and are redemptive because they concentrate devotion on a central symbol in a master story. In that vein we might suppose that Atwood's heroine gave herself "bad news" because her story had no such focus. The thread was autobiographical but the images of self used to assemble the relevant episodes could not carry the burden put on it by the heroine. Daughter, mistress, artist, mother, none of these was rich enough or realistic enough to liberate her from the weight of past experiences which kept her from living freely in the present. But would a central symbol for her life story have been enough to save her? Obviously not, if the center in question had been demonic rather than divine.

Exponents of classical cultures tell us that the sacred stories by which our ancestors lived were life-enhancing because they provided a point of orientation, a way of building a cosmos when chaos threatened, which gave stability to life in the face of death, disease, and famine.[2] Through the story a sacred center was established in the life of a tribe, around which perceptions of space and time could be grouped having some semblance of order. The highest mountain, the tallest tree, the meeting of the waters, provided a central reference point on which to concentrate expressions of the heights and depths of human experience. Likewise full moon and high noon provided focal points in time.

As human visions of life turned inward and ideals were rationalized, people drew inspiration more from human figures than from natural objects. So we have the stories of the gods, goddesses, and their artifacts, the laws, the rituals, the structures of civilization. If we treat these myths as truths told in story form, not as literal history, then they may still be powerful for us. But if, like Atwood's heroine, we are not initiated into their vision of life, we lose all sense of the dynamics of religion. We are left to the mercy of our own uninterpreted dreams with their quasi-mythological figures and undecoded messages. Our scientistic fathers will have failed us because they ignored the needs of the "body" in the stories they spun out of their heads.[3] They did not educate us in the healing power of the old myths, and so we are left to cope with inadequate myths of our own contriving.

In accounts of mythological thinking the organizing center of perception is often described as a "hierophany," a manifestation of the sacred, in which is expressed the awesome majesty of the power of life and death. Seen for what it is, it is no ordinary experience. It is the occasion on which we receive our vision of beginnings and ends. It is the day of days in the place of places from which thereafter we venture out into the profane world, secure in the possession of a home base. All the elaborate rituals, taboos, codes, and seemingly trivial rules relating to this base have as their meaning the reinforcement of this sacred center. Its story is scripture and its message is life and truth. We who have forgotten our scriptures have only the errors of our own versions of life to live by, only a vision of the plague or war in terms of which to structure our memories and our aspirations.

But in the atomic bomb we seem to have a symbol which fits

the requirements of sacred stories that brings bad news rather than good. Its explosion is an awesome expression of scientific power which is, however, life-negating. For the people of Hiroshima, since the first bomb was dropped, it has provided the pivotal event by reference to which all that has happened since must be understood.[4] It is a constant feature of the past on which their identity is based and through which they realize a vision of their end-state. And about it we may cluster stories of the H-bomb and subsequent world history, whereby our destiny may become one with theirs. If we are looking for a new myth for "technopolitan" man should we not begin here? Should we speak no longer of the era of the Buddha's enlightenment, of the Christ's birth, or the Muslim Hegira, but, as we do, of the Atomic Age? Must not changing religious thinking change its central symbol system, if it is to be relevant to our times? If so, is not this the most potent force on which to concentrate our attention?

Given such questions I find it instructive to read the diary of Michihiko Hachiya.[5] It is the record of his impressions and experiences as Director of the Communications Hospital in Hiroshima at the time of bombing. It covers the period from August 6, when the first atomic bomb was dropped, to September 30, 1945. Much of its detail reflects medical puzzlement over the unfamiliar symptoms of what came to be known as radiation sickness. But through his narrative of this we share something of Hachiya's sense of situation and destiny, of how he tries to restore meaning to a life turned to chaos. For purposes of exposition we can consider his story in two parts, one concerning the immediate impact of the bomb and the second concerning the subsequent work of reconstruction. What is of interest to us is the way in which new and old symbols come together to express both reaction to the bombing and concern for the future of the Japanese people. Throughout we should remember that, for them, theirs was a holy nation with a sacred destiny symbolized by the person of the Emperor, the descendant of the Sun Goddess.

The atomic bomb completely destroyed the world in which the people of Hiroshima had previously found meaning and value. For a time they lost all contact with the rest of Japan. As it became apparent that proximity to the "hypo-center" of the blast meant greater likelihood of fatal illness, exactly where each individual had been relative to that center on "the day" became the single most important fact for his or her thoughts about the future. "Where were you on the day?" they asked each other afterwards. Even Hachiya, who used the conventional calendar for his diary, naturally fell into that manner of speaking. "This way" and "that way" now meant direction to or from the hypocenter. The tale of his or her actions since the bombing became the framework for each individual's subsequent thoughts of survival. All were left to wonder why they had lived while the ones next to them had died. The earth had trembled. Fires had raged and a great wall of water had washed through the city. It was an apocalyptic time in which to be alive.[6]

By comparison with downtown, places of refuge like the Communications Hospital seemed a veritable "paradise." Whereas most Japanese homes were and are of wood—the Allies had counted on this to dramatize the power of the bomb[7]—the concrete walls of the hospital had withstood the shock and protected its inhabitants from the worst of the radiation. The familiar faces of doctors and nurses moving among the burnt timbers and broken glass reassured the injured and their attendant relatives. To appreciate the scene we have to remember how highly Japanese culture places honor and beauty, how deeply the culture expresses feelings of shame. To men like Hachiya, who was at home and had been injured by the blast, the disgrace of defeat and fear of disfigurement were far more destructive of the old order than the physical impact of the bomb.[8]

Running naked from his crumbling home Hachiya had felt no shame. But soon he was hiding his scars in embarrassment and worrying that he had neglected "proper greetings" for those who brought gifts of supplies. He grieved over the family *gaku* (scroll) destroyed by billeted militiamen and sought to console his staff by saying, "We were defeated in a scientific war." Privately he hoped that their ancestors and descendants would forgive them for their blind patriotism and useless sacrifices. Doctors and patients cheered when it was rumored that Japan also had the mystery weapon and that San Francisco had been bombed. They panicked when it was whispered that Hiroshima would be uninhabitable for the next seventy-five years. At the sound of a new air raid warning only fear of disgracing his hospital kept Hachiya at his post. Life as it had been lived was transfigured by the experience of the bombing. Many lacked even the will to survive. For those who had the will, while it served for a time as their central reference point, and gave meaning and direction to their daily tasks, the significance of the bomb was not redemptive but corrosive. Its story was not sacred but profane.[9]

Like the Nazi Holocaust the bombing of Hiroshima was an experience for the people involved which transformed their previous understanding of life in terms of sacred history. But the bomb as a central symbol lacked life-giving power. It offered no hopeful vision of a less ambiguous future. In the immediate aftermath of the explosion its presence was overwhelming and its consequences were seen everywhere. But its scope was insufficient as a basis for restoration. Death might make room for new life but is not of itself life-giving. And, above all, the bomb was a symbol of death.

Consequently, as the Allied planners anticipated when they allowed him to retain his position, the Emperor became the rallying point for the people's morale.[10] Surrender became acceptable when it was announced in the Emperor's Voice. The man who saved the Emperor's Portrait from the flames was a greater hero than those who rescued the wounded. The army was denounced for abusing the Emperor's Name in its lust for power. Prayers for his safety expressed tremendous veneration as well as fears for the safety of self and country. Hachiya wondered what the Emperor must think of the looting. He consoled himself with the thought that it was for the sake of his people that the Emperor had voluntarily broadcast the message of defeat. Now the future depended upon the actions of the victorious enemy, as immoral young girls were not slow to realize.[11]

Hachiya's story is not entirely typical in that he had an unambiguous role to play as a doctor, once he had recovered from his own wounds.[12] Offsetting the opportunism of some were the humanitarian gestures of others that he witnessed. Orphans were given new mothers, mothers new children. Sometimes he felt more like a soothsayer than a healer. His published observations on radiation sickness soon brought him into professional contact with the Americans, who offered curious sidelights on the situation. When one asked his thoughts on the bombing Hachiya replied:

> I am a Buddhist and since childhood have been taught to be resigned in the face of adversity. I have lost my home and my wealth, and I was wounded, but disregarding this I consider it fortunate my wife and I are alive. I am grateful for this even though there was someone to die in every home in my neighborhood.[13]

Echoing in his words are centuries-old attitudes to the chances and changes of life which made this latest outrage, if not acceptable, yet bearable. By comparison Hachiya found the American's attitude incomprehensible when the latter replied, "If I were you I'd sue the country."[14]

On the level of religion and ethics, Buddhist ritual and traditional protocol began to restore some sense of balance among the people. Concern for individuals and respect for authority were shown through the giving of gifts and the amenities of the tea ceremony. It would be "a sin against heaven" not to be thankful for one's friends and their gifts. For the dead one could later go the rounds of remaining shrines. For oneself one could meditate on the transiency of things and the virtue of fewness of desires. Abhorrence of pollution meant that to give water to the dying was more than an act of charity. Prompt disposal of corpses was more than a medical necessity. Whether to use much needed blankets to cover the dead reflected a real conflict in priorities. Almost as soon as they regained consciousness, people began making their funeral arrangements.[15] Reflecting on the *Lotus Sutra* a bereaved father wrote this verse on August 9:

> I am grateful for this cigarette,
> > For in this darkness the faint light
> > Brightens reality.[16]

Allied strategists had pictured the Japanese masses as kamikazes (warriors of the divine wind) who would act out the rhetoric of their war leaders. On this basis the U.S. military had calculated the potential casualties of an invasion of the main island and justified the bombing as a way of saving lives.[17] They glossed over the fact that the lives saved were those of their own combatants, while those sacrificed would include Japanese women and children.[18] In fact the majority of Japanese like Hachiya dissociated themselves from the military, just as the majority of Germans dissociated themselves from the Nazis and we dissociate ourselves from those who dropped the bomb. We are shocked to find that the Canadian Prime Minister of the time privately expressed gratification that the bomb had been dropped on Asians rather than on Europeans.[19] Somehow we like to think that we know enough not to take our own leaders' rhetoric literally. Yet we take our opponents' slogans at face value. The typical result is that the combatants come to resemble each other and fulfill each other's worst predictions.[20] Had the Allies understood "kami" they might have known better.[21] We shall return to this point shortly.

In later years only members of the peace movement kept the bombing at the center of their thinking. Some never regained their equanimity. The young especially had to face the stigma of contamination when the time came for them to consider marriage. Some rediscovered their Buddhist heritage and most found in the Emperor a bridge figure to carry them over from war to peace. But no great literature came out of the devastation, and it was not long before Japanese politicians were wavering on the question of procuring their own nuclear armaments against the Chinese.[22] *If we look for a single master story molded by this experience we shall not find it. If we look for renewed moral vision we shall be disappointed. The extraordinary order imposed on Japanese perceptions by the bombing was a demonic order of death without release.* The symbol of the Emperor used as a rallying point for peace had previously been used as a rallying point for war. Even the scientific genius expressed in the doctors' efforts to tend the wounded had, as its other side, the technological skill which had produced the bomb. *No single unambiguously life-enhancing figure emerges from under the mushroom cloud.*

The shattering of his world does not make a revolutionary of Hachiya. He can make nothing of the American's remark about suing the country. He transcends his situation through resignation and so retains a measure of personal freedom. But he does nothing himself to alter the conditions which had led to the war. No call for liberation rings out at the end of his book. Rather his story illustrates the kind of chaos associated with life-denying forces and the need for a symbolic center, around which people can gather their thoughts of self and nation. The bomb does not last as a transfiguring symbol because its meaning is too frightening and disruptive of basic relationships. The Emperor serves for a time because he represents for his people their beloved islands. Also he shares in their shame and betrayal by the army.[23] To this extent we find confirmation of what social scientists and historians of religion had said about the stabilizing effect of traditional myths and rituals. But Hachiya proves to be more "polytheistic" than academic accounts of Emperor worship had allowed.

There is no doubt that Hachiya's greatest veneration was for the "kami" (divine power) of the Emperor. But his feeling for his ancestors and refuge in the Buddha gave him other points of spiritual reference about which to coordinate his thoughts of life and death. In medicine he found sufficient power for good in the present. In the community of his hospital he found sufficient moral support and occasion for his leadership to give him hope. In James's sense, he thought of a tribunal judging his social self which was not just that of the army, the national leaders, or his profession but his posterity. Thus *if there was no single unambiguously divine presence in his life there was, nevertheless, a collectivity of positive influences.* From this he drew the strength not only to survive but also to give aid to others.

Implicit in Hachiya's accounts of his experiences is a "polysymbolic" set of references which frees him from absolute dependence on any one sacred story or any one central symbol. If we look for a single sacred order arising from the chaos of Hiroshima we shall be imposing on his data a Western perspective which is contrary to fact. But if we look to the many sources of his spiritual resilience, rather than for some supposedly eternal order or hierarchy of gods, we may yet see the power of transcendence revealed through his experiences.

According to James Hillman, the monotheistic consciousness which informs most Western religious thinking fosters egocentricity at the expense of other valid archetypes of the psyche. It would be healthier for us to acknowledge, with Hachiya, the many-in-the-one and the one-in-the-many. We should "focus intensively upon the *plurality* of the self, upon the many Gods and the many existential modes of their existence." We should "leave to one side theological fantasies of wholeness" and celebrate in the death of God the rebirth of the gods. Then we would no longer be enthralled by one dominant force in our thinking. Instead, our theory could reflect "the empirical fact that consciousness moves . . . through a multiplicity of perspectives and ways of being." In order to affirm the tragic depths of the therapeutically more powerful myths, we must give up our single-minded commitment to the ordering Logos, symbolized by Apollo, and acknowledge the divinity of the mad god Dionysius. These myths do not simply reveal human feelings. They provide "the objective aspect for the subjective meanings in psychic events," without reference to which we should be reduced to chronicling the particularities of individual case histories.[24]

In the view of Hillman and others, if we fail to appreciate the variety of characters emerging in our consciousness, we shall coalesce all the symbols contrasted with that of a central rational order into one composite stereotype, that of the Devil. Then we would miss the creative possibilities in the "shadow" side of our experience. For example, we might merge the Shadow with the feminine and reject as silly fantasies those outlets for our emotions which are oppressed by male images of the Ego. For the sake of a questionable ideology of manliness and rationality we might thereby destroy our natural ability to transcend disaster. Not listening to silly women, for example, we should fail to hear the message of hope in the story of the empty tomb.[25] Worse, we might fall into the assumption that the only meaningful stories expressing value in life are those with a definite plot to them, in which victory over evil is represented as the outcome of war. Then, for the sake of our victories, we would cast our enemies in the role of devils and play out, at their and our expense, a myth which expresses our very worst feelings.[26]

When we abandon our penchant for stereotyping what seems extraordinary, we shall be better able to react to events around us. In particular, says Hillman, we should recognize that not all that is called mad is insane. Then we should be able to draw on the divine power in our imagination. With reference to religious practices, for instance, we should realize that the "madness of ritual enthusiasm is clearly to be separated from disease and insanity." Instead of diagnosing it as hysteria, we should recover the symbolic significance of "borderline" behavior. Only so shall we nurse the vitality of "childish" trust which enables us to realize mystic freedom beyond the one and the many.[27] (Somehow the vision of Hitler youth chanting *"Sieg Heil"* mars our appreciation of this insight, and the thought that the gods run things like a committee of senators dampens this vision.) At this point we have to remember that Hillman is striving to redress an imbalance in popular thinking, which has not yet caught up with the "new" polytheism.

Part of this message is that we have to resurrect the body from its traditional religious suppression by the rational soul. We must restore the wisdom of the "feminine" to its place beside the will of the "masculine." The way to liberate our puritanical Calvinistic consciences is said to be to convert our thinking to the deep levels of classical polytheism.[28] Here Hillman is speaking directly to the Western heirs of those who bombed Hiroshima and murdered the European Jews. In place of wholeness, he seems to set the ideal of fully rounded experience, shifting the scene of religiously healing action from the center to the circumference of our symbol systems. If this takes on the characteristics of a giddying merry-go-round, it may be simply because we have forgotten the names of most of the players and cannot join in the divine sport.[29] However, as we noted in Chapter Four, *if plot is de-emphasized in redemptive stories then character becomes more important.* We shall have to consider the question of the character of the gods and goddesses before we can greet their resurrection in our stories as good news.

The mushroom cloud and the death camps are demonic symbols of a culture which is low on final priorities. But the demonic stories associated with them are not stories of the Japanese and the Jews. *The demonic stories are stories of German and American "Christians" whose ideologies led them to call evil good and to justify what, with hindsight, we recognize to have been depraved acts.*[30] No doubt most preconceived murders are rationalized as justifiable homicides.[31] Since World War II there has even been some suggestion that its victims were somehow accomplices in their own deaths.[32] The idea that the inheritors of a Christian civilization could arbitrarily have eliminated hundreds of thousands of peo-

ple not for what they had done but because of what they represented to others is not one that we readily entertain. Yet to the
extent that we consent to such acts, or fail to dissent openly, we
share responsibility for the kind of culture that engenders
them.[33]

*The truly demonic element in the stories of Hiroshima and the German
death camps is their denial of humanity to the victims.* They had no
opportunity to become responsible and responsive selves in the
moment of their deaths. They were treated only as means to
other people's ends. There were in fact more deaths from bombing in Dresden or Tokyo than in Hiroshima. But in Hiroshima
the people had no warning. Certainly they realized that, living
near a military base, they must expect to be bombed. But the
Allies had lulled them into assuming that a single plane overhead
meant only a reconnaissance flight, not bombing. Also the after-
effects were unlike anything that anyone had ever known. They
were especially devastating for a people to whom pollution is the
paradigm of evil.

Again, no doubt others today are being similarly treated in
Belfast and Beirut. At this minute, as I write, and in the minute
that you read this, someone somewhere is dying accidentally on
a highway, probably because of someone else's carelessness. But
to risk such a death is part of our choice when riding in a car.
Those who entered the gas chambers at Belsen and elsewhere
were told that they were simply going to the showers.[34] The first
to go had no inkling that it might be otherwise and no opportunity to say the prayers of the dying.

It is important to remember that these victims experienced the
ultimate in degradation not because of an "act of God" or a
natural disaster, not from attack by wild animals, but at the hands
of technologically sophisticated and educated men. *What was demonic was not the fact of their deaths but the manner of their dying.*
Whether defeated in a scientific war or herded into camps, they
had no say in, and therefore no responsibility for, their fate.
Those who did were the demonic ones. They exercised their
freedom to deprive others of theirs, to the point where their
victims' lives and deaths were completely without dignity. What
was demonic was not just the loss of the future, but the denial
of a dignified past.

If we call the atomic bomb or the gas chamber a negative symbol, we must bear in mind that it belongs in stories of active negation, of perversity, not deficiency.[35] Bullies act out of boredom as much as out of deprivation. Master manipulators, by contrast, are men with power whose priorities have gone astray. A psychology of needs is not adequate to account for their behavior. If we take the interaction process as our model, then we may say that what they were denied in early life was education in restraint and respect for other people. They are bad news for others because they are unable to cope with the shadow side of nature, their own included. To this extent, Hillman is right in saying that we have to educate such people to a different way of thinking from the linear and convergent models favored in the past.[36] We have to become educated to values and principles nurturing characters that can cope with our shadow lives.

Critics like Hillman suggest that our culture is an expression of male domination. It reflects that loss of harmony with nature which results from failure to admit the inherent weaknesses of our superiority complex. In the American story, this weakness was not fully revealed until the war in Vietnam. But already, in the assumption that the lives of American fighting men should be saved by the sacrifice of Japanese civilians, we see the premises of an argument for ruthlessly "defending" American interests on Asian shores. The consequences were so alien to what we like to think of as our own best instincts that, like Bethune, we are led to wonder at the extent of the self-deception involved. What led ordinary, average Germans and Americans to *allow* their leaders to burn and bomb in their names as much as they did? In reply to this question I quote R. D. Laing:

> The condition of alienation, of being asleep, of being unconscious, of being out of one's mind, is the condition of the normal man.
>
> Society highly values its normal man. It educates children to lose themselves and become absurd, and thus to be normal.
>
> Normal men have killed perhaps 100,000,000 of their fellow normal men in the last fifty years.[37]

Laing often overstates his case in order to unhinge his fellow psychiatrists and to draw our attention to schizophrenic behavior as an expression of schizoid experience. In terms familiar from the theme of *One Flew Over the Cuckoo's Nest* he relates definitions of madness as deviance to the power of the psychiatric profession over its "patients." In *Surfacing* we noted that "madness" is perceiving the other party to a relationship as well as oneself in "unrealistic" ways. In *The Divided Self* Laing defines insanity as the result of your failure to acknowledge my version of my identity or my failure to acknowledge yours. Whenever that happens, whoever has "common consent" on his side is sane and the other is "psychotic."[38]

In *The Politics of Experience* Laing adds that what is "common" or "normal" is to reify the other. Thus, if insanity is due to the dissociation of the "subjective" self from what the "objective" self is doing "out there," then we must say that a kind of collective insanity came over the German and American military in the twentieth century. It follows that *whose version of events is "realistic" cannot be determined simply by reference to majority opinion.* Large segments of society may be acting insanely for much of the time. One trick of insanity then is to lock up those who are behaving sanely for their "deviant" behavior. But the plane which is flying out of formation is not necessarily the one which is lost.[39]

The story of a disintegrating or destructive relationship told by the "patient" may well be more true to his experience than the objective "case history" written up by the doctor. More, it may be a logical function of the way the patient is being treated, as when in *Surfacing* the heroine's first lover was playing "husband" to her "wife." Only when he defined her out of the game, by insisting on an abortion, did her vision of the finale prove totally unrealistic. In her situation then the path of sanity lay in the direction of a "divided self," since the alternative was to allow the other's behavior to define "reality" for both of them. For the heroine, in Atwood's words, the experience at the abortionist's was enough reality for the time being. To have accepted his view of what was "best" might have meant the death of any separate self for her.[40] Only a fantastic version of what had happened could express what had been to her a fantastic betrayal. This experience is what determines the "logic" of the stories which she told to her parents and her "friends," as well as to her conscious self.

As Hillman and Laing point out, a story portrays the reality of the situation from the perspective of one of its protagonists. The reality is not just their behavior but the experience which it expresses. Thus Malcolm X, for example, followed Elijah Muhammad in describing their tormentors as "white devils."[41] In Atwood's story, the woman *had* been a victim and was reacting accordingly. Not until healing time had passed was she able to see herself as *no longer* a victim. Only then was she ready to come out of her private world. That she had this opportunity was not entirely of her contriving either. It was a consequence of her interaction with Joe.

In Laing's view the difference between psychotics and the rest of us is not that we never withdraw into our private worlds, but that we are fortunate enough to be able to come out of them. Those who remain locked away in the supposed security of their psyches, treating their bodies as tenuous, tend to lose both. Applying this insight to society we see people like the Japanese locking themselves into martial myths of domination, which are finally shattered by the superior force behind the American war story. One difference between the Japanese leaders after World War II, or the American leaders after Vietnam, and the Germans after World War I, may be that the former are developing stories which enable them to acknowledge defeat. In this respect Watergate may have been a blessing.

William James reminded us that, when our education is formally concluded, we do still have to choose. Atwood adds that, in order to become "creative ex-victims," we have to accept responsibility for the roles that we have been playing. We have to see our childhood "gods" as fallible adults like ourselves. If attaining adulthood is like a promotion, then part of this experience is the discovery that the gods too experience death and rebirth. Traditionally, a personal deity was not just a protection against bewitchment. It was also an aid to self-transcendence. By identifying with a god and acting as gods, people participated in a common world. In the process, they played roles whose characters were already established. But the price that they paid was a loss of individuality.[42]

It may be that, in order to become fully free, we have to see through the masks of the gods. If, in later life, we become again as little children, what is meant is not just that we are again dependent on others for physical support.[43] It means also becoming as egocentric as children, preoccupied with our bodies and our private, inner space. By then our choice of roles is over. Our task is to realize some sort of integrity in the identity which is ours.[44]

Because the earliest psychologists worked in medical contexts with "abnormal" conditions, they tended to assume that "maladjusted" or sick individuals are so because they are "unstable." In a time when mechanics gave physical theory its models they looked for mechanical equilibrium and equated health with balance or a state of rest. By Laing's time, however, psychiatrists have become aware that stability may spell stagnation. It all depends on the state and stage of development of the individuals involved. Abnormal times may require unbalanced people. It seems true that we need a relatively stable and secure "home" environment when young if we are to face the future confidently. But religion is concerned with ends as well as beginnings, and religious thinking, we have argued, turns on symbols of our end-state and the ways in which we realize them. The nucleus of such ways is a core of character and cluster of images in terms of which we integrate our living and accept our dying. It may be that at present we need symbols of a future which reverses the overly regimented routines of "normal" experience.

What depth psychology and mystical awareness add to our discussion is the realization that *"reality" is multidimensional in ways which require more than one version of events if the truth is to be known. The truth about ourselves and our worlds cannot be told in any one story because worlds are places where many stories are being lived simultaneously.* In such places, we do not wish encounters with the demonic on anyone. But we can use demonic stories to recall us to what is divine or life-enhancing. As we shall observe in the next chapter, religious master stories do not explain the demonic away. They acknowledge the reality of evil. But they put this in a context of a transfiguring symbol which gives our experience a different, more redeeming significance.

As James also observed, each of us plays bit parts in innumerable stories. However, it is misleading to conclude from this that we can only find health in polytheism. We may in fact be living in a "polytheistic" society. But in traditionally polytheistic cultures each individual is devoted to his or her own particular saint or deity. For insurance we may leave offerings at more than one altar. But we have our own personal image enshrined in our own home sanctuary. Especially in this age of anti-heroes we, like Atwood's "heroine," may be betrayed by our expectations of parent, lover, partner, or boss. Laing suggests that our greatest need then is for knowledgeable guides. We do not want them to dictate the story of our lives. But we do need maps and cues concerning the kinds of characters that we are likely to meet on the way. Even the author of a plotless play, one without an "ending," has to give us a sense of situation and interacting characters if he is to make his "No Exit" sign plausible.[45]

Whether we follow the Way of Resurrection or some other, our central symbol has to express, as Tillich insisted, an affirmation of self in spite of the negativities of existence. In this connection, the demonic is seen in the kiss of betrayal or the cup of poison, precisely because its intentionality perverts the normal meaning of kissing or passing the cup. In response, divine power has to be seen in the conversion of the negating move into an occasion for the release of the "spirit" or principled personality in the body or company of the faithful. What is central here is the freedom of the spirit to find new forms of physical presence. What is subordinated are the orders or structures or systems of existence —physical, psychological, and social—which are the necessary but not sufficient conditions of meaningful human life. For this reason I place freedom above order in the conception of goodness. But this freedom is life-enhancing for ever-widening circles of individuals, as they are touched by the spirit of the central figure in our master story. It is not a license to infidelity on the part of egotistical individuals. It is good news for the beloved as well as the lover. It is not a warrant to murder by those possessed by a will to power. It means release also for the captive and peace for the enemy.

Against the background of recent work, we may understand how decentralization may seem bad news for the tender ego but good news for the overly centered self. If we assume that both polytheistic and monotheistic stories are colored, if not engendered, by projections of our personal perspectives on self and world, then we can see how monotheistic stories might express a strong sense of personal identity. A person called by one name or a people chosen by one god may be supposed to have a relatively heightened awareness of unity. By contrast, a denizen of a pluralistic modern city may experience as many role changes a day as he or she receives calls on the telephone. Which experience is more liberating depends largely on the quality of the experience that went before. A single figure at the center of a pattern of faith may not be contributing to our spiritual health. But if that figure is a transfiguring symbol which deepens our understanding of life, it may be our key to the problem of interpersonal relationships. *What is important is not the singularity of the figure but the integrative effect of the stories told around it.*

If we follow Maslow we shall look for insight less in studies of deficiency motivations and more in the self-expression of self-actualizing people.[46] In their moments of "peak" experience they appear to be "non-dual," neither one nor many, neither egocentric nor consciously altruistic, spontaneously interacting in their milieu in life-enhancing ways. For them to be as they are they have to be able to presuppose a degree of social stability and physical security. As James remarked, they have to think in terms of an ideal social order by reference to which present uncertainties are of less account. But part of their self-expression is a self-transcendence which makes any moment of equilibrium just a step along the way. The ultimate state is represented by the freedom from convention of a Zen master, or the atonal compositions of a maestro, not the recollections or vain repetitions of would-be timeless beings.

The process of self-transcendence requires a kind of consciousness-raising whereby each image of self is relativized by the next.[47] In this connection a polytheistic pantheon may at times be more fruitful than a saintless Protestantism. In any case the demonic conditions are those which obliterate consciousness for both agents and patients. The divine are those which enable us to realize an end-state in which we are free to be ourselves and to let others be themselves.

As we have presented them, monotheistic traditions have been as "polysymbolic" as polytheistic traditions in religion. Their master stories have enabled countless individuals to surmount the handicaps of their family histories and personal relationships.

If the freedom to which we aspire is the freedom of "love's body," we have, nevertheless, to recognize that the body is the individuating principle for the spirit.[48] The limiting force of physical conditions cannot be ignored. Through the telephone I may have links around the world. But in order to receive one call I must put another on "hold." In short, there is an inescapable time-frame to life, which fosters a linear image of one "way" at a time.

We may theorize that all ways lead eventually to the same "end," so that final freedom means letting go also of particularizing traditions with their separate communities. But this is one theory among others whose truth has yet to be tested.[49] It involves the exclusion as unimportant of symbols which other traditions have regarded as primary. Unless we advocate a kaleidoscope of symbols, whatever master story we tell will introduce some pattern of development. The phases of bodily existence—birth, youth, maturity, and death—impose on our thinking a limit to our relativism. Relativism has its season, following the absolutistic positivism of youth. But truth depends on our ability to see through the claims of relativism as well. How this may be so we shall consider in the final chapter.

In summary, we note that according to Tillich the demonic is known by its parasitic negation of the self, whereas the divine fulfills the self even in its moment of dying. The demonic hides, whereas the divine transforms. A polysymbolic story of faith does not deny this truth. It widens our horizons concerning the means and ends in view. Where religious master stories guide us through the dynamic interplay of past and future, demonic stories confront us with the prospect of no future and the memory of a degrading past. Decentralization as such is neither divine nor demonic. Again in this connection we observe that freedom is not anarchy. It is the realization of a responsive and responsible self. To deny others their right to such freedom is one sure mark of the demonic. Here those of us who prefer our own stories, must ask: is *our* master story good news for others?

CHAPTER TEN

Good News and
Priority Thinking

WE HAVE been reflecting on the cycles of stories in which religious people express their sense of situation and value, their
feelings and intentions, by reference to the margins and centers
of ultimate concern. We shall concentrate now on three tenden-
cies toward falsehood in the telling of religious stories and the
kind of thinking which frustrates their redemptive purpose. We
shall consider what so far has been touched on only in passing:
the archaizing, the stereotyping, and the rationalizing which vitiate too many judgments in the dynamics of religion. In the process we shall be summing up our conclusions concerning what
constitutes good news in religion and what guidelines we have
for critical religious thinking in times of diversification and
change.

Religious stories have included myths, histories, records of
witnesses, and prescriptive parables. They have offered us spir-
ited visions of the good life, if not in this world then in the next,
if not on the ordinary level of perception, then above the stars or
between the eyes. But because great visions are rare we tend to
fasten on them, lifting them from the contexts in which they
once showed people the creative possibilities in their situation.

We tend to transform them into fossils of faith. We collect them in sacred books and frame them in traditional styles of thinking, from which we may deviate only on pain of excommunication. In short, we fall victim to the archaistic fallacy of supposing that the only truth in religion is old truth, turning what was true for our forefathers into falsehood for ourselves. As the changing structures of our consciousness make it more and more difficult to enter into the spirit of the original visions, we turn what should be words of life into symbols of decay.

Examples of fossilization abound in all traditions. Compare, for instance, the lively birth stories of Theravada Buddhism, their parade of elephants, tigers, birds, and fishes, with the stifling canonical rules (Vinaya), the lists of precepts and catalogues of virtues, the three this and the five that, dull mnemonic recitations of proximate causes and penultimate effects according to the tradition of the Elders. The latter may structure the lives of monks and laymen but the former give them joy and hope. As is well known, a Jewish rabbi is not teaching Judaism unless he tells good stories. A glance at the Talmud shows that the Protestant caricature of Judaic legalism is simply a one-sided Christian device for prefacing good news (Gospel) with bad news (Law).

Yet caricatures have some foundation in fact. Consider the impact of codification and classification revealed in this excerpt from an argument between a son and his parents:

"... just because it's your religion doesn't mean it's mine. ... I don't believe in God."

"Get out of those dungarees, Alex, and put on some decent clothes."

"They're not dungarees, they're Levis."

"It's Rosh Hashanah, Alex, and to me you're wearing overalls. Get in there and put a tie on. ..."

"I'm not going to act like these holidays mean anything when they don't. ..."

"Maybe they don't mean anything because you don't know anything about them, Mr. Big Shot. What do you know about the history of Rosh Hashanah. One fact? Two facts maybe ... ?"

"There is no such thing as God, and there never was, and I'm sorry, but in my vocabulary (the Jewish tradition) is a lie."

"Then who created the world, Alex? ..."[1]

A number of issues are raised by this exchange. What is the connection between fact and theory in religion? What is the role of dialogue between exponents of conflicting views? Whose is the decisive judgment concerning the weight to be given to the various factors mentioned? And so on. But here let us consider the basic level of religious vision and first principles touched on in the argument. To do this, we need to learn something more of Alex's point of view. We find this expressed after an interlude, during which his mother goes to hospital to have a growth removed. For a while he inconsistently lapses into prayer for her recovery. But when she regains her health, he regains his skepticism. His basic story is a salacious satire on psychotherapeutic obsessions with sex. In the course of this Alex says to his doctor:

> "What else, I ask you, were all those prohibitive dietary rules and regulations all about to begin with, what else but to give us little Jewish children practice in being repressed. . . . Why else, I ask you, but to remind us three times a day that life is boundaries and restrictions, if it's anything, hundreds of thousands of little rules laid down by none other than None Other, rules which either you obey without question, regardless of how idiotic they may appear (and thus remain, by obeying, in His good graces), or you transgress, most likely in the name of outraged common sense—which you transgress because even a child doesn't like to go around feeling like an absolute moron and schmuck—yes, you transgress, only with the strong likelihood (my father assures me) that comes next Yom Kippur and the names are written in the big book where He writes the names of those who are going to get to live until the following September . . . lo your own precious name ain't among them. Now who's the schmuck, huh? And it doesn't make any difference (this I understand from the outset, about the way this God who runs things, reasons) how big or small the rule is that you break, it's the breaking alone that gets His goat —it's the simple fact of waywardness . . . that He absolutely cannot stand, and which He does not forget, either, when He sits angrily down . . . and begins to leave the names out of that book. . . ."[2]

If we ask from this what is Alex's ideal image of himself, we should reply, negatively, not to be a "schmuck" and, positively, to be an individual who acts with integrity. The idea of blind obedience offends his sense of personal dignity. To tell him three more facts about Rosh Hashanah, or even to challenge the authority of his personal experience, would not meet the core of his concern. If we want to argue on the religious level, and not to assert the authority of the past simply for the sake of our own traditional sense of identity, we should have to relate Alex's sense of self to a more life-enhancing vision of God's ways with humanity. We should have to confirm the integrity of Alex's judgment, not try to undermine it for the sake of conformity to our own preconceptions. Then we should have to ask whether his primary symbols of self in the world are in fact bringing him good news. If we ourselves found the good news in the history of Israel, we should have to testify to him what is for us its master story, not to the book-keeping character of atonement but to the life-giving promise of fulfillment in Israel. That is to say, we should have to ally the internal pressure of his own set of intrinsic values with the principles of community which have become obscured, rather than exemplified, by his father's story of rules and precepts.

What changed the minds of many Alexes in our time was the Six Day War between Israel and the Arab countries. That is to say, the heirs of Belsen and Auschwitz were suddenly confronted by the possibility that, regardless of how they chose to identify themselves, others in the world still regarded them as Jews who stood in the way of a national dream. External rather than internal pressures challenged their private stories and threw them into the kind of debate noted earlier among Neusner, Fackenheim, and Rubenstein. One lesson from all this is that who we are depends as much on how others see us as on how we see ourselves. Our future is not simply a matter of our choice. In times of plague or war this may be brought home to us brutally and abruptly. But in more peaceful circumstances we learn this from interacting with our community, including discussions among friends. To find the truth we must engage in personally challenging situations and meaningful relationships with those around us.

At the end of *Surfacing*, Atwood's heroine realizes that if she decides to go with Joe, in future they will have to talk.[3] Their earlier minimal level of conversation and commitment will no longer be adequate as a basis for their relationship. She is not under the illusion that talking things out is always therapeutically beneficial. But she will not simply be talking over with Joe their feelings about the past. Theirs will have to be self-involving talk of a shared future. They will have to exchange ideas expressing commitment to the constitutive principles of their life together. They will have to mesh visions of life in ways that are complementary rather than competitive. Theirs will have to be different from the dialogue between Alex and his father. It will have to be the kind of talk that leads to love-making, not the slamming of doors. In short, it will have to bring good news.

In a similar situation, the alternative to war between nations is to enter into negotiations around a bargaining table. Where visions of the future are in conflict, there have to be peace talks and argument, reverting to principles of justice not simply in the context of a recitation of past grievances, but on the basis of a search for policies and programs promising justice in the future. The reiteration of one fact or two to bolster a one-sided argument will not do, since the other party will be equally one-sided. In order to argue well, each side will have to anticipate the other's positions and, in the process, begin to see something of the other's point of view. Internal pressures alone will probably not lead to commitment to a common destiny. But geography seldom supports the luxury of permanently suspended negotiations.

In religion as in life, we find truth only through the exchange of ideas in which we come to see ourselves as others see us. Through mutual discussion we learn to discern principles of relationship expressing our vision of a shared future. Part of the process is indeed a clearing away of disputes over facts. Thus debates concerning genesis and geology, sin and psychology, superstition and sociology, are a necessary step toward an acceptable story of our lives. Especially in our dialogues with the past, as Atwood's story again reminds us, we are tempted to deceive ourselves.[4] If our concern is to find out where our vision was distorted, when we lost our way and what story promises truth to live by, the stakes are so high that our memory soon plays tricks on us. We select only what sounds like good news and gloss over the rest. Thus if someone disputes our version of the master story, we become demon defenders of what at bottom are debatable points. We lose sight of the redemptive vision. We twist principles to serve our special pleading. But if we are to survive we must still reach beyond recitations of facts for constitutive principles on which to build for the future.

A genuinely religious dialogue with history looks at history whole. That is to say, it does not lift proof-texts out of context to marshal one-sided lines of thought. Instead, it looks for witnesses to the realizability of the vision shared by those whose master story is concentrated on the same central symbol. Thus among Christians, for example, we may look with hindsight at the debate between Platonic and Aristotelian Christians and realize that the truth lay somewhere between them. We see the wisdom and the special pleading expressed by *both* sides. So we learn not how to repeat their arguments but how, in our own way, to adhere to first principles and primary symbols in the adjudication of disputes. We do not, for instance, think creatively by quoting every author who shares our conclusion—say, that the Christ is fully divine and fully human. Rather we look at the redemptive significance of telling a story in terms of God-men and see what kind of love it expresses. In this process our own egotism may begin to be less central to our vision. But this will happen only if we learn to enter into genuine dialogue with the past and learn from past dialogues how to find the intersecting point of present truth. We need others' versions of the truth to correct ours.

When properly conducted the Anglican liturgy illustrates what I mean by seeing history whole. It includes not only rhythms of contrition and celebration, expressing the range of possible feelings of wayfarers. It also assembles a symbolic sequence of voices from the past. There are readings from the Hebrew Bible and the singing of psalms, readings from the New Testament and the recitation of a traditional creed. The prayers blend in the Reformation-Renaissance language of faith. The hymns exude eighteenth and nineteenth century piety. If the congregation is fortunate, there will be a sermon relating some of the insights from the past in a challenging and inspiring way to twentieth century problems. For those who know what they are tuning into, the tone of the whole will juxtapose present concerns with past testimonies in a way that gives confidence for the future. Needless to say, for "internal" and "external" reasons it is not always so. But a similar kind of liturgical balance can be found among most of the major traditions. At their best they serve the redemptive purpose of ego-transcendence.

The spirit of the liturgy is destroyed if we construct a kind of score-card of approved verses, excising those judged to be making statements contrary to our conception of the facts or our standards of morality. If David's descendants sang the Hebrew equivalent of "Lord bash their bloody heads in," we distort that witness by leaving this out. For, as has often been said of David, the point is not that he was perfect but that, imperfections and all, his faith in his God (Yahweh) outshone that of the Goliaths of his day. Looking for wisdom from that part of our past, we keep fresh the memory of his story, not that of the Philistines. This is not because we applaud all that he said and did—the story does not do this—but because we share the intentional system of the Kingdom of God, however understood. Through his story we see how, on *his* understanding of the facts and according to his moral lights, the ways of God and men may be followed. Similarly in reciting the Apostles' Creed or saying "Amen" to Cranmer's prayers, we declare ourselves to be standing in the tradition of those who, seeing things as they did, expressed themselves in that way. In a culture which believed that virgins give birth miraculously, or divine ransoms are paid to redeem slaves, then those were ways in which the Christ story could be told. We should respect the terms in which they told the story while retelling it in our own way. Neither their story nor ours expresses the whole truth. But in the juxtapositions of such patterns we may know the living faith.

According to our theory, what establishes the identity of our faith with others from the past is the underlying intentionality of our central symbol system and its core of traditional stories. Most often there is a single central reference to which we can allude when evoking the spirit of the master story. But we have also seen that symbols can become stereotypes, which obscure rather than inform our vision. As Alex's story reminds us, the characteristics of Yahweh which inspired some can come to seem demonic to others. If the character at the core of the story becomes demonic then the faith begins to sour. On the other hand, if we simply replace it with an image of ourselves we may be living idolatrously, that is, putting in the saving pivotal position something which equally lacks redemptive power. Making our own egos the sole reference point can be just as destructive of our future as focusing on an alienating presence. The constitutive characteristics are thus crucial if our story is to become good news.

One suggestion coming out of the last chapter is that we leave the central position vacant and move around the horizon of our interests according to need. In reaction against demonic stories we may find freedom for a time in the telling of no story. In reaction against substantivist definitions of saving power we may welcome emptiness and silence. There is truth in the "death-of-God" stories of liberation, the truth affirmed by Alex against an arbitrary and unjust judge. But even so there is a central theme, a set of principles for along the way, and a vision of some end that help to determine the context in which we judge particular symbols. Images of chaos juxtaposed with images of regimentation are only meaningful in a sequence whereby we appreciate statements based on one set of images by contrast with the preceding set.[5] Thus, the validity of any one primary symbol or of the absence of such symbols may be entirely relative to our progress along the way. But that our movements constitute some kind of pattern is not a contingent fact. It is a necessary condition of their expressing meaning in life. Skipping from place to place can itself become a symbol, perhaps of fear, lest like stones crossing the water we sink if we stop moving.[6]

At issue here is our judgment concerning the signposts used along the way and our judgment whether, in fact, what our movements describe is a way at all. In this process it would seem that we have at least four choices. We may judge from the signs that there is no way. We may suspend judgment. We may follow what are traditionally religious ways. Or we may try to make our own way without religious involvements of any kind, alone or in the company of other nonreligious naturalists or humanists.

In our assessment of redemptive stories our choice should be determined by whatever policy we consider to be wisest according to our perception of our circumstances. In particular, *our judgment will depend upon how we weigh good news against bad.* If at the forefront of our thinking is an experience of radical evil, we may never believe in the redemptive possibilities of those who would have us hear good news. Yet, as William James remarked, those whose versions of good news have stood the test of time are all witnesses to the seriousness of evil, as well as to the joy of the truly good life. So how are we to validate our judgments concerning the weight of good and evil in religious thinking?

When we confront experiences of radical evil, such as we recalled in the last chapter, we may adopt, on the one hand, a policy of suspecting that all claims to hear good news are vicious nonsense or products of wishful thinking.[7] For example, against traditional Christian stories of God's power and goodness, we may assert that it is nonsense to say that such a God loves all people equally. If we are forced to admit that we have no idea what a loving God with unlimited power should do—for instance, creating harmless robots rather than defective human beings, or resisting the creative urge altogether[8]—then we may have to say that the evidence leaves us with an unresolvable mystery at the center of any true story of life.[9] In short, our perception may be of unavoidable ambiguities, which make acting on any religious vision psychologically impossible and morally suspect.[10] The only courses open to one with integrity therefore may be to say "No way" or to suspend judgment.

On the other hand, traditional religious stories put the spotlight on what seems best in our experience. They avoid unprofitable questions not by denying the mystery of evil but by concentrating on our prospects for realizing the good. Accordingly, at the center of their stories is always a figure whose policy is not to escape from suffering but to achieve victory through suffering —figures such as Socrates, Jesus, and Mao. *Religious convictions come not when we can explain evil but when we know good.* How such convictions are interpreted depends in part on how we see evil. If we suspect its root to be human pride, then we choose stories of humility and obedience to a higher law. If we suspect its root to be apathy in the face of death camps, then we emphasize stories of the active defense of a new homeland. If we suspect radical ignorance of our basic identity then we collect stories of enlightenment, and so on.

While we have our theories of good and evil we also know that we must live with many unanswered questions. We may choose to suspend judgment concerning explanations of evil rather than withhold assent to promises of good. At the heart of our master story may still be an experience of betrayal or bureaucratic incompetence. But this will be part of the scene which the story shows us to be leaving behind. It will not be the conclusion. Rather than speculate why Judas kissed Jesus, for instance, we may testify to what the spirit of the Risen Christ has done to transform not only individual lives but whole societies into communities with new hope. The last word will be one of promise.

However, the sincerity of believers as they tell stories of good and evil is no guarantee of wisdom and truth. Philosophers who sincerely believe that ambiguities and inconsistencies vitiate religious judgments, and theologians who sincerely believe that understanding is impossible apart from faith may all be equally prejudiced. They may all be taking the easy route of reflection on paradigm cases which support their views and thus be falling into religiously sterile arguments. They will be prejudiced because their favorite paradigms have become stereotypes—of omnipotence, benevolence, and evil—which prevent them from seeing the actual problems of people like Alex. A stereotype is too removed from everyday experience to serve as a guide to reflections on life's ambiguities. Those of us who are trained in both philosophy and theology are in double jeopardy. As often as not, we accept terms for discussion laid down by archaizing critics and lose touch with the community whose current consensus defines our tradition for today. Then indeed our language "goes on holiday."

If we adopt a developmental-dialectical-process view of the dynamics of religion, we have to recognize that *judging the correctness of our faith is not a matter of weighing up pros and cons and then choosing the better bet*. We do not, for example, simply balance doubts against certainties. Rather we *go through periods* of doubting and believing. We wonder whether our earlier faith or our irreligion holds up against disconcerting changes in our perspective on events. We wonder whether W. K. Clifford was right against William James in asserting that suspended judgment is always a virtue in cases of insufficient evidence.[11] Then we wonder whether James was right in insisting that there is a time to doubt and a time to believe.[12] James's point against Clifford was that in religion the faith or doubt concerns ourselves. Thus the subject of uncertainty changes according to the attitudes and policies on which we act. This is especially true of the question of evil, when we wonder whether the problem is in the paradigm or in ourselves. Am I my own worst enemy, my only true guide, or neither? *I can only know in retrospect,* judging by results whether my self-confidence or my submission to traditional authority was misguided. Further, as Kierkegaard reminded us, faith, hope, and love are not once-only affairs such that we can say, "There I have hoped and that's an end of it!" *The truth is in the process.* It cannot be prejudged.

It is a mark of immaturity to rush into certitude on the basis of stereotyped thinking and insufficient evidence. *The mature judges are those who can live with ambiguity and uncertainty.*[13] But how do we become mature judges in matters of faith, if not on the basis of an initial trust as the background for later doubts? Given that we generalize from some central facet of experience to frame our perception of what follows, is there any compelling reason why we should generalize from our experience of radical evil rather than of unsullied good? Given a beginning in trust do we trust our own experience, our gurus, or what? And given the need to suspend some judgments, do we suspend those concerning explanations of evil or those concerning aspiration toward bliss? Might not wishful thinking be the only relevant kind for people in our situation?

This last question brings us back to James's insight that *all* thinking is colored by directed attention and emotion. *The question in religion is not whether our conclusions are based on wishful thinking but whether our particular wishes are realistic.*[14] Furthermore, there can be no question of going against our own experience, since gurus, laboratories, moments of panic and prayer, all are parts of that experience. The question, once more, is how we weigh some aspects of our experience against others. And here what is most revealing is the story that we tell ourselves about whence we have come and whither we are going. For we tend to select those incidents in our experience which fit our preferred story. Whether our central symbol in this story is Jesus of Nazareth or ourselves in Tennessee, for example, there creeps into any narrative a tendency to rationalization which runs partly contrary to fact. Let us think for a moment about religious stories in this respect.

When all is said and done, *religious stories are slices of life and not our whole experience.* Despite our best efforts at religious education, to the effect that myths are truths told in story form, in popular parlance "myth" still connotes fiction. Of course every story is true in the sense that an octogenarian's statement "I am thirty-nine" is true. It truly expresses a fear of growing old or some other sentiment. But, by the same token, it can be a falsehood if taken literally. Thus, as we remarked in Chapter Two, what is expressed in religious stories based on symbolization is not literal truth. Most importantly, it presents an unambiguous vision of what is otherwise a scene of uncertain character. A story based on symbols rationalizes our experience in favor of one course of action rather than another. In doing so, as Atwood's woman discovered, it may put us on a collision course with events in our common world.

To defend against an infinite regress of rationalizations about rationalization or stories about stories,[15] and to ensure that those of our wishes which involve others will not founder on theirs, we need fixed points of reference in our present world and bridges to understanding in visions of our future commonwealth. Atwood's heroine found her fixed points in her cottage. The voices of those who had shared her past were stilled. The voices of her companions were uncomprehending. But in her immediate environment were reference points to scenes about which she could regroup her thoughts. In addition, in her vision of life with Joe was a potential social self who could integrate feeling with thinking and hold meaningful conversations. Are there similarly fixed points on our cultural horizon, by reference to which we can differentiate hard news from soft? And are there visions of potential social relations which promise some resolution of our conflict between autonomy and heteronomy?[16] What comes to mind among the topics discussed in this book in answer to these questions are three aspects of our religious situation.

First, there is the realization that the *principles* governing our way must be congruent with our ideal end. *Second* is the fact that *death* comes to each of us. And *third*, for religious thinking, is *the priority given to transcendent ends.* The first two are common to nonreligious philosophies of life, and we shall deal with them only cursorily. What we think of the third affects our decision whether or not to be formally religious, and to it we shall direct our concluding thoughts on rationalization and changes in religious life and thought.

Concerning principles I refer the reader back to Chapter Five. To that we must now add that not everyone in a tradition is fully able to make judgments of principle. A developmental view of religious thinking leads us to recognize degrees of maturity which are reflected in the fact that profound and wise judgments are rare.[17] This is one reason why tradition has such weight in the major world religions. Collectively we depend upon the insights of our wisest men and women. We do not lightly set them aside in favor of untested contemporary opinion, even though their tone is archaic and their cosmology antiquated. The gift of prophecy or even the interpretation of prophecy is less frequent than claims to prophecy (by about 1:850 according to 1 Kings 18:19). Nevertheless, once someone has rendered a superior judgment we can enter into the thinking which went into it. We can follow those ahead of us, even though we could not initially have made such judgments ourselves.[18] In moments of inspiration especially, we may make astute assessments of a situation which ordinarily would be difficult for us to imagine. Thus, our choice concerning whose judgment to follow is not one between our own feeble opinions and blind faith. It is rather one of working through the best available patterns of thought to the point where we can develop our own patterns and confirm, by our own judgments, those principles which are constitutive of our common life.

It is consistent with this understanding of developing judgments that in religious studies we school ourselves in the classic authors and the classic arguments. We do this not with a view to regurgitating their conclusions but in order to learn how to think clearly for ourselves. In the literature there may be relatively few moments of great insight. But there *are* insights which we can share.[19] Only psychotics who are completely locked away in their own private worlds are unable to enter at all into the thinking expressed in the sayings of Confucius or the other giants of intellectual history. Yet most of us find that the richness of their wisdom is such that it takes much rereading to appreciate all that they have to say to us.

A creative thinker or great teacher in the traditions is one who takes us through the familiar stories and earlier expressions of principle and points us to new conclusions, which we can then see to be congruent with what has gone before. Thus Mahatma Gandhi, for example, could transpose the concept of non-injury *(ahimsa)* from private morals to political thinking and invent the concept of truth-force *(satyagraha)*. Jesus could transform Jewish messianic thinking in his parables of the Kingdom, and so on.[20] In this connection we have to remember that *the typical conclusion to genuine religious thinking is not more thought but action*.[21] What is sought are not more beautiful thoughts on love and justice but just and loving lives. Consequently, communication in religion is often "indirect." Like modern plays, in which the action occurs between the players on stage and the audience, the verses of the prophets engage the imagination of their followers at a given time. Taken out of context their words may seem trivial. We may, for example, match up equivalents of the Golden Rule in most of the world's religions. But unless we hear them in their setting of stories and sequels, we may not hear them as invitations to a nobler way of life.

This last point leads us to one further observation concerning principles and stories. *The principles are the relational thoughts implicit in our master stories.* Even if we put at the center the ideal of being an authentic individual we find in his or her story principles of trust and risk in I-You relationships, which take us out of purely self-regarding ways of thought. When a central symbol transfigures rather than obscures our thinking, it serves this self-transcendent purpose. To be able to serve such a purpose is thus one test of a religiously satisfying primary symbol. How such principles may be interpreted by the religious crowd can still amount to distorting rationalization, as Laing reminded us. But the proverb "You can fool some of the people all of the time and all of the people some of the time, but not all of the people all of the time" applies to religious traditions also. In particular it applies to the ways in which the master stories in traditions teach us to cope with the experience of evil and the fact of death.

An unsympathetic critic might comment here that the Christian tradition, for instance, is proof that you can fool some of the people all of the time on the subject of Christ's resurrection. Psychologists may even help us to understand why the first disciples rationalized the stories of Jesus' death in this way.[22] But what motivated the disciples to carry on in the Way of Resurrection is not, of itself, decisive for an evaluation of their testimony.[23] As we recalled with reference to Bethune, motives may be mixed. What is religiously significant is the level of vision and intentionality that directs our thinking. Here again we must guard against taking beliefs out of context and learn to read our history whole. Thus we must remember that, although there was disagreement from the beginning of the Christian era concerning the possibility of resurrection, there *were* those who regarded it as a distinct possibility. Among them there was further disagreement concerning the kind of place to which resurrected persons might go.

A resurrection appearance could be news without necessarily being good news. Indeed, many stories of life after death were predicated on the assumption that such a state might be bad news. Especially the spirits of those who died violently and before their time might be expected to remain near their earthly haunts until a more peaceful departure could be arranged for them.[24] Thus, in context, *what was good news for the first disciples was not the thought that Jesus' body had been raised again but the realization that his spirit was still alive in their midst.* Their natural way of symbolizing this realization was to tell resurrection stories modeled on stories of the Assumption of Moses and Elijah, leaving the mechanics of the process to God and his angels. But what was decisive for their subsequent courses of action was the character of the Christ, the kind of spirit in which he had *both* lived *and* died.

On the level of vision and intentionality the good news of Jesus' resurrection is best expressed in John's Gospel.[25] Anyone who visits a country where gurus are still revered cannot escape the sense of their living presence among their disciples.[26] The latter know that their master has realized "samadhi" (final enlightenment) in such a way as never again to be physically alive in the old form. They can point to where his body sits in yoga position. But his presence is no longer restricted to that one spot. He lives through their teaching, in their common vision of life, treasured in words and stories and active in healing and worship throughout the community. Thus Socrates lives in Plato, Jesus in

John, and so on, not in any psychologically reductionistic sense but in the religiously relevant sense that their patterns of behavior, their character and constitutive principles, now shape ways of life which previously were unstable or distinctly different. Their old haunts are historic reference points for their disciples. But it is not by lingering at these that the disciples are inspired.

To keep our feet on the ground while thinking resurrection thoughts we need not only realistic reminders of fate and death, such as the stories of Moses' failure to reach the Promised Land or Socrates' death at the hands of some of his students but also realizable policies for attaining the good life. These, we have said, must be consistent with the kind of end envisioned in the thinking of the community of the faithful. But what counts as realizable varies according to the horizon of our expectations—this world with a heavenly superstructure, a supernatural spirit state, a place of non-returning, or whatever. And it is at this point that we find a parting of the ways between religious and nonreligious thinkers. Faith, we said earlier, engenders a hope for impossible possibilities, which probabilistic thinking and statistical forecasting will not honor with the label "reasonable." The hope is not necessarily unreasonable—this depends upon how "reason" is defined—but it is not guaranteed in advance. Its realization depends in part upon our acting on it. Such action requires the kind of decision elicited by the question of death: on what are we willing to stake our life? To what and for what, if anything, would we give our life? Is there anything that could happen to us in history that could so compromise our integrity as living human beings that we would rather be dead?

The testimony of Socrates, of Jesus, of Gandhi, of Martin Luther King, of Malcolm X, and countless others is that *there are conditions under which life is worth risking.* This is not to say that they had a death wish or were accomplices in their own murders. It is to say that the threat of death was not sufficient to deter them from their basic policies and ultimate goals. They were consistent in their priorities and values so that, *whether they lived or died, their cause became a movement not restricted to their physical presence among their supporters.* What lives, what is resurrected, if and when we would talk this way, is the saving identity which sees through the threat and even the fact of dying the possibility of a better life than that which had been known before. The same realism, the same priorities, the same principles of compassion and justice are found in stories about them and their way, after their deaths, as in the stories which they told when they were on their way.

When reflecting on realizable ends we have to recognize in the history of religious thinking a continuum of more or less transcendent references. What is perhaps not sufficiently acknowledged in current theories is that such references always had both a "vertical" and a "horizontal" thrust. The latter is seen not only in Hebrew stories of God's Kingdom in history but also in Indian realizations of Nirvana in samsara, Chinese expressions of the Tao, and so forth. The vertical thrust seems to change direction according to the ways in which we interpret dreams. When these were thought to be messages from the gods above their movement was upward. Now that dreams are regarded as symptoms of inner psychic states their movement is said to be down into the depths of our souls. Here whether we talk of Man with a capital *M*, Nature with a capital *N*, or God with a capital *G*, our reference is to a level of interactions which involves us in a different system or structure of meanings from that signified by a mere aggregation of life forces or human purposes. The whole is not reducible to the systems studied in physics, social psychology, economics, and related disciplines.[27] How we may think of it is the task of religious theorists to explicate. *Whatever transcendent references we allow in our stories serve to raise our sights to whatever force we consider capable of carrying our sense of meaning and value in life beyond the physical limitations of our present personal situation.*[28]

Where along the continuum we mark the cut-off point between nonreligious and religious references is somewhat arbitrary. Fastidious thinkers who prefer pure categories object to such apparent arbitrariness.[29] However, the fact that we can debate the precise point of demarcation does not mean that there is no difference between nonreligious and religious thinking. It just means that there are religiously significant aspects of nonreligious movements, such as Marxism, and there is a secular side to all religious activities, which should not be ignored for the sake of our categories. Earlier we cited Camus as an example of a nonreligious thinker. But if his only absolute force is demonic rather than divine, in relation to "the plague" even he gives priority to I-You over I-It relationships in the definition of authentic human being. In our conceptions of our situation in life, an aggregation of I-Its does not make an I-You. An aggregation of I-Yous does not make a We. An aggregation of "We's" does not make a life-world. And an aggregation of worlds does not make an unambiguously life-enhancing and universal presence, if not at the beginning then at the end of our story.[30] When such a presence is directly or indirectly evoked by a story then we are without doubt dealing with religious thinking. Between that and Camus, however, is a network of connected hopes and fears, myths and symbols, which can only be unraveled case by case. There is no a priori limit to the range of possible family resemblances in patterns of faith.

In any case, what controls the dynamics of argument on the religious level of life and thought is the unambiguous vision of the good life. This is evoked by our preferred systems of symbols. Its character is shaped by priorities implicit in the principles governing our way of self-realization. As long as this realization remains incomplete, its orientation is future.

To illustrate these points and conclude our discussion, I refer the reader finally to a debate between Mahatma Gandhi and Rabindranath Tagore concerning the pace of industrialization in India.[31] Gandhi's ideal for man was an inner strength which would be expressed in personal freedom from external pressures, unrelenting even to the point of death. To foster this he advocated, among other things, economic self-sufficiency, symbolized by the spinning wheel in the home as opposed to the importing of processed material from the industrial nations of Europe. "The hungry millions ask for one poem—invigorating food. They cannot be given it. They must earn it." They are deprived of their earning power if wealthy Indians prefer to patronize Manchester cotton mills. At issue was a question of priorities. Industries would come in time. But more immediately important was Indian independence. Neither economic nor political independence would be good news, however, unless Indians were spiritually prepared to cope with its complexities. To this end they must all "experiment with Truth," live *ahimsa* (nonviolently), express love by giving their neighbor work while renouncing their fancy European clothes. To become free they must repudiate the spiral of aggressions evident among the warring nations of Europe which had already drawn Japan into its orbit.[32]

Tagore's vision of Truth was more universalistic. He questioned Gandhi's nationalistic version of the truth of independence and his repudiation of Western technology in his development of means. Tagore's bent was aesthetic and his conception was of the underlying unity of all life. In fact it was Gandhi the holy man not Tagore the poet who mobilized the masses. But the Europeanized Indians were the ones who later led the government.

Do we conclude from the fact that India today hardly realizes the vision of either Gandhi or Tagore that neither was correct? Like all prophets, Gandhi tended to foreshorten the time-span in which he hoped that his countrymen might realize his way for themselves. Like all universalists Tagore glossed over the individuating characteristics of incarnated truth. In short, we can see now that neither one had the whole truth, and neither one was wholly mistaken.

What we have been presenting in this book is a dialectical or "alternating" model of the truth according to which no one version of the ultimate vision is true when taken in isolation. *Truth comes at the intersecting point between code and character, between impersonal, universal ideas and personal, particular passions. The truth comes in silence.* Not the silence of unresponsiveness, but the silence of realization provoked by the testimony of others to their vision of the truth. If in the beginning is "the Word," at the end is a quality of self-realization which words cannot adequately express. This realization comes from seeing, through the interweaving witnesses of other life stories, that pattern of faith which can be true for us. Because the vision is of an unambiguously good life for us, it is not yet true. Whether it becomes true depends partly on our decision. In this context, to defer judgment on the vision is itself a decision which will delay the dawning of the day on which our dreams come true.

When we talk of judgment and testimony we adumbrate a legal model for reasoning in religion. We suggest that we must cross-examine history for realistic reference points on our way. And we must cross-examine ourselves in the light of history to see whether our images of self and integrating principles are consistent with our ends. But here the judgment differs from the legal, since at issue is not the assessment of past responsibility and ordering of penalties. Now rather we are concerned with acceptance of present and future responsibility and promises of liberation. Hence our talk is not only of precedents but also of priorities, not only of realistic histories but also of realizable dreams, not only of actualities but also of possibilities. To sum up, we must ask of any life story:

What are its primary symbols and does it have a central core?

If so, what are the constitutive principles articulated in its master story?

What are the realistic reference points acknowledged in elaborations of this story?

And what are the realizable ends in view consistent with the way which is being proposed?

With regard to Gandhi we might answer that the primary symbols were drawn from the ways of devotion and action *(bhakti* and *karma yoga)*. The master story was an idiosyncratic reading of the *Bhagavad Gita* applied to India's political destiny. The constitutive principles included non-injury *(ahimsa)*, freedom *(swaraj)*, and the superiority of moral to physical force *(satyagraha)*. The references were realistic concerning the effects of industrialization on a village culture and concerning the political intentions of the British. However, the vision was realizable by the master but not so easily by his followers. For he left no structures to sustain his movement.[33] Instead, he has himself become a primary symbol for contemporary religious thinkers, more perhaps outside India than at home. By contrast, Marxist activists have shared Tagore's universalistic vision and moved to absorb the illiterate masses into cadres of workers in the cities. "To a people famishing and idle," Gandhi wrote, "the only acceptable form in which God dare appear is work and promise of food as wages."[34] By this criterion we should have to say that God has appeared recently more often in China than in India, even though God has been invoked by name more often in the latter place. But Indians such as Gandhi and Tagore take a much longer view of history than we are accustomed to taking in the West. The facets of truth to which they bore witness may yet be realized by the majority of their countrymen.

By whose hand redeeming power will come to those who are no longer hungry and idle, however, is a question for other leaders with other visions of the truth for all. What Gandhi admonished us to do, when we are not *sure* that ours is the right way, is so to act that the probable consequences of our miscalculations and lack of feeling may fall more on us than on others. In his "experiments with Truth" he never doubted that he had more to learn, even from those whom he saw to be in the wrong. He tried never to compromise his principles. But he also sought always to accept personal injury without retaliation, rather than let this become an occasion for future discord. He never accepted the partiality of his perspective as an excuse for inaction. In the face of so much misery and ill-will in the world around him, he believed in acting on his incomplete conception of the good rather than in waiting to clear up every ambiguity in his theory of good and evil.

To be true, a way of life has to be both *the* way and *our* way. It has to be the way in the present which is consistent both with our tradition and with the future being shaped by our hopes. It has to be our way of expressing the interplay of past and future in the faithful formation of tradition in the present.

The world religions, even in their ideal and normative modes of expression, set before us no *single* way, to which we must all be true. There is in each a demand for personal participation, personal adaptation, personal judgment concerning the priorities at stake in moments of decision. But all the ways taught by the traditions agree that whatever is presented as true for us must be recognized by us to be good news.

As we make our personal judgments, we may draw on guidelines from the master stories of the major traditions. These are the Jesus story, the Buddha story, the Passover story, the May Day story and the rest, which set the contours of our common cultural world. My argument in this book has been that, properly understood, each master story is incomplete if it is thought to refer only to the past. The True Church, the True Community, the True Israel, the Permanent Revolution, Nirvana and the like are present to experience in religion, certainly, but present as demands to do and be better in the future. Without this hope of future development the traditions alone, as often as not, warrant only the kind of negative judgment that Alex made on his parents' faith. As presented to him, their tradition was bad news. He did not want to say "We" when he thought of Israel in the future.

How the redemptive themes and tests for truth must be worked out in each tradition are topics not just for another paragraph or chapter but for another book. In this book I have considered concrete instances of problems encountered on each "way." But I have concentrated primarily on the general spirit in which religion at its best is a continually developing force in our individual and collective experience. Insofar as we are never always at our best, and religions are *our* ways of life, what I have discussed remains an ideal never fully realized. But insofar as what is real is not just the literal experience of past and present faith but also the symbolic thrust of living hope, no account of religion is accurate which looks only at past failures. A Grand Inquisitor or a Stalin indeed stands as a negative symbol undermining the credibility of a tradition for a time. But each tradition develops from the *good* news that its adherents have known, precisely at points where the mystery of evil most confronted them. The master stories are focused not on negative symbols of dispersal and despair but on positive symbols, which transfigure the experience of failure and transform faith into hope.

What the *whole* truth is in religion is not fully articulated in any master story because, in addition to stories, life is constituted by moments of silence, feelings, unconscious urges, inexpressible ecstasies preceded by painful stretches of emptiness, in short by far more than we can ever put into words. It is, finally, only in the wisdom that knows the silences as well as the stories, that we may live according to the "ways" of which we have been thinking.

My contention has been that, whatever our way, we understand true faith when we think through our priorities, from rules to principles and from means to ends, so that, even when we lose confidence in the plot-line of a traditional master story, our character will be such as to carry us through to new or renewed hope. As Tillich pointed out, the dynamics of faith always includes doubt, not as an unwelcome threat but as a needed instigation to personal growth. The dynamics of religion similarly includes both judgment on our past and affirmation of our future as signs of our increasing maturity. The good news about religion in our day is that such affirmations are still being made among the traditions. The good news of religion is that such affirmations can indeed be based on realistic appraisals of past performance and on authentic visions of present promise.

Notes to Chapters

NOTES TO PREFACE

1. See Paul Tillich, *Systematic Theology*, 3 vols. (Chicago: University of Chicago Press, 1951, 1957, 1963) esp. vol. 1 pp. 59–66. During a graduate seminar at Harvard, Tillich once remarked that the label was a late suggestion from one of his graduate assistants at Union Theological Seminary in New York. His own preferred term was "dialectics," not in the Hegelian-Marxist pattern of thesis-antithesis-synthesis, but as in Schelling, the German idealist philosopher on whom Tillich wrote two dissertations. With reference to the use of religious symbols the important point is that we see in and through them the living process whereby we bring together, and go beyond, what in abstract thought we treat as polar opposites, for example, life and death or faith and doubt. In this respect, dialectical thinking is not simply "phenomenological," that is, restricted to an orderly description of phenomena. On phenomenology in relation to theology see Edward Farley, *Ecclesial Man: A Social Phenomenology of Faith and Reality* (Philadelphia: Fortress Press, 1975) esp. pp. 25–29, and in regard to Tillich, pp. 263–66.

2. I am indebted to my colleague Robert Polzin for my introduction to these concepts. See Robert M. Polzin, *Biblical Structuralism: Method and Subjectivity in the Study of Ancient Texts* (Missoula, Mont.: Scholars Press, 1977) chap. 1.

NOTES TO CHAPTER ONE

1. See, e.g., Leslie Dewart, *The Future of Belief: Theism in a World Come of Age* (New York: Herder & Herder, 1966); Maurice Wiles, *The Remaking of Christian Doctrine* (London: SCM Press, 1974); and Walter Holden Capps, *Hope Against Hope: Moltmann to Merton in One Theological Decade* (Philadelphia: Fortress Press, 1976).

2. On this subject see what Gadamer says concerning representation, as con-

trasted with copying an "original," in Hans-Georg Gadamer, *Truth and Method,* translated from the second German edition (New York: Seabury Press, 1975) esp. pp. 123–27.

3. For some of the problems here see Peter Winch, "Understanding a Primitive Society," in D. Z. Phillips, ed., *Religion and Understanding* (New York: Macmillan, 1967) chap. 1.

4. In this connection see William James's critique of "medical materialism" in *The Varieties of Religious Experience* (New York: Longmans, Green & Co., 1902; London: Collins Fontana pb, 1960) Lecture I (p. 35 pb).

5. See Walter H. Capps, ed., *The Future of Hope* (Philadelphia: Fortress Press pb, 1970) for essays and discussions by Ernst Bloch, Emil Fackenheim, Jürgen Moltmann, Johannes Metz, and others; or Carl Braaten and Robert Jenson, *The Futurist Option* (New York: Paulist Press pb, 1970).

6. For argument on this point see Gadamer, *Truth and Method,* p. 106 concerning tradition and p. 195 concerning experience as "that strange fusion of memory and expectation." In conversation, Gadamer once acknowledged that he gives less weight to the futurist orientation, as found in Bloch, than to the interplay of past and present.

7. See, e.g., the eight "ways" described by Frederick Streng, Charles Lloyd, and Jay Allen in *Ways of Being Religious* (Englewood Cliffs, N.J.: Prentice-Hall, 1973) which are labeled as follows: rebirth through personal encounter with the Holy, creation of community through myth and ritual, living harmoniously through conformity to cosmic law, spiritual freedom through discipline (mysticism), attaining an integrated self through creative interaction, achievement of human rights through political and economic action, the new life through technocracy, and enjoyment of the full life through sensuous experience. For argument on the unity of religious ways see Huston Smith's introduction to Frithjof Schuon, *The Transcendent Unity of Religions,* rev. ed. trans. Peter Townsend (New York: Harper & Row, Harper Torchbooks pb, 1975).

8. See, e.g., D. Z. Phillips, *The Concept of Prayer* (London: Routledge & Kegan Paul, 1965); Donald D. Evans, *The Logic of Self-Involvement* (London: SCM Press, 1963); and William A. Christian, *Meaning and Truth in Religion* (Princeton, N.J.: Princeton University Press, 1964).

9. On relevant similarities and differences in this context see Langdon Gilkey, *Religion and the Scientific Future* (New York: Harper & Row, 1970) and Ian Barbour, *Myths, Models and Paradigms* (New York: Harper & Row, 1974).

10. For the legal model see Stephen Toulmin, *The Uses of Argument* (Cambridge: Cambridge University Press, 1958) and application of his concept of warrants to theology in Van Harvey, *The Historian and the Believer: The Morality of Historical Knowledge and Christian Belief* (New York: Macmillan pb, 1966) pp. 49–64, pp. 191–94; David H. Kelsey, *The Uses of Scripture in Recent Theology* (Philadelphia: Fortress Press, 1975) pp. 125–46, and on Toulmin's notion of "limiting questions" (from his earlier book on ethics), see Schubert Ogden, *The Reality of God and Other Essays* (New York: Harper & Row, 1963) pp. 27–39 and David Tracy, *Blessed Rage for Order: The New Pluralism in Theology* (New York: Seabury Press, 1975) pp. 101–4. Innovative use of legal patterns is found in Robert A. Evans and Thomas D. Parker, eds., *Christian Theology: A Case Method Approach* (New York: Harper & Row, 1976).

11. On this subject see Wilfred Cantwell Smith, *The Meaning and End of Religion: A New Approach to the Religious Traditions of Mankind* (New York: Harper & Row, 1978 chap. 3. For an introduction to and bibliography of Smith's publications

see *Religious Diversity*, ed. Willard G. Oxtoby (New York: Harper Forum Book pb, 1976).

12. Robert Monk et al. use the concept of pivotal values in their textbook *Exploring Religious Meaning* (Englewood Cliffs, N.J.: Prentice-Hall pb, 1973). In this they are following H. Richard Niebuhr.

13. See Paul E. Johnson, *Psychology of Religion: A Psychological Analysis of What It Means to Be Religious* (Nashville: Abingdon Press, 1959) pp. 47–48, "In the name of religion what deed has not been done?"

14. For an earlier account of this see my article "Religion as an Academic Discipline," *Bulletin of the Council on the Study of Religion* 2:4 (October 1971) pp. 2–7, and in Claude Welch, ed., *Religion in the Undergraduate Curriculum* (Washington, D.C.: Association of American Colleges, 1972) pp. 26–36. See also Frederick Ferré, "The Definition of Religion," *Journal of the American Academy of Religion* 38:1 (March 1970) pp. 3–16 and Frederick J. Streng, "Studying Religion: Possibilities and Limitations of Different Definitions," *Journal of the American Academy of Religion* 40:2 (June 1972) pp. 219–37.

15. See, e.g., Charles Davis, "Towards a Critical Theology," *1975 Proceedings of the American Academy of Religion: Philosophy of Religion and Theology*, comp. James W. McClendon, Jr. (Missoula, Mont.: Scholars Press, 1975) esp. pp. 221–22. On praxis see, e.g., Jürgen Habermas, *Theory and Practice*, trans. John Viertel (Boston: Beacon Press, 1973) Introduction and chap. 7.

16. See Ludwig Wittgenstein, *Philosophical Investigations* (New York: Macmillan, 1973; Oxford: Blackwell & Mott, 1958) par. 339–40, concerning "private" language. On the more debatable relation between thinking and speaking see Jean Piaget, *Six Psychological Studies*, trans. A. Tenzer (New York: Vintage pb, 1968) pt. III, 1.

17. For a contemporary account of the ceremony see Melford Spiro, *Buddhism and Society* (New York: Harper & Row pb, 1972) chap. 10.

18. See, e.g., Harvey Cox, *The Secular City* (New York: Macmillan pb, 1966) chap. 1.

19. See, e.g., Gregory Baum, *Religion and Alienation: A Theological Reading of Sociology* (New York: Paulist Press pb, 1975) chap. 12.

20. Note the sentiment inscribed on a Buddhist monument in Pagan for Queen Caw of Burma: "Meantime, *before I reach Nirvana* by virtue of this great work of merit which I have done, may I prosper as a man. . . . More especially I would have a long life, freedom from disease, a lovely complexion, a pleasant voice and a beautiful figure. I would be the loved and honoured darling of every man and spirit. Gold, silver, rubies, corals, pearls and other lifeless treasure—may I have lots of them. . . . Wherever I am born, may I be filled with noble graces, charity, faith, piety, wisdom, etc., and not know one speck of misery; *and after I have tasted and enjoyed the happiness of men and the happiness of spirits,* when the noble law of deliverance called the fruit of sanctity blossoms, may I at last attain the peaceful bliss of Nirvana." A. S. Burma, List of Inscriptions, no. 334, quoted in Robert Lawson Slater, *Paradox and Nirvana: A Study of Religious Ultimates with Special Reference to Burmese Buddhism* (Chicago: University of Chicago Press, 1951) p. 45, R. L. Slater's italics.

21. William A. Christian, *Meaning and Truth in Religion*, speaks of what is *very important* among our interests, rather than of ultimates or absolutes, chap. 4.

22. On the importance of the process of conversion to religious thinking, see Bernard Lonergan, *Method in Theology*, 2d ed. (New York: Seabury Press, 1972; London: Darton, Longman & Todd, 1973) pp. 130–32, chap. 10.

23. C. G. Jung, *Psychology and Religion* (New Haven: Yale University Press pb, 1972) chap. 3, p. 99.
24. On the related concepts of focal and subsidiary awareness see Michael Polanyi, *Personal Knowledge: Towards a Post-Critical Philosophy* (Chicago: The University of Chicago Press, 1958) pp. 55–65.
25. I have in mind here the example of Karl Barth's theologizing in the many volumes of his *Church Dogmatics* (New York: Allenson, 1936–69; Edinburgh: T. & T. Clark, 1936–69). On the value-laden nature of a linear order of perception see Dorothy Lee, "Codifications of Reality: Lineal and Nonlineal," reprinted in Robert Ornstein, ed., *The Nature of Human Consciousness* (San Francisco: W. H. Freeman, 1973) chap. 10. See also Ray L. Hart, *Unfinished Man & The Imagination* (New York: Herder and Herder, 1968) chap. 2, concerning "the Hermeneutical spiral."
26. See my papers "From World to God and Back Again," *Philosophy of Religion and Theology: 1974 Proceedings AAR*, comp. James William McClendon, Jr. (Missoula, Mont.: Scholars Press, 1974) pp. 86–103 and "Christian Talk of God," in George F. McLean, ed., *Traces of God in a Secular Culture* (New York: Alba House, 1973) pp. 345–79, for argument on this point. For a critique of Peter Berger's concept of world-building in this connection see Ninian Smart, *The Science of Religion and the Sociology of Knowledge* (Princeton: Princeton University Press, 1973) chap. 4.
27. See Leon Festinger et al., *When Prophecy Fails: A Social and Psychological Study of a Modern Group that Predicted the Destruction of the World* (New York: Harper Torchbooks pb, 1964). For my general thesis I am indebted here to H. H. Farmer's lectures on the philosophy of religion at Cambridge University, 1955–57.
28. On the need for "demythologizing" in this context see Rudolf Bultmann, "New Testament and Mythology," in H. W. Bartsch, ed., *Kerygma and Myth* (New York: Harper Torchbooks pb, 1961) chap. 1.
29. Smith, *The Meaning and End of Religion.*
30. See William James, *The Will to Believe, Human Immortality and Other Essays on Popular Philosophy* (New York, 1898, reprinted as a Dover pb, 1956) pp. 2–4.

NOTES TO CHAPTER TWO

1. See the story of Noah, Gen. 9:11–17. For other examples see e.g., Jean Daniélou, S. J., *Primitive Christian Symbols*, trans. Donald Attwater (London: Burns & Oates, 1964) and Edwyn Bevan, *Symbolism and Belief* (Boston: Beacon Press pb, 1957), the Gifford Lectures for 1933–34.
2. See Luke 10:38–42.
3. On institutional racism see Stokely Carmichael and Charles V. Hamilton, *Black Power: The Politics of Liberation in America* (New York: Random House, 1967) pp. 40–49 and pass. In general, see Patrick Kerans, *Sinful Social Structures* (New York: Paulist Press, 1974) and, on symbolism and ethics, Gibson Winter, *Elements for a Social Ethic: The Role of Social Science in Public Policy* (New York: Macmillan, 1966).
4. A useful account of current conceptions is given by W. R. Comstock in *Religion and Man: An Introduction* (New York: Harper & Row, 1971) pt. I. The philosophy of symbolic forms is associated especially with the work of Ernst Cassirer, e.g., his popular *Language and Myth*, trans. Susanne K. Langer (New York: Harper & Brothers, pb 1946). See also the essays by Tillich, Kenneth Burke, Whitehead, and others in Rollo May, ed., *Symbolism in Religion and Literature* (New York: George Braziller, 1961).

5. Piaget, *Six Psychological Studies* speaks of indices, signifiers, signs, and symbols, of which the last barely reaches the range of connotations assumed, for example, by Tillich.

6. For example, A. J. Heschel, *God in Search of Man* (New York: Harper Torchbooks, pb 1955) p. 103. Heschel speaks of a level of meaning "deeper" than concepts, utterances, and symbols, which is both "immediate" and "metasymbolic." A contrasting position, related to studies in religious uses of language, is found in Langdon Gilkey, *Naming the Whirlwind: The Renewal of God-Language* (Indianapolis & New York: Bobbs-Merrill, 1969) pp. 266–76. On some of the problems involved see John Meagher, *The Gathering of the Ungifted: Toward a Dialogue on Christian Identity* (New York: Herder & Herder, 1972) chap. 4.

7. For example, Austin Farrer in *The Glass of Vision* (London: Dacre, 1948) and Stephen C. Pepper, *World Hypotheses* (Berkeley: University of California Press, 1942).

8. I. T. Ramsey, *Religious Language* (New York: Macmillan, 1963; London: SCM Press, 1957) chap. 2 and Battista Mondin, *The Principle of Analogy in Protestant and Catholic Thought* (The Hague: Martinus Nijhoff, 1963). On analogy and symbol see John Macquarrie, *God-Talk* (New York: Harper & Row, 1967) chaps. 9 and 10.

9. See Gadamer, *Truth and Method* p. 69 in regard to Schelling. For Tillich see Sidney Hook, ed., *Religious Experience and Truth* (New York: New York University Press, 1961) chap. 1, the comment by W. P. Alston in chap. 2, and the Appendix. See also W. L. Rowe, *Religious Symbols and God* (Chicago: The University of Chicago Press, 1968) for criticism of Tillich.

10. Paul Ricoeur, *The Symbolism of Evil*, trans. E. Buchanan (New York: Harper & Row, 1967) p. 5.

11. See, e.g., Mircea Eliade *The Sacred and the Profane*, trans. Willard Trask (New York: Harper & Row pb, 1959). For a critical appreciation of Eliade which develops the concept of centering see Jonathan Z. Smith, "The Wobbling Pivot," *Journal of Religion* 52:2 (April 1972) pp. 134–49.

12. Ricoeur, *Symbolism of Evil*, Conclusion.

13. A shaman, on the contrary, might regard his psychic experiences as more "objective" than hallucinations of his "profane" environment. Consider the discussions of "reality" in Carlos Castaneda, *A Separate Reality: Further Conversations with Don Juan* (New York: Pocket Books pb, 1972) pp. 25–29 and the philosophical commentary by David Silverman, *Reading Castaneda* (London: Routledge & Kegan Paul, 1975).

14. What counts as "literal" is usually less well defined than what is meant by "symbolic." See D. Hoitenga, "The Symbolic Theory of Religious Language" (Ph.D. diss., Harvard University, 1959). On metaphor in religious usage see Sallie McFague TeSelle, *Speaking in Parables: A Study in Metaphor and Theology* (Philadelphia: Fortress Press, 1975) chap. 3 and Paul Ricoeur, "Biblical Hermeneutics," in *Semeia* 4 (1975) pp. 75–106. Ricoeur's recent views on symbol and metaphor are given, e.g., in Paul Ricoeur *Interpretation Theory: Discourse and the Surplus of Meaning*, (Fort Worth: The Texas Christian University Press, 1976). For present purposes I am drawing from his earlier work.

15. Ricoeur, *Symbolism of Evil*, p. 15

16. Ibid., p. 309.

17. Ibid., p. 11.

18. For critical comment on Lévi-Strauss concerning nature and culture see Jacques Derrida, *Of Grammatology*, trans. G. C. Spivak (Baltimore: The Johns

Hopkins University Press pb, 1974) p. 104. In this connection note especially Mary Douglas's work on bodily symbols. She suggests that the contrast between spirit and matter is more important to many societies than that between culture and nature, *Natural Symbols* (New York: Random House, 1970) p. xiii and pass.

19. See, e.g., Paul Lutz and Paul Santmire, *Ecological Renewal* (Philadelphia: Fortress Press, 1972) pp. 110–12 and pass.

20. On "seeing as" consult Virgil C. Aldrich in Sidney Hook, ed., *Religious Experience and Truth* and John Hick, *God and the Universe of Faiths* (London: Macmillan, 1973) chap. 3, "Religious Faith as Experiencing-as." My own critical comments will appear in more detail in *Sophia*, 1978/9, on "Seeing As, Seeing In and Seeing Through."

21. On "hard" and "soft" perspectivism see James William McClendon, Jr., and James M. Smith, *Understanding Religious Convictions* (Notre Dame: University of Notre Dame Press pb, 1975) pp. 6–7 and pass. and Harvey, *Historian and Believer*, chap. 8.

22. Martin Buber, *I and Thou*, trans. W. Kaufman (New York: Charles Scribner's Sons, 1970).

23. In many anthologies, for example, *Classical and Contemporary Readings in the Philosophy of Religion*, ed. John Hick (Englewood Cliffs, N.J.: Prentice-Hall, 1964) chap. 30, p. 434, reprinted from *Proceedings of the Aristotelian Society*, 1944–45.

24. Ibid., chap. 32, pp. 464–65, reprinted from *New Essays in Philosophical Theology*, ed. Antony Flew and Alasdair MacIntyre (New York: Macmillan, 1955).

25. See Milton K. Munitz, *The Mystery of Existence* (New York: Meredith, 1965) and Wilfrid Desan, *The Planetary Man* (New York: Macmillan, 1972) chap. 3, "Truth as Angular."

26. See Wittgenstein, *Philosophical Investigations*, pt. II, xi. He warns against imposing finer distinctions than ordinary usage allows concerning "seeing," p. 200e, and sharply separates conceptual from psychological analysis. However, I find psychological studies of yoga helpful here, e.g., Robert Ornstein, *The Psychology of Consciousness* (New York: Viking, 1974) pp. 124–27.

27. See the criticism of Flew by R. M. Hare and Basil Mitchell in the "Theology and Falsification" debate (also in Hick, ed., *Classical and Contemporary Readings*) and Donald Evans's discussion of onlooks, *Logic of Self-Involvement* pp. 124–41.

28. On "vision of life" see T. Patrick Burke, *The Reluctant Vision* (Philadelphia: Fortress Press pb, 1974), pp. 18–19.

29. On this concept see Gadamer, *Truth and Method*, who speaks of "two extremes . . . pure indication (the essence of sign), and pure representation (the essence of symbol)" p. 134. Concerning intending, compare Lonergan, *Method in Theology*, pp. 10–11 and pass.

30. See, e.g., Paul van Buren, *The Edges of Language* (New York: Macmillan, 1972) pp. 101–3; Joseph C. McLelland, *The Clown and the Crocodile* (Richmond, Va.: John Knox Press, 1970) p. 27; and, in general, Arthur Koestler, *The Act of Creation* (New York: Macmillan, 1964; London: Pan pb, 1971) pt. one.

31. Note the lyrics for Joni Mitchell's "Big Yellow Taxi": "They paved paradise . . . ," reprinted in *Listen! Songs and Poems of Canada*, ed. Homer Hogan (Toronto: Methuen, 1972) p. 109.

32. On "passing over" from one viewpoint to another see John S. Dunne, *A Search for God in Time and Memory* (New York: Macmillan, pb 1969) 1.

33. On dancing in this connection see, e.g., Janheinz Jahn, *Muntu: The New African*

Culture, trans. Marjorie Grene (New York: Grove Evergreen pb, 1963) chap. 3 and Harvey Cox, *The Feast of Fools: A Theological Essay on Festivity and Fantasy* (New York: Harper & Row, 1970) chap. 3.

34. On Buddhist images see, e.g., Giuseppe Tucci, *The Theory and Practice of the Mandala*, trans. A. H. Brodrick (New York: Samuel Weiser, 1973). On garden symbolism note, e.g., T. S. Eliot's "Burnt Norton" from *Four Quartets, Collected Poems 1909–1962* (New York: Harcourt, Brace & World, 1963), pp. 175–76.

35. See the argument in Richard Creel, *Religion and Doubt: Towards a Faith of Your Own* (Englewood Cliffs, N.J.: Prentice-Hall, 1977) pp. 70–80.

36. On the contrast between seeing and looking at, note Castaneda, *A Separate Reality*, pp. 36–37. On seeing things differently note Annie Dillard, *Pilgrim at Tinker Creek* (New York: Harper & Row, 1974) chap. 2. However, I would dispute the interpretation on p. 26: "For the newly sighted, vision is pure sensation unencumbered by meaning. . . ." What becomes clear from the accounts given is that formerly blind people have different contexts from the conventional ones, into which they bring their first experiences of seeing.

37. In this connection note Frederick Streng's discussion of the Buddhist doctrine of "skill in means" as applied to the descriptive and transformative uses of language, "Mystical Awareness, Or How To Be in the World but Not of It," *Philosophy of Religion and Theology: 1976 Proceedings*, American Academy of Religion, comp. Peter Slater (Missoula, Mont.: Scholars Press, 1976) pp. 224–29.

38. The need for "dehellenization" is argued by Leslie Dewart, *Future of Belief*, chap. 1 with reference to the relationship between Christian theology and Hellenistic philosophy, pp. 49–51 and pass.

39. On this point see Thomas Luckmann, *The Invisible Religion* (New York: Macmillan, 1967) pp. 42–43.

40. Ibid., chap. 6. But I agree with Victor Turner, against such authors as Luckmann, in saying that, religiously speaking, tribal groups are no "simpler" than others. See Victor W. Turner, *The Ritual Process* (Chicago: Aldine, 1969) p. 3.

NOTES TO CHAPTER THREE

1. See, e.g., Victor Turner, *Ritual Process*, p. 8; *The Forest of Symbols: Aspects of Ndembu Ritual* (Ithaca, N.Y.: Cornell University Press, 1967) chap. 1 and elsewhere. Turner speaks of "dominant" and "instrumental" symbols, *Forest*, p. 45.

2. See, e.g., James B. Wiggins, ed., *Religion as Story* (New York: Harper Forum Book pb, 1975); James William McClendon, Jr., *Biography as Theology: How Life Stories Can Remake Today's Theology* (Nashville: Abingdon Press pb, 1974); Michael Novak, *Ascent of the Mountain, Flight of the Dove* (New York: Harper & Row, 1971) chap. 2, "Autobiography and Story"; Stanley Hauerwas, with Richard Bondi and David B. Burrell, *Truthfulness and Tragedy: Further Investigations into Christian Ethics* (Notre Dame: University of Notre Dame Press, 1977) esp. chaps. 1, 4, and 5; and John Dominic Crossan, *Raid on the Articulate: Comic Eschatology in Jesus and Borges* (New York: Harper & Row, 1976). See especially Monika Konrad Hellwig in Gregory Baum, ed., *Journeys: The Impact of Personal Experience on Religious Thought* (New York: Paulist Press, 1975) p. 127:

I am equally convinced that without recourse to the cumulative wisdom of one's own tradition, one cannot be creative. I also believe one must be very much steeped in tradition to be at all innovative.

Secondly, I am deeply convinced that the traditional wisdom is not passed on primarily by purely intellectual connections. When I reflect on my own experience I am aware that although I am in many respects a "head person" with aptitude and inclination for abstraction, logic, and rational discourse in general, I was born from the womb of sculpture and music and fairy tale, and my head has always had much deeper levels of tradition to draw upon than the purely intellectual.

3. Sam Keen, *To a Dancing God* (New York: Harper & Row, 1970) chap. 1 and *Beginnings Without End* (New York: Harper & Row, 1975) esp. pp. 40 and 45–53.

4. For a useful survey of the relevant literature see Barbour, *Myths, Models and Paradigms*.

5. We are reminded of this especially by the structuralists. See Polzin, *Biblical Structuralism*, Dan O. Via, Jr., *Kerygma and Comedy in the New Testament: A Structuralist Approach* (Philadelphia: Fortress Press, 1975); and Edmund Leach, ed., *The Structural Study of Myth and Totemism*, A.S.A. Monograph 5 (London: Tavistock, 1967) including essays by Claude Lévi-Strauss, Mary Douglas, and Kenelm Burridge. Emphasis on symbol systems in religion is noteworthy especially in Clifford Geertz, "Religion as a Cultural System," reprinted in W. Lessa and E. Vogt, eds., *Reader in Comparative Religion*, 3d ed. (New York: Harper & Row, 1973) and Robert N. Bellah, *Beyond Belief: Essays on Religion in a Post-Traditional World* (New York: Harper & Row, 1970) pp. 9–12, 175–79, and pass.

6. See the discussion in TeSelle, *Speaking in Parables* pt. I. My own earlier observations on this point appear in "Parables, Analogues and Symbols," *Religious Studies* 4:1 (October 1968) pp. 25–36.

7. See, e.g., Gustaf Aulén, *Christus Victor*, trans. A. G. Hebert (New York: Macmillan, 1969; London: SPCK, 1953). For a critique of Aulén and other theories of atonement see George Rupp, *Christologies and Cultures: Toward a Typology of Religious Worldviews* (The Hague: Mouton, 1974) pt. one.

8. This point was brought home to me by George Widengren's account of the conflict between Karl Barth and the German church in the 1930s, University of Pennsylvania public lecture, 1968.

9. See, for example, the selection in *Writings of the Young Marx on Philosophy and Society*, ed. and trans. Loyd Easton and Kurt Guddat (New York: Anchor pb, 1967).

10. On stages in life see, e.g., John S. Dunne, *Time and Myth: A Meditation on Storytelling as an Exploration of Life and Death* (Notre Dame: University Notre Dame Press, pb 1973) chap. 2.

11. See Gordon W. Allport, *The Individual and His Religion* (New York: Macmillan, 1954) p. 25.

12. Consider the salmon in Margaret Craven, *I Heard the Owl Call My Name* (New York: Doubleday, 1973; London: Pan pb, 1974).

13. For Indian Buddhist thought see Hajime Nakamura, *Ways of Thinking of Eastern Peoples: India-China-Tibet-Japan*, rev. ed. and trans. Philip P. Wiener (Honolulu: East-West Center Press, 1964) pt. I.

14. See Luckmann, *Invisible Religion* and Peter Berger, *The Sacred Canopy: Elements of a Sociological Theory of Religion* (New York: Doubleday, 1967) chap. 6.

15. On the psychotherapeutic aspects of the need for "external" links to symbolic significance see William F. Lynch, *Images of Hope: Imagination as Healer of the Hopeless* (Notre Dame: University of Notre Dame Press, 1974) pp. 40–41.

16. Concerning "key" words see I. T. Ramsey, *Freedom and Immortality* (Naperville, Ill. : Allenson, 1960; London: SCM Press, 1960) p. 49 and pass.

17. See, for example, the story of Sariputta's conversion in H. C. Warren, ed., *Buddhism in Translations* (Cambridge: Harvard University Press, 1953) par. 10.

18. On the link between physical and spiritual in such a context see Douglas, *Natural Symbols.*

19. See Raimundo Panikkar, *The Unknown Christ of Hinduism* (New York: Humanities, 1968; London: Darton, Longman & Todd, 1964). I have discussed Panikkar's thought in "Hindu and Christian Symbols in the Thought of Raimundo Panikkar: Reflections on a Religious Transposition of Traditions," forthcoming in *Cross Currents* (paper delivered at the conference on cross-cultural religious understanding, Santa Barbara, 1977).

20. Below, Chapter Eight, p. 118.

21. See Evans, *Logic of Self-Involvement,* chap. 5.

22. See the critique of Rudolf Otto's *The Idea of the Holy,* rev. ed. & trans. John W. Harvey (London & New York: Oxford University Press, 1950), by John Oman, *The Natural and the Supernatural* (Cambridge: Cambridge University Press, 1931) pp. 60–69 and elsewhere. For a more recent discussion see John P. Reeder, Jr., in Gene Outka and John P. Reeder, Jr., eds., *Religion and Morality* (New York: Doubleday, 1973).

23. See W. D. Davies, *Paul and Rabbinic Judaism* (New York: Harper Torchbooks pb, 1967) chap. 7 and the quite different perspective in Richard Rubenstein, *My Brother Paul* (New York: Harper & Row, 1972).
Concerning the death of Jesus see John G. Gager, *Kingdom and Community: The Social World of Early Christianity* (Englewood Cliffs, N.J.: Prentice-Hall, 1975) pp. 39–43.

24. On this see also below, p. 86.

25. George Foot Moore, *Judaism in the First Century of the Christian Era: The Age of the Tannaim,* 3 vols. (Cambridge: Harvard University Press, 1959).

26. On this see, e.g., John F. Miller, "Science and Religion: Their Logical Similarity," *Religious Studies* 5:1 (1969) and the replies by John King-Farlow et al. (and the discussion in turn by Barbour, *Myths, Models and Paradigms,* chap. 7, p. 132).

27. On differentiation see Bellah, *Beyond Belief,* chap. 2, "Religious Evolution."

28. See the discussion of family resemblances in Wittgenstein, *Philosophical Investigations,* par. 67, where the image is of threads and fibers (*"wie wir beim Spinnen eines Fadens Faser an Faser drehen . . ."*—"as in spinning a thread we twist fiber on fiber . . ." p. 32e). Ninian Smart, *Reasons and Faiths* (New York: Humanities, 1958; London: Routledge & Kegan Paul, 1958) applies the notion of strands to incarnational and other streams in religious thought.

29. The classic reference for the West is Max Weber, *The Protestant Ethic and the Spirit of Capitalism,* trans. Talcott Parsons (New York: Charles Scribner's Sons pb., 1958). On the Japanese parallels see Robert N. Bellah *Tokugawa Religion* (Glencoe, Ill.: Free Press, 1963).

30. John Dominic Crossan, *The Dark Interval: Towards a Theology of Story* (Niles, Ill.: Argus, 1975) pp. 47–67, sharply distinguishes between the functions of myth and parable in this connection. For David and Nathan see 2 Samuel 11–12.

31. See, e.g., Berger, *Sacred Canopy,* chaps. 1–3.

32. For example, Victor Turner.

33. On this see John Dillenberger, *Protestant Theology and Natural Science* (New York: Doubleday, 1963).

34. For recent philosophical discussions, especially of conceptual relativism, see Ernest Gellner, *Legitimation of Belief* (Cambridge: Cambridge University Press, 1974) and Roger Trigg, *Reason and Commitment* (Cambridge: Cambridge Univer-

sity Press, 1973). On social theory see Jürgen Habermas *Legitimation Crisis,* trans. Thomas McCarthy (Boston: Beacon Press, pb 1975; London: Heinemann, 1976) esp. pt. III. On conceptual changes in the sciences see Stephen Toulmin, *Human Understanding,* vol. 1 (Princeton: Princeton University Press 1972; Oxford: Clarendon Press, 1972) esp. chap. 8 with regard to relativism.

NOTES TO CHAPTER FOUR

1. In addition to authors mentioned in note 2 to Chapter Three, see James Barr, "Story and History in Biblical Theology," pp. 1–17 and Ted Estess, "Elie Wiesel and the Drama of Interrogation," pp. 18–35 in *Journal of Religion* 56:1 (January 1976); Hugh Jones, "The Concept of Story and Theological Discourse," *Scottish Journal of Theology* 29 (1976) pp. 415–33; and John E. Zuck, "Tales of Wonder: Biblical Narrative, Myth and Fairy Stories," *Journal of the American Academy of Religion* 44:2 (June 1976) pp. 299–308. With reference especially to setting see Lonnie D. Kliever, "Story and Space: The Forgotten Dimension," *Journal of the American Academy of Religion* 45:2 (June 1977) abstract p. 221, supplement pp. 529–64.
2. See, e.g., Via, *Kerygma and Comedy,* pp. 10–14. Via's remark that narrative is an extended "sentence" (p. 11) needs to be modified by what he says later concerning different genres.
3. This point is well illustrated from the Chinese cited in Derk Bodde, *China's Cultural Tradition* (New York: Holt, Rinehart & Winston, pb, 1963) chap. A:3.
4. See the chapter by Wiggins in *Religion as Story.* As used by Wittgenstein, *Philosophical Investigations* par. 7 and elsewhere, the notion of language-games is helpful for bringing out different rules of usage and/or action, or sets of rules. In my usage "story" includes whole series of "games." Where patterns of action are meant, Wittgenstein spoke of "forms of life" as distinct from language-games. On the difference see John H. Whittaker, " 'Forms of Life' and Religious Belief," *Philosophy of Religion and Theology: 1971 Proceedings,* ed. David Griffin (Chambersburg, Pa.: American Academy of Religion, 1971) pp. 228–40.

Whittaker characterizes a form of life *(Lebensform)* as "a way of thinking and living"—for example, hoping or grieving *(Philosophical Investigations,* II, i, p. 174e)—founded on a community's perception of the nature of things. In this sense it corresponds to what others call "mythos" or the foundational presuppositions of a particular culture. See, for instance, Bernard Meland in *Fallible Forms and Symbols: Discourses of Method in a Theology of Culture* (Philadelphia: Fortress Press, 1976), p. 102:

I described "mythos" as "the pattern of meaning and valuations arising from within the structured experience of a people which has been imaginatively projected through drama or metaphor, expressing the perceptive truths of the historical experience of a people bearing upon man's ultimate nature and destiny." I think I should now add the words, "as these perceptive truths of experience express themselves within the culture as psychic energy in the form of hopes, expectations, attitudes of trust or apprehension. . . ."

Mythos is the pattern presupposed by a given cycle of myths and sagas or, in my usage, the set of constitutive principles related to realization of the transcendent end articulated in a particular "master story." By contrast, language-games help us to ponder more or less arbitrary rules which exemplify principles of judgment, and so on (on principles versus rules see the beginning of Chapter Six). Whittaker's paper, incidentally, is a refutation of Kai Nielsen's well-known critique of "Wittgensteinian fideism" (in *Philosophy* 42 [1967] pp. 191–209).

5. On this see Stephen Crites, "The Narrative Quality of Experience," *Journal of the American Academy of Religion* 39:3 (September 1971) pp. 291–311. For critical comment see Ted L. Estess, "The Inenarrable Contraption: Reflections on the Metaphor of Story," *Journal of the American Academy of Religion* 42:3 (September 1974) pp. 415–34 and the reply by Dale W. Cannon, "Ruminations on the Claim of Inenarrability," same journal, 4:3 (September 1975) pp. 560–85. (Except for their titles both papers are highly readable.)

6. On poet-statesmen see W. Montgomery Watt, *Muhammad, Prophet and Statesman* (London: Oxford University Press, 1961) esp. chap. 6. On the more mystical side of Muhammad as Seal of the Prophets see Earle Waugh, "Following the Beloved," in Frank Reynolds and Donald Capps, eds., *The Biographical Process* (The Hague: Mouton, 1976) pp. 63–85.

7. See the quote from Monika Hellwig (cited in note 2 to Chapter Three above).

8. On this see C. H. Dodd, *According to the Scriptures* (London: Nisbet, 1953) and *The Apostolic Preaching and Its Development* (London: Hodder & Stoughton, 1951).

9. For fuller treatment of this example see my essay "Religion as Story: The Biography of Norman Bethune," in Peter Slater, ed., *Religion and Culture in Canada/Religion et Culture au Canada* (Waterloo, Ont.: Canadian Corporation for Studies in Religion, at Wilfrid Laurier University Press, 1977) pp. 289–314. On Maoism see Ninian Smart, *Mao* (London: Collins Fontana pb, 1974).

10. See Ted Allan and Sydney Gordon, *The Scalpel, the Sword: The Story of Doctor Norman Bethune* (Boston: Little, Brown & Co., 1952; rev. ed., Toronto: McClelland & Stewart, pb, 1971) pp. 32–40.

11. Ibid., pp. 68 and 85–87.

12. Ibid., p. 217.

13. Ibid., p. 278.

14. Ibid., pp. 315–16, Bethune's italics.

15. Ibid., pp. 267–270. For a more factually oriented biography see Roderick Stewart, *Bethune* (Toronto: New Press, 1973; Don Mills, Ont.: General Publishing, Paperjacks, 1975). For Bethune's collected papers see Roderick Stewart, ed., *The Mind of Norman Bethune* (Don Mills, Ont.: Fitzhenry & Whiteside, 1977).

16. See Luckmann, *Invisible Religion*, chap. 1.

17. Consider, e.g., Margaret Laurence's *The Stone Angel* (Toronto: McClelland & Stewart, 1968). Only at the very end does the heroine, Hagar, say a redeeming word (a "true" lie) to her less favored son Marvin. See p. 304.

18. On setting, plot, and so forth see Wesley A. Kort, *Narrative Elements and Religious Meaning* (Philadelphia: Fortress Press, 1975) pp. 57–58 and pass. While I have adopted Kort's terms I have generally put my own construction on their meanings. The basic concepts go back to Aristotle (*Poetics* 1450–53). On the sacred and the profane see Eliade, *The Sacred and the Profane*.

19. For Gnostic redeemer myths in this connection see Hans Jonas, *Gnostic Religion*, 2d ed. (Boston: Beacon Press, pb 1958).

20. See John S. Dunne, *A Search for God in Time and Memory*, chap. 6.

21. See Andrew Weil, *The Natural Mind: A New Way of Looking at Drugs and the Higher Consciousness* (Boston: Houghton & Mifflin, 1972) chap. 2; R. E. L. Masters and Jean Houston, *The Varieties of Psychedelic Experience* (New York: Holt, Rinehart & Winston, 1966) chap. 7; and Herbert Fingarette, *The Self in Transformation: Psychoanalysis, Philosophy and the Life of the Spirit* (New York: Basic Books, 1963; Harper Torchbooks pb, 1965) chap. 5, "Karma and the Inner World."

22. For an anthropologist's assessment concerning Marxism and millenarianism see Kenelm Burridge, *New Heaven, New Earth: A Study of Millenarian Activities* (New York: Schocken, 1969; Oxford: Basil Blackwell, pb 1969) pp. 130–36.

23. On the genetic and many other fallacies see David Hackett Fischer, *Historians' Fallacies: Toward a Logic of Historical Thought* (New York: Harper Torchbooks pb, 1970).

24. On this see Rudolf Bultmann and his critics in Bartsch, ed., *Kerygma and Myth*, and the profound comments of Amos Niven Wilder, *Theopoetic: Theology and the Religious Imagination* (Philadelphia: Fortress Press, 1976) chap. 6.

25. In Wiggins, ed., *Religion as Story*, pp. 26–40.

26. Ibid., p. 135, the essay by James Hillman.

27. See Northrop Frye, *Anatomy of Criticism: Four Essays* (Princeton: Princeton University Press, 1957) third essay. Sam Keen adopts the same schema for *Beginnings Without End.*

28. These are the subject of a separate book. Briefly, each "way" promises transcendence of our present ambiguous situation and realization of ultimate peace or bliss. It may be analyzed with reference to the kind of setting presupposed, the nature of the saving power invoked, the vision of the transcendent end, and so on. The Way of Resurrection may be worldly or otherworldly but must rely on the transcendent presence of God. The Way of Renunciation sacrifices a part for the sake of that within us which is thought to be of lasting value. The Way of Revolution looks to collective action for the salvation of the group. For a different division of "ways" see Streng et al., *Ways of Being Religious.*

29. On the possibility of the impossible and other matters in this connection see Kierkegaard's analysis of the "sacrifice" of Isaac in *Fear and Trembling,* trans. Walter Lowrie (New York: Anchor pb, 1954) p. 57.

30. See below, Chapter Ten, p. 162–163.

31. See the discussion of terms by James M. Robinson and Helmut Koester, *Trajectories Through Early Christianity* (Philadelphia: Fortress Press, 1971) pp. 13–14. Robinson speaks of overarching trajectories and trajectory patterns. With reference to early Christianity he argues the same basic points which I have made generally concerning the dynamics of religious history and the interplay of religion and culture. On the latter the classic discussion of subsequent Christian history is H. Richard Niebuhr, *Christ and Culture* (New York: Harper Torchbooks, pb, 1957).

32. The theological point is that only God can judge whether any given individual is "saved" or "damned." Against the Calvinist doctrine of "double predestination" (some to be saved, some to be damned, regardless of what they seek to will independently, because of some mysterious "eternal decree"), this is argued at length, in Karl Barth, *Church Dogmatics: The Doctrine of God,* trans. G. W. Bromiley et al. (Edinburgh: T. & T. Clark, 1957) vol. II, pt. 2.

33. Concerning character see McClendon, *Biography as Theology,* chap. 1.

34. See the story of her uncle's organ in Jessamyn West, *The Friendly Persuasion* (New York: Harbrace pb, 1945).

35. On Freud in this connection see Paul Ricoeur, *Freud and Philosophy,* trans. D. Savage (New Haven: Yale University Press, 1970) pp. 536–43. In Harvey Cox note the change of tone between *The Secular City* and *The Feast of Fools* pt. two. On imagination see Amos Wilder *Theopoetic,* chaps. 4 and 5.

NOTES TO CHAPTER FIVE

1. For discussion of the philosophical/theological problems see, e.g., Gordon Kaufman, *God the Problem* (Cambridge: Harvard University Press, 1972) chaps.

3 and 4; Robert H. King *The Meaning of God* (Philadelphia: Fortress Press, 1973) chap. 2; and William L. Power "The Notion of Transcendence and the Problem of Discourse about God," *Journal of the American Academy of Religion* 43:3 (September 1975) pp. 531–41.

2. In this connection note the definition favored by Streng, "Studying Religion" (cited in note 14 to Chapter One). For a critique of a static conception of God and an alternative discussing reality as process see Alfred North Whitehead, *Process and Reality: An Essay in Cosmology,* the Gifford Lectures for 1927–28 (New York: Macmillan, 1929) pt. V, chap. 2 and esp. pp. 134–35. For critique by a process philosopher of John Wisdom's "Gods" (discussed in Chapter Two) see Charles Hartshorne, *The Logic of Perfection and Other Essays in Neoclassical Metaphysics* (LaSalle, Ill.: Open Court, 1962) chap. 5. Whitehead's concluding chapter is included in Ewert H. Cousins, ed., *Process Theology* (New York: Newman Press, pb 1971).

3. See Robert Bellah, "Transcendence in Contemporary Piety" in Donald R. Cutler ed., *The Religious Situation: 1969* (Boston: Beacon Press, 1969) pp. 896–909. The basic reference is Abraham H. Maslow, *Toward a Psychology of Being* 2d ed. (New York: Van Nostrand Reinhold pb, 1968) especially pts. II and III. Less useful is Maslow's *Religions, Values, and Peak Experiences* (New York: Viking pb, 1970).

4. See also Burridge, *New Heaven, New Earth,* p. 11, concerning prestige.

5. For critical comment on Maslow see Lucy Bregman, "Maslow as Theorist of Religion. Reflections on His Popularity and Plausibility," *Soundings: An Interdisciplinary Journal* 59:2 (Summer 1976) pp. 139–63.

6. For example, Ernst Bloch, *A Philosophy of the Future,* trans. John Cumming (New York: Herder & Herder, 1970) pp. 143–44; Jürgen Moltmann, *Religion, Revolution and the Future* trans. M. Douglas Meeks (New York: Charles Scribner's Sons, 1969) IX, "The Future as New Paradigm of Transcendence," esp. pp. 196–99; Johannes B. Metz *Theology of the World,* trans. William Glen-Doepel (New York: Seabury Press, 1973) chap. V; Letty M. Russell, *Human Liberation in a Feminist Perspective* (Philadelphia: Westminster Press, 1974) pp. 41–49; Gustavo Gutiérrez, *A Theology of Liberation,* trans. and ed. Sr. Caridad Inda and John Eagleson (Maryknoll, N.Y.: Orbis, 1973) chap. 11. See among earlier works Reinhold Niebuhr, *The Children of Light and the Children of Darkness* (New York: Charles Scribner's Sons, 1944 and pb 1960) pp. 79–85. Note also the theses in Peter Berger, *Pyramids of Sacrifice: Political Ethics and Social Change* (Garden City, N.Y.: Doubleday, 1974).

7. Martin Heidegger, *Being and Time,* trans. John Macquarrie and Edward Robinson (New York: Harper & Row, 1962; London: SCM Press, 1962) I.5.A.29.

8. For a Christian reading of this situation see Arend Theodoor van Leeuwen, *Christianity in World History: The Meeting of the Faiths of East and West,* trans. H. H. Hoskins (New York: Charles Scribner's Sons, 1964) p. 416.

9. In addition to references already given above note also the historical data adduced by Eric Voegelin, *Order and History;* see, e.g., *Israel and Revelation,* vol. I (Baton Rouge, La.: Louisiana State University Press, 1956) pp. 5–8. For a view less wedded to Western presuppositions concerning being and order see Raimundo Panikkar, *The Trinity and the Religious Experience of Man* (Maryknoll, N.Y.: Orbis, 1973) p. xiii.

10. See Paul Tillich, *The Courage to Be* (New Haven: Yale University Press, 1952) chap. 6.

11. On the concept of presence in this connection see, e.g., Dewart, *Future of Belief*

chap. 5. In philosophy see Gabriel Marcel, *The Mystery of Being*, 2 vols. trans. G. S. Fraser and René Hague (Chicago: Henry Regnery, 1960) vol. 1, Lecture 10.

12. For a comparison of God and Nirvana as ultimate terms see Slater, *Paradox and Nirvana* chap. 5. See also the discussion of changing concepts of heaven by Ninian Smart in G. N. A. Vesey, ed., *Talk of God* (London: Macmillan, 1969) chap. 14.

13. See the story of the Buddha's younger brother in Warren, *Buddhism in Translations* par. 55.

14. Herbert Marcuse, *One Dimensional Man* (Boston: Beacon Press pb, 1964; London: Routledge & Kegan Paul, 1964) chaps. 5, 6, and 10.

15. For my earlier argument on this see "Christian Talk of God" (cited in note 26 to Chapter One). On the need for conceptually "vague" symbols compare Herbert W. Richardson, *Toward an American Theology* (New York: Harper & Row, 1967) p. 24:

> The total cybernetic system must be fortified by an eschatological symbolism which can provide it with general goals and assist men to make the continual transitions an increasingly complex system requires. A cybernetic system determines a rate and form of change, but it does not determine the ultimate end of change. Rather it is guided by some encompassing social vision of the good society. This vision cannot be conceptually precise—for then it would be static rather than dynamic. But it must be symbolically precise if it is to give real direction to the social process.

What gives direction and symbolic precision, in my view, is the developing set of secondary symbols, parables, and so forth, adduced by the leaders in each new generation. On conceptual change in the sciences compare Toulmin, *Human Understanding*, p. 206:

> The task of improving the concepts themselves . . . is by no means as positive or straightforward as checking the truth or falsity of an empirical proposition, or measuring the frequencies required as measures of probability: rather it is a subtle and imaginative task, of conceiving how our concepts might be reordered so as to yield a "better"—i.e., a more exact, more detailed, and generally more intelligible—picture of the objects, systems, and events involved.

Toulmin then stresses that innovations occur only when there is collective dissatisfaction with the previous conceptual scheme and agreement concerning the potential worth of the changes proposed.
Failure to do justice to the communal dimension is a weakness in Kaufman's personal models of transcendence (note 1 above). For Josiah Royce's potential contributions on this subject see Wayne Proudfoot, "Conceptions of God and Selfhood," *Journal of Religion* 55:1 (January 1975) pp. 57–75.

16. With reference to slavery in this connection see, e.g., Peter C. Hodgson, *New Birth of Freedom: A Theology of Bondage and Liberation* (Philadelphia: Fortress Press, 1976) pp. 22–25.

17. On utopian thinking and the role of protest movements see Rosemary Ruether, *The Radical Kingdom: The Western Experience of Messianic Hope* (New York: Paulist Press, 1970) esp. pt. III and Peter C. Hodgson, *Children of Freedom: Black Liberation in Christian Perspective* (Philadelphia: Fortress Press, 1974) chap. 2, "The Dynamics of Oppression."

18. See Gadamer, *Truth and Method* p. 101 concerning transformation, pp. 295–97 concerning interpretation and revelation. For a counter to fundamentalist

views see H. Richard Niebuhr, *The Meaning of Revelation* (New York: Macmillan, 1941, Macmillan pb 1967) p. 131.

19. For the critique from Sartre applied to theology see, e.g., Keen, *To a Dancing God* chap. 1, "An Existentialist Interlude—Projecting the Future and Discovering the Past."

20. More philosophically the point was established by Immanuel Kant, *Fundamental Principles of the Metaphysics of Morals*, trans. T. K. Abbott (New York: Liberal Arts Press, 1949) p. 53, #3. For Gandhi's views see M. K. Gandhi, *An Autobiography or the Story of My Experiments with Truth*, trans. Mahadev Desai (Ahmedabad: Navajivan, 1927; Boston: Beacon Press pb, 1959) and the comments by Thomas Merton, *Conjectures of a Guilty Bystander* (New York: Doubleday and Image pb, 1968) pp. 117–20.

21. Concerning Christianity and universality in this regard see H. Richard Niebuhr, *Radical Monotheism and Western Culture*, with supplementary essays (New York: Harper & Brothers, 1943; Harper Torchbooks pb, 1970) pp. 62–63. Note the emphasis on "hope" and "goal."

22. See Book 19 of Augustine's *City of God*. Text, translations, and commentary on Book 19 are in R. H. Barrow, *Introduction to St. Augustine's City of God* (London: Faber & Faber, 1950).

23. On ritual see Jahn, *Muntu* and Turner, *The Ritual Process*. For Confucius' emphasis on the importance of ritual see, e.g., Alfred Bloom in W. R. Comstock ed., *Religion and Man: An Introduction* p. 280.

24. See Charles Davis, *The Temptations of Religion* (London: Hodder & Stoughton, 1973) pt. IV.

25. See Reinhold Niebuhr, *Moral Man and Immoral Society* (New York: Charles Scribner's Sons, 1932) p. xv.

26. See TeSelle, *Speaking in Parables* p. 113 on Corita Kent, for some of the better current examples.

27. See, for example, Burridge, *New Heaven, New Earth*, chap. 9 and D. H. Lawrence, *Apocalypse* (New York: Viking pb, 1966) pp. 10–13.

28. For critical comment on B. F. Skinner in this respect see J. E. Barnhart, "B. F. Skinner and Cultural Design," in Henry B. Clark, comp., *Religion and Social Sciences: 1973 Proceedings* (Tallahassee, Fla.: American Academy of Religion, 1973) pp. 2–10 and Peter C. Hodgson, *New Birth of Freedom* pp. 90–5. Skinner's position is given in *Beyond Freedom and Dignity* (New York: Knopf, 1971). Failure to consider the paradigm shift is a serious flaw in the contributions to Peter L. Berger and Richard John Neuhaus, eds., *Against the World For the World: The Hartford Appeal and the Future of American Religion* (New York: Seabury Press pb, 1976).

29. See Vittorio Lanternari, *The Religions of the Oppressed: A Study of Modern Messianic Cults*, trans. Lisa Sergio (New York: Knopf, 1963) p. 240, Conclusion.

30. On the interweaving of strata in this connection see James M. Robinson, *The Problem of History in Mark* (Naperville, Ill.: Allenson, & 1957; London: SCM Press, 1957).

31. On Mara see James W. Boyd, *Satan and Mara: Christian and Buddhist Symbols of Evil* (Leiden: E. J. Brill, 1975) pt. two, and Trevor Ling, *Buddhism and the Mythology of Evil* (London: George Allen & Unwin, 1962), chap. 3.

32. See, e.g., Gilkey, *Naming the Whirlwind*, p. 423. For critical comment on Tillich and a positive appraisal of Whitehead here see Ogden, *Reality of God* pp. 54–61.

33. For an attempt to bring the two together see Herbert Marcuse, *Eros and Civilization: A Philosophical Inquiry into Freud* (Boston: Beacon Press, 1955) pt. 2.

34. On this subject I have benefited from recent discussions with Schubert Ogden and Gordon Kaufman. Note, e.g., Schubert Ogden, "The Meaning of Christian Hope," in H. J. Cargas and B. Lee, eds., *Religious Experience and Process Theology* (New York: Paulist Press, 1976) pp. 196–212 and Gordon D. Kaufman *An Essay on Theological Method* (Missoula, Mont.: Scholars Press, 1975).

35. On Mao see Robert Jay Lifton, *Revolutionary Immortality: Mao Tse-Tung and the Chinese Cultural Revolution* (New York: Peter Smith, & 1969; London: Weidenfeld & Nicholson, 1969).

36. On this see John S. Dunne, *The Way of All the Earth: Experiments in Truth and Religion*, pp. 223–24.

37. See Robert Bellah's comment on Wallace Stevens in "Transcendence in Contemporary Piety," in Cutler, ed., *The Religious Situation: 1969*, p. 904.

38. Soren Kierkegaard, *Fear and Trembling.*

39. This is fully argued in Charles Taylor, *The Explanation of Behaviour* (New York: Humanities Press, 1964) chap. 10: 2 and 3.

40. In addition to authors cited in note 34 to Chapter Three and note 33 above see the bibliographical data in Edward Cornish et al., *The Study of the Future: An Introduction to the Art and Science of Understanding and Shaping of Tomorrow's World* (Washington D.C.: World Future Society, 1977).

41. See the discussion of the *Bhagavad Gita* in Robert Lawson Slater, *Can Christians Learn from Other Religions?* (New York: Seabury Press, 1963) chap. 2, "How Much Truth Can a Man Stand?"

42. On transcendent presence as critique see Gregory Baum, *Man Becoming: God in Secular Experience* (New York: Herder & Herder, 1970) chap. 8. Concerning love and partnership see Kahlil Gibran, *The Prophet* (New York: Knopf, 1923 and 1971) "On Marriage."

NOTES TO CHAPTER SIX

1. On this see William Frankena, *Ethics* (Englewood Cliffs, N.J.: Prentice-Hall, 1962) chap. 2.

2. Hence Barth's insistence on discussing ethics as part of dogmatics throughout the *Church Dogmatics.*

3. Karl Potter, *Presuppositions of India's Philosophies* (Englewood Cliffs, N.J.: Prentice-Hall, 1963) chap. 1, pp. 6–7. Potter calls these "attitudes" and "orientations" but also remarks *"moksa*, or complete freedom, is a state. . . ."

4. See, e.g., Viktor Frankl, *Man's Search for Meaning: An Introduction to Logotherapy* (New York: Washington Square, 1969) pp. 118–20.

5. This applies both to "natural" family groups and to voluntary associations which are more than transitory in an individual's life. Concerning Christian community see James M. Gustafson in G. Outka and P. Ramsey, eds., *Norm and Context in Christian Ethics* (New York: Charles Scribner's Sons, 1968) pp. 34–35 and pass.

6. Douglas, *Natural Symbols* distinguishes between grid and group, p. viii and thereafter.

7. So Paul Mus, *Barabodur*, vol. II (Hanoi, 1935) p. 702 with reference to the Buddha and the Dharma in the *Lotus Sutra.*

8. On charisma and prophetic figures see Gager, *Kingdom and Community* pp. 28–32.

9. For example, with reference to "the true individual" in existentialist writing.

10. For concepts of kingship in Israel see A. R. Johnson, *Sacral Kingship in Ancient Israel* (Cardiff: University of Wales Press, 1955).

11. I am indebted here to an unpublished paper by Richard Luman. See, e.g.,

Norman Sykes, *Old Priest and New Presbyter* (Cambridge: Cambridge University Press, 1956) and for dramatization of the issues George Bernard Shaw, *Saint Joan* (Baltimore: Penguin pb, 1954).

12. See, e.g., Daniel Day Williams, *The Spirit and Forms of Love* (New York: Harper & Row, 1968); Gene Outka, *Agape: An Ethical Analysis* (New Haven: Yale University Press, 1972); C. S. Lewis, *The Four Loves* (New York: Harbrace, & 1960; London: Geoffrey Bles, 1960, & Collins Fontana pb, 1963); and José Míguez Bonino, *Christians and Marxists: The Mutual Challenge to Revolution* (Grand Rapids: Eerdmans, 1976; London: Hodder & Stoughton, 1974) esp. Chap. 7.

13. See the selections in H. Gollwitzer ed., *Church Dogmatics: A Selection*, trans. G. W. Bromiley, (New York: Harper Torchbooks pb, 1962) chap. 6 (from *Church Dogmatics* IV, 2). The classic discussion is by Anders Nygren, *Agape and Eros*, trans. P. S. Watson (Philadelphia: Westminster Press, 1953).

14. Barth's critique of the Calvinist doctrine in *Church Dogmatics* II, 2 is a classic example of transformation within a tradition.

15. On the differences in dualism see D. Z. Phillips *Death and Immortality* (London: Macmillan, 1970) p. 47. In general see A. O. Lovejoy, *The Great Chain of Being* (Cambridge: Harvard University Press, 1936).

16. See James, *The Varieties of Religious Experience*, Lecture X.

17. Paul Tillich, *Love, Power and Justice* (New York: Oxford University Press, 1960) chap. 2.

18. See Dietrich Bonhoeffer, *Prisoner for God: Letters and Papers from Prison* ed. E. Bethge, trans. R. H. Fuller (New York: Macmillan, 1957) pp. 160, 178–80.

19. On the archetypal significance of Jesus in this context see Hans Küng, *On Being a Christian*, trans. Edward Quinn (New York: Doubleday, 1976; London: Collins, 1976) B.I.1. For critique of Nygren's theses see John Burnaby, *Amor Dei* (London: Hodder & Stoughton, 1947) chap. 1.

20. Note in this connection the essays in John Hick, ed., *The Myth of God Incarnate* (London: SCM Press, 1977) and the wide range of recent reviews of these.

21. On Paul see W. D. Davies, *Paul* chaps. 8–10.

22. Consider the examples which fired Augustine's enthusiasm prior to his conversion, cited in his *Confessions VIII*, 2 and 6. On Augustine see David Burrell, *Exercises in Religious Understanding* (Notre Dame: University of Notre Dame Press, 1974) chap. 1.

23. See the selections from his anti-Pelagian writings in Augustine, *Later Works*, selected and trans. John Burnaby, Library of Christian Classics, vol. 8 (Philadelphia: Westminster Press, 1955) pp. 182–250. On Augustine as bishop see Peter Brown, *Augustine of Hippo* (Berkeley: University of California Press, 1968).

24. See, e.g., Gordon Rupp *The Righteousness of God* (London: Hodder & Stoughton, 1953) pt. 2.

25. See Tillich, *The Courage to Be*, chap. 6. Note the use of this concept by Thomas A. Harris in *I'm O.K.—You're O.K.* (New York: Avon pb. 1969) chap. 12 and the experiments described by James Dittes, "Justification by Faith and the Experimental Psychologist," in L. B. Brown, ed., *Psychology and Religion* (Baltimore: Penguin pb. 1973) VI.20.

26. See the comment by David Tracy, *Blessed Rage for Order* pp. 6–7, concerning Tillich and theological loyalty. Typical of those who dismiss Tillich for "baptized atheism" is Alasdair MacIntyre, for example in *Secularization and Moral Change* (London and New York: Oxford University Press, 1967) p. 69. Most critics fail to take seriously what Tillich meant by "the God above 'God,'" (in

The Courage to Be), or to keep in mind his philosophical roots in German Classical idealism and especially the German connotations of "ultimate" *(unbedingt)* in his description of religion as "that which concerns me ultimately" *(das mich unbedingt angeht)*. On specific doctrines Tillich is certainly suspect. But my interest is in the central thrust of his thinking, which comes from within "the theological circle" (see the Introduction to his *Systematic Theology*, vol. 1).

27. On this topic see the critique of J. N. Findlay by John Hick in his *God and the Universe of Faiths: Essays in the Philosophy of Religion* (London: Macmillan, 1973) chap. 6.

28. For critical reviews of Flew's recent work, *The Presumption of Atheism and Other Philosophical Essays on God, Freedom and Immortality* (New York: Barnes & Noble, 1976), see Schubert Ogden and Kai Nielsen in *Religious Studies Review* 3:3 (July 1977) pp. 142–50.

29. See Gager, *Kingdom and Community,* pp. 32–36.

30. See Wilfred Cantwell Smith's suggestion concerning the Bible in "The Study of Religion and the Study of the Bible," *Journal of the American Academy of Religion* 39:2 (June, 1971) pp. 131–40, reprinted in Oxtoby, *Religious Diversity* chap. 3. In this essay, incidentally, Smith explicitly compares the central place of the Qur'an in Muslim thinking with that of the Christ in Christian thinking (in Oxtoby, pp. 45–47).

31. Relevant here is Tillich's concept of "the Protestant principle"; see *The Protestant Era* (Chicago: The University of Chicago Press, 1957, Phoenix pb, 1966) Introduction and chap. 11.

32. On this see Wiles, *The Remaking of Christian Doctrine* chap. 1, concerning criticism of his earlier work *The Making of Christian Doctrine.*

NOTES TO CHAPTER SEVEN

1. See Gager, *Kingdom and Community,* chap. 5. Compare Toulmin, *Human Understanding,* concerning conditions for "effective conceptual innovation," chap. 3.

2. Compare also the Lutherans and Luther at the outset of the Reformation.

3. For a contemporary reading of the issues see Rubenstein, *My Brother Paul* chap. 5.

4. For the background see Tor Andrae, *Mohammed, The Man and His Faith* (New York: Harper Torchbooks pb, 1972) chaps. 1 and 6.

5. See, e.g., Rudolf Otto, *Mysticism East and West: A Comparative Analysis of the Nature of Mysticism* (New York: Meridian pb, 1957); Schuon, *Transcendent Unity to Religions;* (cited in note 7 to Chapter One); Ninian Smart, *Reasons and Faiths* (cited in note 28 to Chapter Three); Harold Coward and Terence Penelhum, eds., *Mystics and Scholars: The Calgary Conference on Mysticism 1976* SR Supplements 3 (Waterloo, Ont.: Canadian Corporation for Studies in Religion, Wilfrid Laurier University Press, 1977); and Huston Smith, *Forgotten Truth: The Primordial Tradition* (New York: Harper & Row, 1976).

6. For example, Dunne, *The Way of All the Earth* esp. chap. 2.

7. For a survey of the issues here see Robin Gill, *The Social Context of Theology: A Methodological Inquiry* (London: Mowbrays, 1975) chaps. 7 and 8.

8. See, e.g., Jacob Neusner, "The Implications of the Holocaust," *Journal of Religion* 53:3 (July 1973) pp. 293–308.

9. Ibid., p. 304, quoting Wyschogrod on Fackenheim.

10. See Emil Fackenheim, *God's Presence in History: Jewish Affirmations and Philosophical Reflections* (New York: Harper Torchbooks pb, 1970).

11. Especially in *After Auschwitz: Radical Theology and Contemporary Judaism* (Indianapolis: Bobbs-Merrill, 1966). Concerning Torah see Chap. 6.

12. For example, in *My Brother Paul.*

13. For a popular literary portrayal of this experience see Chaim Potok, *The Chosen* (New York: Fawcett pb, 1967) chap. 11.

14. See *My Brother Paul,* p. 6 where Rubenstein describes Paul as doing the same. But the categories are ours, not Paul's.

15. I take this figure from Henry Chadwick's Inaugural Lecture as Regius Professor of Divinity at Oxford. His foci were Jerusalem and Rome.

16. See Rubenstein, *My Brother Paul,* concerning fear of the mother, p. 67, referring to his discussion in *The Religious Imagination* (Indianapolis: Bobbs-Merrill, 1968) pp. 69–100.

17. On this see the essay by R. R. Niebuhr in A. R. Bellinzoni and T. V. Litzenburg, Jr., *Intellectual Honesty and Religious Commitment* (Philadelphia: Fortress Press, 1969).

18. For appraisals of Keen see Sallie TeSelle, *Speaking in Parables,* pp. 20–22, 169–72, and an essay in a forthcoming collection by Donald Evans (University of Toronto Press).

19. William C. Shepherd, "On the Concept of 'Being Wrong' Religiously," *Journal of the American Academy of Religion* 42:1 (March 1974) pp. 66–81.

20. On polysymbolic religion entitled "E Pluribus Unum," unpublished. See also his commentary on Norman O. Brown, *Symbolical Consciousness: A Commentary on Love's Body* (Missoula, Mont.: Scholars Press, 1976) chap. 5.

21. See Robert S. Ellwood, Jr., *Religious and Spiritual Groups in Modern America* (Englewood Cliffs, N.J.: Prentice-Hall, 1973) and his comment on David L. Miller in "Polytheism: Establishment or Liberation Religion?" *Journal of the American Academy of Religion* 42:2 (June 1974) pp. 344–49.

22. R. C. Zaehner, *Mysticism Sacred and Profane: An Inquiry into Some Varieties of Praeternatural Experience* (New York: Oxford University Press, 1957) chap. 10.

23. The phrase comes from Walter H. Clark, *Chemical Ecstasy: Psychedelic Drugs and Religion* (New York: Sheed & Ward, 1969). Also on this topic see Andrew M. Greeley *Ecstasy: A Way of Knowing* (Englewood Cliffs, N.J.: Prentice-Hall pb, 1974) pp. 70–72.

24. On Kierkegaard's use of Kantian ideas see the article by George Schrader in Josiah Thompson, ed., *Kierkegaard: A Collection of Critical Essays* (New York: Doubleday, 1972).

25. See Weil, *Natural Mind,* pp. 161–66.

26. David L. Miller, *The New Polytheism: Rebirth of the Gods and Goddesses* (New York: Harper & Row, 1974).

27. See the literature on "civil religion in America," including the essay with that title in Bellah, *Beyond Belief,* chap. 9. See also Robert N. Bellah, *The Broken Covenant: American Civil Religion in Time of Trial* (New York: Seabury Press, 1975). Martin Marty once made some critical remarks concerning overemphasis on this concept, from a podium with a backdrop of at least a dozen U.S. flags (all stars and stripes) immediately behind his head (address to the American Academy of Religion meeting in Chicago, 1975).

28. On Wiesel see Estess, "Elie Wiesel" (cited in note 1 to Chapter Four) and Robert McAfee Brown, "Story and Theology," in James W. McClendon, Jr., comp., *Philosophy of Religion and Theology: 1974 Proceedings* (Tallahassee, Fla.: American Academy of Religion, 1974) pp. 55–72.

29. E. Wiesel, *Gates of the Forest,* trans. Frances Frenaye, (New York: Holt, Rinehart & Winston and Avon pb, 1966) pp. 6–10.

30. With reference to those who survived the death-camps and the "bio-social

roots" of their behavior see Terrence Des Pres, *The Survivor: An Anatomy of Life in the Death Camps* (New York: Oxford University Press, 1976) p. 199, concerning the will to bear witness. Des Pres categorically rejects "teleological" explanations of survival (see p. 193 with regard to Bergson and Teilhard de Chardin), though this seems to be more an expression of his dogmatic presuppositions than anything demanded by his data.

31. On this subject see Thomas Dean, *Post-Theistic Thinking: The Marxist-Christian Dialogue in Radical Perspective* (Philadelphia: Temple University Press, 1975) esp. pt. III and John C. Raines and Thomas Dean eds., *Marxism and Radical Religion: Essays Toward a Revolutionary Humanism* (Philadelphia: Temple University Press, 1970).

32. I discussed this previously in "Evil and Ultimacy," *Sciences Religieuses/Studies in Religion* 4:2 (1974/5) pp. 137–46.

NOTES TO CHAPTER EIGHT

1. William James, *The Principles of Psychology*, 2 vols. (New York: Henry Holt, 1880, and Dover pb, 1950) vol. 1, p. 186.
2. Ibid., pp. 400–1.
3. Ibid., pp. 291–92.
4. Ibid., pp. 294–95.
5. Ibid., p. 311.
6. See also on this John Dewey, *A Common Faith* (New Haven: Yale University Press, 1934) p. 19. Subsequent "ideal observer" theories in ethics have their roots here.
7. See *The Letters of William James*, vol. 2, ed. Henry James (Boston: Atlantic Monthly Press, 1920) pp. 213–14, and William James's Introduction to *The Literary Remains of the Late Henry James* (Boston: Houghton & Mifflin, 1884). The two Henrys here are his son and his father, not his brother.
8. James, *Principles*, vol. 1, pp. 309–10.
9. Ibid., p. 316.
10. James, *The Varieties of Religious Experience* Lecture IX (Fontana pb. p. 194).
11. James *Principles*, vol. 1, p. 317.
12. See David Hume, *A Treatise of Human Nature*, ed. L. A. Selby-Bigge (Oxford: Clarendon, 1958) I.iii.8: p. 102, regarding custom; p. 105, regarding habit.
13. James, *Varieties*, IX, p. 200
14. William James, *Psychology (Briefer Course)* (London: Collier-Macmillan, 1962; New York: Collier pb, 1962) p. 159.
15. James, *Varieties*, IX, p. 201.
16. Ibid., pp. 201–3. See the comment to Flournoy in *Letters*, vol. 2, pp. 327–28 (September 28, 1909).
17. James, *Varieties*, X, p. 239
18. Ibid., pp. 234–35.
19. For Maslow, *Religions, Values, and Peak Experiences* For C. G. Jung see his *Memories, Dreams, Reflections*, rev. ed. Aniela Jaffé (New York: Random House, Vintage pb, 1962) pp. 196–97 regarding mandalas and centering. For Kohlberg see, e.g., Lawrence Kohlberg and E. Turiel, *Moralization Research, the Cognitive Developmental Approach* (New York: Holt, Rinehart & Winston, 1971) and T. J. Bachmeyer, "Ethics and the Psychology of Moral Judgment," *Zygon* 8:2 (June 1973) pp. 82–95. Note also David Elkind on Piaget and religious development in Brown, ed., *Psychology and Religion*, sec. 4.11.
20. Margaret Atwood, *Survival: A Thematic Guide to Canadian Literature* (Toronto: Anansi, 1972) pp. 36–39.

21. Margaret Atwood, *Surfacing* (New York: Simon & Schuster, 1973 Popular Library pb, 1976; Toronto: McClelland & Stewart, 1973).
In *The Edible Woman* (Toronto: McClelland & Stewart, 1969) Atwood uses the device of a nameless woman who switches from first to third person pronouns, during periods of alienation.

22. Atwood, *Surfacing*, p. 73.

23. Ibid., p. 104.

24. Ibid., p. 105 and pp. 107–8. See also p. 76.

25. Ibid., pp. 130–32. See also p. 162.

26. Ibid., pp. 143–44.

27. Ibid., p. 169. Concerning "geometrical sex" see pp. 152–4.

28. This quote is from *Selected Poems* (Toronto: Oxford University Press, 1976), "Book of Ancestors," pp. 239–40.

29. See Carol P. Christ, "Margaret Atwood: The Surfacing of Women's Spiritual Quest and Vision" and Judith Plaskow, "On Carol Christ on Margaret Atwood: Some Theological Reflections," *Signs: Journal of Women in Culture and Signs* 2:2 (Winter 1976) pp. 316–39. Atwood's reply, pp. 340–41, remarks that whereas American reviewers have emphasized the feminist and ecological issues raised by the novel Canadian reviewers have stressed the nationalist viewpoint. In support of Atwood's novel, one of my students pointed out that the "solution" is what makes sense to the "heroine" at the time, that is, it follows the logic of the character in that setting, whatever we or the author may think about it. For a critique of Jungian presuppositions see Naomi R. Goldenberg, "Jung after Feminism," in Rita M. Gross, ed., *Beyond Androcentrism: New Essays on Women and Religion* (Missoula, Mont.: Scholars Press, 1977) pp. 53–66. In teaching I use *Surfacing* in correlation with D. H. Lawrence's *Apocalypse*.

30. Compare, for example, the atmosphere in Nathanael West's *Miss Lonelyhearts* (New York: New Directions pb, 1962). The autobiographies that I have in mind are Eldridge Cleaver, *Soul on Ice* (New York: McGraw Hill, 1967) and Pierre Vallières, *White Niggers of America*, trans. Joan Pinkham (New York: Monthly Review Press, 1971).

31. On this subject see George Woodcock, *Anarchism* (Cleveland: Meridian pb, 1962). For insight into the Canadian urban guerrillas' thinking see the semi-fictional account in Brian Moore, *The Revolution Script* (Richmond Hill, Ont.: Pocket Books pb, 1972) and the political analysis in Denis Smith, *Bleeding Hearts . . . Bleeding Country: Canada and the Quebec Crisis* (Edmonton, Alberta: M. G. Hurtig, 1971).

32. See, for example, the analysis of Bruno Bettelheim, *The Children of the Dream* (New York: Avon pb, 1968).

33. On this subject see William Sargant, *Battle for the Mind: The Mechanics of Indoctrination, Brainwashing and Thought Control* (Baltimore: Pelican pb, 1957) and Robert Jay Lifton, *Thought Reform and the Psychology of Totalism: A study of "Brainwashing" in China* (New York: W. W. Norton, 1961). Sargant gives more physiological, Lifton more psycho-social data.

34. See also the work of Frantz Fanon. On this see David Caute, *Fanon* ed. Frank Kermode (Baltimore: Penguin, pb 1976; London: Collins Fontana Modern Masters,pb, 1970). Fanon's main titles are *The Wretched of the Earth*, trans. Constance Farrington (New York: Grove, 1963) and *Black Skin, White Masks* trans. Charles L. Markmann (New York: Grove, 1967).

35. See Tillich's comment on fanaticism in *The Courage to Be*, p. 50 and the essay cited earlier by James Dittes.

36. See Lifton, *Thought Reform* and Frankl, *Man's Search for Meaning.*
37. On fact-gathering and shared paradigms generally see Thomas S. Kuhn, *The Structure of Scientific Revolutions,* 2d ed. (Chicago: The University of Chicago Press, 1970) chaps. 3–5 and 10. For application of Kuhn's findings to theology and discussion of "eschatological verification" see Wolfhart Pannenberg, *Theology and the Philosophy of Science,* trans. Francis McDonagh (Philadelphia: Westminster Press, 1976; London: Darton, Longman & Todd, 1976) pp. 334–45.
38. With the assistance of Alex Haley (New York: Grove, 1964). I have benefitted here from reading James W. Fowler's Thirkield-Jones Lectures for 1974, given at Gammon Theological Seminary. Fowler outlines a structural analysis of faith as exemplified by Malcolm X, based on Piaget and Kohlberg.

NOTES TO CHAPTER NINE

1. For Tillich on the demonic see *Systematic Theology,* Index entries.
2. See, e.g., Mircea Eliade, *Cosmos and History: The Myth of the Eternal Return,* trans. Willard R. Trask (New York: Bollingen Foundation, 1954; Harper & Row, 1959) chaps. 1 and 2.
3. On this theme see, besides Atwood and Jung, Joseph Campbell, in *Myths to Live By* (New York: Viking pb, 1972) esp. chap. 1.
4. See the material recorded in Robert Jay Lifton, *Death in Life: Survivors of Hiroshima* (New York: Vintage, 1969), chaps. 7, 9–12. More journalistic is John Hersey, *Hiroshima* (New York: Knopf, 1946).
5. Michihiko Hachiya, *Hiroshima Diary,* trans. and ed. Warner Wells (Chapel Hill: University of North Carolina Press, 1955; New York: Avon pb, 1955).
6. Ibid., pp. 24, 30, 46, 56, 62, 103–4.
7. See Robert C. Batchelder, *The Irreversible Decision: 1939–1950* (New York: Macmillan, 1961) pp. 53, 65–66, 90.
8. Hachiya, *Hiroshima Diary,* p. 59. On the Japanese sense of shame and honor see Ruth Benedict, *The Chrysanthemum and the Sword* (Rutland, Vt.: Charles E. Tuttle, 1965).
9. Hachiya, *Hiroshima Diary,* pp. 15, 56, 70, 72–73, 75.
10. See Batchelder, *Irreversible Decision,* p. 77. I am also indebted here to conversations with Hugh Borton, who was among those advising against trying the Emperor as a war criminal.
11. Hachiya, *Hiroshima Diary,* pp. 86–89, 91–93.
12. This thought applies similarly to Rieux in Albert Camus' *The Plague.*
13. Hachiya, *Hiroshima Diary,* p. 217.
14. Ibid.
15. Ibid., pp. 62, 68, 33, 139.
16. Ibid., p. 212. This was for a thirteen-year-old son. Customarily the son would be expected to make the funeral arrangements for the father.
17. Batchelder, *Irreversible Decision,* chap. 13.
18. Ibid., pp. 158–59.
19. The Diaries of William Lyon Mackenzie King for August 1945 (Public Archives of Canada).
20. An early example of this is given in Holmes Welch, *Taoism: The Parting of the Way* (Boston: Beacon Press, 1957) pt. 3, chap. 4 and H. G. Creel, *Confucius and the Chinese Way* (New York: Harper Torchbooks pb, 1960) chap. 13.
21. On this see, e.g., Robert Bellah, *Tokugawa Religion,* chap. 1.
22. On the Japanese peace movement see Lifton, *Death in Life,* pp. 300–302.
23. See Joseph M. Kitagawa, *Religion in Japanese History* (New York: Columbia University Press, 1966) pp. 11–19, 66–69, 160–176 and chaps. 5 and 6.

24. James Hillman, *The Myth of Analysis: Three Essays in Archetypal Psychology* (Evanston: Northwestern University Press, 1972) pp. 264–65, 267.
25. So Edmund Leach during a public lecture in Ottawa, April 1976.
26. Hillman, *Myth of Analysis,* pp. 268–69.
27. Ibid., pp. 273, 276.
28. Ibid., p. 380 and David L. Miller, *The New Polytheism,* chap. 1, regarding H. Richard Niebuhr's radical monotheism and Eric Voegelin's account of Greek religion, *Order and History,* vol. 2.
29. For a review of the literature on this subject see David L. Miller, *Gods and Games: Toward a Theology of Play* (New York: Harper Colophon Books pb, 1973) Introduction to the Colophon edition.
30. See Rosemary Ruether, *Faith and Fratricide: The Theological Roots of Anti-Semitism* (New York: Seabury Press, 1974).
31. On justification in war see Ralph B. Potter, *War and Moral Discourse* (Richmond, Va.: John Knox Press, 1969) chaps. 4–6.
32. Refutation of this idea is found in Lucy Dawidowicz, *The War against the Jews 1933–1945* (New York: Holt, Rinehart & Winston 1975).
33. So Denis de Rougemont, "On the Devil in Politics," in Wayne Cowan, ed., *Witness to a Generation,* trans. Edward M. Maisel, (Indianapolis: Bobbs-Merrill, 1966) pp. 6–12.
34. For a vivid portrayal see the closing scenes in André Schwartz-Bart, *The Last of the Just,* trans. Stephen Becker (New York: Athenaeum, 1960), chap. 8.4.
35. On the nuances which derive from Augustine, see Reinhold Niebuhr *The Nature and Destiny of Man,* 2 vols. (New York: Charles Scribner's Sons, 1946) vol. 1, chaps. 6–9.
36. On this subject see Edward de Bono, *The Use of Lateral Thinking* (Baltimore: Pelican pb, 1971) and Koestler, *Act of Creation.*
37. See R. D. Laing, *The Politics of Experience* (New York: Ballantine pb, 1967) p. 28.
38. R. D. Laing, *The Divided Self* (Baltimore: Pelican pb, 1965) p. 36. I have written on "The Kerygma and the Cuckoo's Nest" in the *Scottish Journal of Theology,* forthcoming, 1978.
39. Laing, *Politics of Experience,* pp. 118–19.
40. See again Atwood, *The Edible Woman,* who reverts to third person pronouns when she becomes engaged (cited in note 21 to Chapter Eight).
41. See, e.g., *The Autobiography of Malcolm X,* chap. 10. This point was emphasized by Muhammad Ali during a television interview on his life story, March 1977.
42. On role-playing I am indebted to a lecture by H. Sundén at Lancaster University, U.K., August 1975 (XIIIth International Congress for the History of Religions). For a selection of papers on the general topic see Alan C. Elms, ed., *Role Playing, Reward, and Attitude Change* (New York: Van Nostrand Reinhold pb, 1969).
43. The sense of mutual dependency is the key to the Confucian concept of filial piety *(hsiao).* On this see, e.g., Bloom in Comstock, *Religion and Man* pp. 280–81.
44. See Jung, *Memories, Dreams, Reflections.*
45. Jean-Paul Sarte, *No Exit and Three Other Plays,* trans. Stuart Gilbert (New York: Knopf, 1949; Vintage pb, 1960). Note also the article by Ted Estess, "The Inenarrable Contraption."
46. Maslow, *Religions, Values, and Peak Experiences.*
47. See Dunne *A Search for God in Time and Memory* chap. 5.
48. See, e.g., Charles Davis, *Body as Spirit: The Nature of Religious Feeling* (New

York: Seabury Press, 1976) chap. 2. For the Hebrew conception see H. Wheeler Robinson, *Inspiration and Revelation in the Old Testament* (Oxford: Clarendon Press, 1953) pt. II, chaps. 4 and 5.

49. See Frithjof Schuon, *Transcendent Unity* and Huston Smith, *Forgotten Truth*.

NOTES TO CHAPTER TEN

1. Philip Roth, *Portnoy's Complaint* (New York: Bantam pb, 1969) pp. 66–68.
2. Ibid., pp. 88–89. See also pp. 72–73.
3. Atwood, *Surfacing*, p. 192.
4. Note also Harvey, *Historian and Believer* and T. A. Roberts, *History and Christian Apologetics* (London: SPCK, 1960) chap. 1.
5. Compare, for example, appreciating the paintings of Jackson Pollock.
6. The image comes from a talk on theologies of hope by Van Harvey, unpublished. On escapism see Philip Slater, *The Pursuit of Loneliness* (Boston: Beacon Press, 1972).
7. For literature on this see Nelson Pike, ed., *God and Evil* (Englewood Cliffs, N.J.: Prentice-Hall, 1964).
8. See Ninian Smart, "Omnipotence, Evil and Supermen," *Philosophy* 36:137 (April–July 1961) pp. 188–95 (reprinted in Pike, ed., *God and Evil*) and J. L. Mackie, "Theism and Utopia," *Philosophy* 37:140 (April 1962) pp. 153–58.
9. See the essay on evil in Gabriel Marcel, *Philosophy of Existence*, trans. M. Harari (London: Harvill, 1948) and John Hick, *Evil and the God of Love* (New York: Macmillan, 1966) pt. IV. Hick's reply to his critics is in *God and the Universe of Faiths* chaps. 4 and 5.
10. So H. D. Aiken, *Reason and Conduct* (New York: Knopf, 1962) chap. 9, a reprint of "God and Evil: A Study of Some Relations Between Faith and Morals," *Ethics* 68:2 (January 1958) pp. 77–97.
11. On Clifford see James Livingston, *The Ethics of Belief: An Essay on the Victorian Religious Conscience* (Missoula, Mont.: Scholars Press, 1974).
12. James, *Will to Believe*. See also Ralph Barton Perry, *In the Spirit of William James* (New Haven: Yale University Press, 1938) chap. 5.
13. On maturity see Gordon W. Allport, *Individual and His Religion* chap. 3 "Justification by Faith."
14. So Sigmund Freud, *The Future of an Illusion*, trans. W. D. Robson-Scott (New York: Anchor pb, 1964) chaps. 6 and 10. See the discussion by Peter Homans, *Theology after Freud: An Interpretive Inquiry* (Indianapolis: Bobbs-Merrill, 1970) chap. 3 and Paul Ricoeur, *Freud and Philosophy*.
15. See Jorge Luis Borges's "The Circular Ruins," trans. N. T. di Giovanni, in *The Aleph and Other Stories 1933–1969* (New York: Bantam pb, 1971).
16. These terms come from Tillich, *The Protestant Era* and elsewhere. Tillich's solution is a "theonomous" ethics. Autonomous is self-regulated, heteronomous is other-regulated and theonomous is God-regulated.
17. So Fowler, Thirkfield-Jones Lectures (cited in note 38 to Chapter Eight), adapting Kohlberg.
18. In Kohlberg's idiom, one whose own judgments reflect "Stage 4" thinking may nevertheless appreciate "Stage 5" judgments, and so forth.
19. See Buber's discussion of the "I-Thou" of Socrates, Jesus, and Goethe in *I and Thou* pp. 115–16.
20. On the problem of interpreting these see, e.g., Norman Perrin, "Historical Criticism, Literary Criticism, and Hermeneutics: The Interpretation of the Parables of Jesus and the Gospel of Mark Today," *Journal of Religion* 52:4 (October 1972) pp. 361–75. For comparison of Jesus with Kafka and others see

Robert W. Funk, *Jesus as Precursor* (Philadelphia: Fortress Press, and Missoula, Mont.: Scholars Press, 1975).

21. See, e.g., Miguez Bonino, *Christians and Marxists* esp. chap. 2.

22. See Hugh Jackson, "The Resurrection Belief of the Earliest Church: A Response to the Failure of Prophecy?" *Journal of Religion* 55:4 (October 1975) pp. 415–25.

23. This point is well made by William James, *Varieties*, Lecture I.

24. See, e.g., John V. Taylor, *The Primal Vision: Christian Presence Amid African Religion* (New York: Allenson pb, 1966; London: SCM Press, 1965) p. 155. In an interview Margaret Atwood described *Surfacing* as a ghost story: see Graeme Gibson, *Eleven Canadian Novelists* (Toronto: Anansi, 1973) pp. 28–31.

25. See Miguez Bonino, *Christians and Marxists*.

26. I have in mind here the ashram of Ramana Maharshi in South India. The ratio of genuine gurus to charlatans is about that of true to false prophets: see the wry portrait by R. K. Narayan, *The Guide* (Mysore: Indian Thought Publications, 1963).

27. Piaget, *Six Psychological Studies* makes this general point concerning genesis and structure; see chap. 6. In theology see the introduction to the works of Teilhard de Chardin by N. M. Wildiers, *An Introduction to Teilhard de Chardin*, trans. Hubert Hoskins (New York: Harper & Row, 1968).

28. For the spectrum as perceived in contemporary thought see Robert Jay Lifton, *Boundaries* (New York: Vintage pb, 1970). For criticism of "modernist" prejudices see Berger and Neuhaus, eds., *Against the World For the World*.

29. What is crucial here is some recognition of the "non-dual" nature of religious experience. See Raimundo Panikkar, *Worship and Secular Man* (Maryknoll, N.Y.: Orbis, 1973; London: Darton, Longman & Todd, 1973) pp. 70, 90–93.

30. On this subject, in addition to Teilhard de Chardin and others, see William Temple, *Nature, Man and God* (London: Macmillan, 1935) Lecture XIX.

31. Found in W. T. DeBary, ed., *Sources of Indian Tradition* (New York: Columbia University Press, 1958) chap. 26.

32. For a general introduction to Gandhi see George Woodcock, *Gandhi*, ed. Frank Kermode (Baltimore: Penguin & London: Collins Fontana Modern Masters pb, 1972) and on Gandhi's tactics see Joan V. Bondurant, *Conquest of Violence: The Gandhian Philosophy of Conflict*, rev. ed. (Berkeley: University of California Press, 1965) esp. chaps. 1, 2, and 6. See also James W. Douglass, *The Non-Violent Cross: A Theology of Revolution and Peace* (New York: Macmillan, 1969) chaps. 2 and 3.

33. Note, by contrast, the work of Vivekenanda in relation to Ramakrishna; see, e.g., DeBary, ed., *Sources of Indian Tradition*, chap. 22.

34. In DeBary, *Sources* chap. 26.

Index